A THIRD LOOK AT JESUS

A THIRD LOOK AT JESUS

Carlos H. Abesamis

Third and Completely Revised Edition

A Guidebook along a Road Least Traveled

A THIRD LOOK AT JESUS

A division of Claretian Communications, Inc.
U.P. P.O. Box 4, Diliman 1101 Quezon City, Philippines
TE: 921-3984 • Fax: (632) 921-7429
E-mail: cci@claret.org / claret@cnl.net
Website: www.bible.claret.org

Claretian Publications is a pastoral endeavor of the Claretian Missionaries in the Philippines. It aims to promote a renewed spirituality rooted in the process of total liberation and solidarity in response to the needs, challenges and pastoral demands of the Church Today.

Sixth Printing, February 2003

Artwork & cover design: Pia A. Guerrero and Michael V. Cleofe, cmf

ISBN 971-501-879-5

Acknowledgments

Willie Abesamis, Percy Bacani, Letty Bengzon, Raf Borromeo, Bert Cacayan, Leo De Castro, Claretian Management Staff, Bobby and Alice Cuento, Junrey Ente, Richie Fernando (+), Red Fullero, Zeny Gan, Mary Grenough, Dindo and Pia Guerrero, Frances Hardiman, Louie Hechanova, Don Don Irinco, Norlan Julia, Gaston Kibiten, Tess Kong, Bill De Lara, Jolan Lumawig, LHS Kitchen Staff, Pinky Maristela, Joe de Mesa, Reinhard Neudecker, Al Nudas, Vinci & Tere Roco, Alfred Sanchez, Ador Santiago, Bong Silva, Art Shea, Socio-Pastoral Institute

You will recognize the thumb-prints of your person in this guidebook. Hindi masusukat ang aking pasasalamat. – CHA

Mayee Abear, Gina Abesamis, Gilbert Arbis, Rodel Asuncion, Louie Bacomo, Maan Barcelo, Erlie Bragado, Raul Bulalaque, Greg Castilla, Erwin Cuevas, Raul Dael, Ritchie Elot, Mariel Francisco, Dylan Fullero, Gabby Garcia, James Gascon, Gaby Gonzalez, Gabby Lamug-Nañawa, Bembet Madrid, Rowena Maquiling, Zon Moraleda, Rady Olazo, Pacita Polintan, Alec Pizarro, Verne and Annabelle Quiazon, RGS Tagaytay, Karen Sarmiento, Boboy Silerio, Ruben Tanseco, Nora Ulgasan, Richard Vergara

Contents

Stopover 1

The Third Look: What and Why (Mapping Out the Journey)

We Need a Third Look. As we tread our spiritual path, it is imperative that we keep step with Jesus. Nay more, we strive to heighten our bondedness with him. And so we fix our gaze on Jesus in our spiritual retreats and other religious activities. However, it is not enough to keep going back to the same Jesus time after time, simply taking a second look at Jesus. We need a third look.

Three Looks at Jesus. There are at least three ways of fixing our gaze on Jesus. As Jesus himself looks at himself—this is the first look. As Western theology has looked at Jesus – this is the second look. As the poor look at Jesus—this is the third look.

The First Look. The First Look at Jesus was the way Jesus understood himself, his own life and his own work. It was the look at Jesus through Jesus' own eyes. Moreover, many of the first generation Christians, not yet influenced by the later Western outlook, also possessed the First Look at Jesus.

The Second Look. The Second Look at Jesus was the way Graeco-Roman and Western eyes later regarded Jesus, his life and his work. For example, while Jesus' concern was the total well-being of the total human person, the Second Look tended to make redemption of souls Jesus' concern. While Jesus liked to talk in terms of food, the Second Look spoke in terms of sanctifying grace.

This Second Look lasted from approximately 50 C.E.[1] to the 1960s! A very long segment of Church history! And even today, as we enter the third millennium, the Second Look is still the way many Filipino Christians see Jesus. It is the view which early missionaries from Europe and North America, with much good will, taught us. We in turn pass it on to our children, parishioners, students, retreatants. This Second Look is the view that I learned in my youth. It is still prevalent in most of our catechetical institutes, liturgical and spirituality centers—and even seminaries and theological schools!

[1] Common Era.

This view is not wrong. In fact, with it people have reached heroic levels of zeal and holiness. Yet today, we must say that by itself it no longer vibrates with the rhythm of our people's lives. It can no longer provide answers to many of our pain-laden questions. It is time for a Third Look.

The Third Look: Through the Eyes of the Poor. What is the Third Look? It could simply mean a view that follows the Second, once the Second is seen to be inadequate. More significantly, however, the Third Look is the view of the Third World peoples. It is a look at Jesus, his life and his work—by and through the eyes of the poor peoples of the Third World. It is the look at Jesus by the poor and oppressed, the awakened, struggling and selfless poor, who want to create a just, humane and sustainable world. It is also the view of people who themselves are not poor but are in genuine solidarity with the poor.

The next paragraph deserves special attention:

First and Third Looks Are Cousins. The Third Look is very similar to the First. For example, let us see how the First and Third Looks would see Jesus in the face of hunger and hungry people. The Third Look would be ill-at-ease with a Jesus that says: 'Hunger is the will of God, a cross God sends you now in order for you to gain merits for heaven.'

The Third Look would be in search of a Jesus who says: 'I want to see you freed from hunger.' Well, that in fact is the way Jesus sees himself. The Jesus who wants to feed rather than the Jesus who wants to inflict pain is the First Look Jesus. Thus, the concerns and questions of the conscientized poor are similar to those of Jesus – as I hope to re-discover with you, dear reader(s). The First and Third Looks are first cousins. The Second Look is a distant relative.

Jesus and the Poor Share the Same Point of View. Jesus and the poor stand on the same ground and view life from a similar vantage point. This is a fact which will become more and more of an insight as we proceed.

Heaven or New Earth? In this introductory chapter where we are mapping out our journey, I am just offering some examples. Let us take another example. Here is a question that concerns all of us: 'Where are we finally going? What is our ultimate destiny?' The Second Look would answer, 'heaven.' Third and First Looks say: 'new heaven and new earth!' There is a world of a difference between the two goals, and, consequently on the kind of life-journey that one takes to get there. The Second Look wants souls to go to heaven above. The Third and First Looks invite people to journey toward a new world on earth, right here.

Dialogue with Philippine Church. The Second Plenary Council of the Philippines (PCP II) is a cause for celebration in Philippine Church history.[2] The First and Third Looks are echoed in PCP II. None of the desiccated Jesus, abstracted from real life, preserved in immobile theological formulas, but rather a Jesus that has

[2] PCP II was a national gathering of lay, religious, bishops and clerics, held in Manila in January-February 1991.

life and motion and story. PCP II says, in a way uncharacteristic of Church formulations: 'We have to *retell his story* to ourselves, that we may, more credibly, more authoritatively, tell it to others. This is our belief.' [3]

PCP II was more interested in telling Jesus' story than drafting formulas and definitions about Jesus and his nature. Yet, because PCP II is only a document and is only a beginning, the First and Third Looks are still sending beeper messages to much of Philippine catechesis, theology, liturgy, pastoral activity and even spirituality: with what Look do we, the Philippine Church, see Jesus, his message and many other consequential things?

Contact with the Poor. What do we do to understand Jesus properly? The answer is clear ... and hard: We need to see Jesus through the eyes of the poor in struggle. Without living contact with the poor, knowing Jesus is a most difficult task—even for people who have given much thought and study to Jesus. Contact with the poor is not the same as concept of the poor. Once this difficult task is faced and done, however, rediscovering Jesus is easy, even pleasant. After all, Jesus was basically an unsophisticated person, not a metaphysical puzzle. It was only later that followers spun a complex theology around him.

The lives of the poor are like the great rivers Mekong, Ganges, Jordan. Contact with the poor is like contact with a river. When you encounter it, you can wet your feet in it and move on. You can build a bridge or ride a *banca* to cross it. Or you can pause to bathe, to drink, to refresh. I do not mean that the poor are perfect people. I mean that their lives, including their misery, can play the role of baptismal waters in our lives. Some form of immersion in that river can cleanse, nourish and refresh our often uninteresting spiritualities.

This contact with the poor is quite important. Without it, anyone who has read this far, would do well to just put this book aside. The danger is not that of not understanding. The danger is understanding without insight. It is as if someone mistakes dream for reality. The consequences can be fatal. Therefore, to those who, out of a good heart, might be tempted to use this book in teaching Christology, but without some significant immersion among the poor, I say: 'resist and desist.'

Tool for Interpreting the Bible. Biblical scholars use a supermarket of instruments—historical, archaeological, linguistic, literary, form-critical, redactional, structural, sociological. This book makes sober and discerning use of these instruments. But it adds another: the Third Look. Yes, the Third Look is a 'tool' for biblical interpretation. One's world-view, perspective, standpoint—all this makes a difference in one's interpretation of Jesus, of the Scripture, in fact, of life itself. There is indeed a battery of sophisticated tools for dissecting the Scriptures and you might be in control of them, but if your world-view is a mismatch to that of Jesus, you could miss. It is equally possible for someone, with no such bag of tools but possessing a heart and mind similar to that of Jesus, to see.

---

[3] The italics are in the original.

The Third Look and Other Methods. These past 100 years have given the world an outburst of invaluable methods of biblical interpretation. We have learned, for instance, that the gospels are not tape recordings of Jesus' words and deeds but reflect as well the faith meanings of the early Church and the gospel writers. Yet these methods, like most inventions of mice and men, have their limitations and problems. Perhaps it is because hard cold steel is being applied to cut up *life*. And that is what the gospel text is about, life. It is about the life and times of the biblical *people*. The word 'mechanistic' has sometimes been used to refer either to the method or to the user. For example, it is claimed that Jesus never associated with tax collectors and sinners. Is that really so?

Let us use an alternative route. The Jesus-story would certainly have a core. With the judicious use of accepted methods, it is possible to identify such a core. In that core, as we will see, you would find Jesus' Kingdom proclamation, his mission statements, his proclamation of good news to the poor, plus a few other constituents. In that core we will discover a Jesus who is eminently concerned for the poor and marginals. Given such a core, it is easier to see a Jesus who would not mind being seen with tax collectors and the poor, many of whom were tagged 'sinners' in Jesus' time. Association with such marginals would not jar with the *spirit* of such a Jesus, in fact, would be in harmony with it.

Here, by the way, is an important reason why the Third Look is a tool for interpretation: the core of the Jesus-story is Third World in essence; it has all the smells and aura of the Third World. Jesus is a Third World person – this we will see gradually as the story unfolds. Thus, the Third Look together with the other accepted methods, in dialectical complementarity, can give us a better grasp of who Jesus is.

Main Tool. In this book, then, I either use or presuppose contemporary methods, principally the 'historico-critical' and 'sociological' tools of interpretation,[4] but our main tool is the Third Look, a set of eyeglasses, if you will, that looks at Jesus through the prism of the Third World poor ... and thus hopefully through the eyes of Jesus himself. This prism is indispensable for rediscovering the original Jesus. This, of all the instruments for biblical interpretation, is by far the most important ... and the most neglected. In its simplest form, it can take the form of asking: 'what questions or concerns would the poor put to Jesus and to the gospel text?'

Inaccurate Bible Translations. The First and Third Looks also question certain inaccurate translations of the Bible. The Good News Bible, a translation by middle class Americans for middle class Americans, renders: 'Happy are those who are humble for they shall receive what God has promised' (Mt 5:5). What is it that God has promised? This Second Look mis-translation is shy about telling us what it is. Heaven perhaps?

---

[4] Norman K. Gottwald, Richard A. Horsley, Ched Myers, Juan Luis Segundo, Porfirio Miranda, Norman Perrin and Helen Graham will spot my use of their contributions to good biblical scholarship. I hope that it is in the spirit of the Third World to treat their contributions as treasure shared in common rather than as private property to be itemized through individual footnoting.

But Jesus' original version is unequivocal and unmistakable: '... for they shall *inherit the land*' or '... they *shall possess the earth*!' The salvation promised here is the good solid earth! This is Jesus' First Look, and the safest access to it is through Third Look eyeglasses or the eyes of the poor.

Cosmic Christ. One of the significant re-discoveries of the Third Look, especially in Asia, is the Christ of whom it is said: 'in him all things hold together' (Col 1:17). This Christ is hardly discernible in Second Look spirituality. The oneness of all things in Christ is the Christian equivalent to the inter-connectedness of all reality attested to by oriental and indigenous religions and by contemporary physics. The door that opens to this cosmic Christ is internal silence rather than rational religiosity.

The Enemy: Fear. A Third Look reading has one big enemy, fear. We have grown up with a certain tradition in our homes or in the seminary. We are secure and comfortable in it. We fear something which does not look quite like that tradition, even if it is shown to be inadequate. Some years ago, liturgical language was shifting from Latin to the vernacular. A regular church-goer was heard to say: 'I do not go to a vernacular mass because they no longer use the language of Jesus!' We know, of course, that Jesus' language was Aramaic, not Latin! Would that this person did indeed go beyond the Latin and Western tradition, all the way back to Jesus himself. Such is the modest effort in this book—to go back, via the Third Look, not only to the language but also to the original Jesus. Hopefully we will do this with discernment and prudence, but without the fear that cripples. Though perhaps sorely tempted, Jesus had no such fear in the face of the accepted tradition of his day. Could it be because he was in touch with the Source?

Frame of Mind. The following dispositions would be desirable: (1) The open mind of someone in search. One who is happy with the way things are may not find anything here to nourish his/her spirit. (2) A critical mind that says: 'Show me.' This critical attitude would be occupied mostly in scrutinizing the biblical data to check whether the Third Look is the correct reading. (3) A spirit of prayer.

About the First Look Too. Although the title of this book is *A Third Look at Jesus*, it is as much about the First Look. We look through the eyes of the poor, and, in so doing, we rediscover the First Look and the original Jesus of biblical tradition. A rural missionary Sister said it well: 'I understood the Jesus of the Bible through the eyes of the poor.'

Having made the rediscovery, we then have a Jesus who can interact with our lives today. *It is this biblical Jesus, and no other, that we should invite to be in dialogue with us today*.

I believe that the heart of contextual theology is the dialogue between the biblical Jesus and our life today.

Self-Critique. In many ways, this book is about my own passage – or should I say, struggle – from the Second Look to the First and Third Looks. Critique of the Second Look is self-critique as well. It is, however, not an invitation to self-flagellation. It is a spur to move on. Above all, it is Jesus and his invigorating memories that give us the challenge and inspiration to make the passage.

Road Map and Signposts. We need a road map and signposts. Data from the Scriptures will be our signposts. Mark, Matthew, Luke, and Jesus himself will provide the signposts for much of the Jesus-story up until his death on the cross. This portion of the Jesus-story—the pre-crucifixion ministry of Jesus – has to recover the autonomy that it has lost through the centuries, having been made to serve basically as only a preamble to the cross. The Third Look, more than the Second, has the resources for the retelling of this pre-crucifixion story.

From the cross to Christ's coming again, including the risen and cosmic Christ, is another portion of the Jesus-story. For this portion, our main signposts will be supplied by Paul, John, and the rest of the New Testament Scriptures. The Hebrew Scriptures – usually referred to as the 'Old Testament' – will also provide information. We will therefore attempt a *biblical* reporting on Jesus. It is not a 'systematic theology' on Jesus. Although as students, my classmates and I were privileged to study under the reputedly most renowned systematic theologian in the Catholic Church, it was biblical studies that taught me several liberating insights. One of them is that Jesus eludes systems, including the one we have saddled ourselves with today.

A Companion. In this book, I would like to be simply a companion, explaining the road map and pointing to the roadsigns. I hope to be pardoned if most of the conversation seems like a monologue. I will make efforts to remember that with me are co-travelers who one day may sit down and chat with, and even interpellate, me.

A Guidebook along a Road Least Traveled. I was wondering, dear reader, in what way this book might be of use to you. After a season of groping, I realize that this could serve as a guidebook. It is a guidebook not only for us in the Third World but also for anyone who wants to retrace their steps back to the original Jesus and to *re-discover the total story of Jesus*. It is a guidebook *through a road least traveled*.

Indispensable. Indispensable for our journey are the biblical data which will perform the role of *signposts,* and, *the Third Look eyeglasses*. Of course, you, dear co-traveler, will put on these eyeglasses on a trial basis. But hopefully you will come to the happy realization that through them you are looking at the real Jesus.

Let this be an adventure of the scholarly mind, but also of the seeker-heart.

Knowing without Knowing. One vital remark before we set out. In this book, we will need to make use of words and thoughts; and the scholarly mind will be busy at work. However, I wish to remind you of another way of 'knowing' Jesus. It is a way of knowing Jesus *beyond* the mind. It is being *in touch* with 'the Christ who lives in me' (Gal 2:20) *without words, without thoughts*. It must be said emphatically that this silent way of 'knowing without knowing' is infinitely superior. There is no authentic knowing of Jesus without it. Therefore, although this kind of knowing will receive quantitively far less space in this book, I would like to assume that you, dear reader, are or will be engaged in knowing Jesus beyond the mind. As a reminder, there will be a little watchword at the end of each chapter: 'Be still and know ...' (Ps 46:10).

The How. Knowing without knowing, knowing beyond the mind—how to go about this? Well, since it is more a way of being than a discipline, there really is no 'how to.' However, one may speak of facilitating 'methods' and there are a thousand and one such 'methods.'

One simple method is a favorite Eastern practice of being aware of your breath as you inhale and exhale; in so activating your awareness, you minimize the mad circus—thought tumbling after thought—in your mind. Being thus aware of something simple, your breathing, you have more or less evacuated your mind of its clatter, chatter and clutter. You will have gone 'beyond the mind' to a lesser or greater degree. By that very fact you are on the way or already in touch with a silent point in your being, the 'Christ in me' (Gal 2:20). You have made the crossing from thought to simple awareness, from your surface I/me to your deepest self, which is the Divine in you. 'Knowing' without the mediation of word or thought; knowing by being in touch—what better way to know?

You may have fantastic success on first try, like a simple barrio lady I know ... or you may not. No matter. Be patient. Above all, be *playful*. Just a few minutes a day ... or more, as your hunger grows. All you have to do is be aware of your breath ... or of the silent Christ in you. Nothing more. Leave the rest to God. God is your best 'instructor.'

A Way of Becoming. Incidentally, this *way of being* is not just a *way of knowing*. It is also a *way of becoming*. I suppose many of us have entertained, with varying degrees of intensity, the wish to 'change,' to 'be transformed,' to 'make progress' in our spiritual life, 'to *become* better persons.' And we tried many ways and approaches. And perhaps with degrees of success, from pedestrian to phenomenal. Try this simple way of awareness. You might discover with others that it is not only a way of knowing, it is also a way of becoming.

But let us go now to the adventure of the Third Look at Jesus. Put on your Third Look glasses and let us go....

Be Still and Know.

Stopover 2

Where to Start ... Fisherfolk's Village (Jesus' Mission before His Death on the Cross)

OUR HOST: Fisherfolk at a Seaside Village

STARTING POINT: WHERE THE ACTION IS.

With our map as guide, let us start at a fishing village. Here the fisherfolk give us a piece of advice. Begin with this question, they say: 'What was the mission of Jesus?' Avoid questions such as: Who was Jesus? What is the meaning of the titles 'Son of God,' 'Son of Man,' 'Son of David,' etc. These are false starting points. They will take you through circuitous routes and lead to dead-ends. Plunge right away into where the action is. What is the life-purpose of this Jesus? We follow this wise bit of counsel from our hosts, who, like Jesus' first friends, are fisherfolk.

The Mission of Jesus According to the Second Look

The Second Look Looks at Jesus' Mission. What did Jesus want to do with his life? What was his mission? All three Looks will initially agree that his mission had to do with salvation. But what kind of salvation? The Second Look's typical answer is 'to atone for our sins' or 'to save souls' 'to bring us to heaven.' That answer, the First Look would reply, is incomplete. Why? The reason is not only that 'soul' is not the total person but also for a much broader reason. Let us see....

The Second Look Spelled Out. Spelled out in key words, my Second Look answer used to read as follows. 'Jesus came to earth with a mission to *die for my sins,* to gain *divine grace for my soul* in this life, so that after death *my soul may go to heaven,* where *it will see God face to face.'* I later improved this answer. Jesus died not only to save the soul but soul *and* body, I said. Well, this is indeed an improvement, but still a Second Look view; why this is so, we will gradually find out.

Experience tells me that a couple of decades after Vatican II, the Second Look is still held by the average Filipino Christian, including our unsuspecting hosts, the fisherfolk, who have been catechized and preached to by us. At one point in my own life, the Second Look provided excellent fuel for life and spirituality. It fed my desire to continue Jesus' work of saving souls. Today, how do I assess it? I will give a pastoral answer and a biblical answer.

Pastorally Inadequate. In the exercise of pastoral ministry, my Second Look view can not adequately cope with the totality of human needs today. Although belief in Jesus' redemptive death should be part of the faith of our fisherfolk hosts, the Church's ministry to them cannot be limited to saving their souls from sin, providing them sanctifying grace and sending them off to heaven. Food, good health, decent livelihood, fishing grounds, freedom from exploitation, coral reefs and swamps for small fisherfolk are also their concerns. Well, what to do with such concerns?

> According to a typical Second Look view, these concerns are not 'spiritual'; therefore, they are not strictly speaking, part of the business of salvation. Or, they may be conceded some significance, but only because of the needs of the present time – and they are passing needs. Or, they may be vaguely perceived to be a matter of salvation but 'how' or 'why' is not clear to the Second Look. These flawed stances make it difficult to respond adequately not only to the concerns of our fisherfolk but generally to the pastoral challenges of our time.

Biblically Correct but Inadequate. Biblically, this Second Look answer is *basically* correct but *incomplete.* This requires an explanation:

> It is *correct* because, according to a frequent declaration in the New Testament, especially John and Paul, Jesus' mission had to do with atonement for sin through his death. Take a look at our first signpost.

In this is love, not that we loved God but that he loved us and *sent his Son to be the atoning sacrifice for our sins.* (1 Jn 4: 10)[5]

My Second Look view then is correct and biblical. However, it is also, biblically speaking, *incomplete.* Let me explain:

From the Point of View of Eternity. Taking a vantage point in eternity, it can indeed be said that Jesus' mission is to die for sin. Thus, 1 Jn 4:10 says that Jesus was sent to expiate for sins. That is a reading from the vantage point of God's 'eternal now,' outside the space and time of our human history.

Inside History. *However*—and this is the critical point at issue—*inside history*, we must see Jesus' life story in the following way. *On the cross:* When he was hanging *on the cross*, Jesus' mission was indeed to die for sin.[6] *But before that,* in an *earlier phase in his career*, the biblical signposts speak of a mission which is not right away that of dying for sin. What that pre-crucifixion mission was, we will see in a moment. But first, a parallel illustration.

Archbishop Romero: A Parallel. A parallel may help. Archbishop Romero was a defender of the poor in El Salvador, Central America. He was shot and killed at the church altar. Let us say that when he was hit by the assassin's bullet, he made an intention of offering his death in atonement for the sin of his assassin. (This is only one of an infinite number of intentions he could have made. For example: 'I offer this death for those courageously working for the poor in my diocese ... or for victims of child abuse ... or for battered women,' etc.) At that moment at the altar, his mission became that of dying in atonement for his assassin's sin.

But before that, in an earlier phase of his life, Romero's mission was something else. His life-purpose before his death was the defense of the poor of El Salvador. Of course, there is a relationship and continuity between the two, but the earlier mission is not the same as the later one. Can something similar be said about Jesus? Yes, we not only can, but should. The biblical signposts invite, in fact, compel us. So, let us turn to the witness of the New Testament.

---

5 There are numerous other testimonies, such as:
For I handed on to you as of first importance what I in turn had received: that *Christ died for our sins* in accordance with the scriptures (1 Cor 15:3).
Consequently, when Christ came into the world, he said, "Sacrifices and offerings you have not desired, but a body you have prepared for me; in burnt offerings and sin offerings you have taken no pleasure. Then I said, 'See, God, I have come to do your will, O God' (Heb 10:5-7) Also: Rom 5:6-10; Jn 3:16; Mt 1:21; Mk 10:45 and many others.

6 Let us make this more precise: even before the cross—when he became aware of an impending death at the hands of his enemies and accepted and offered it as sin-offering, one can speak of his mission to die for sin. Thus Mk 10:45 depicts Jesus as saying: 'For the Son of man also came not to be served but to serve, and to give his life as a ransom for many.'

Mission, Not Words and Acts. Before we do that, let me interpose a clarificatory note. Our question is: What was the *mission* of Jesus? Our question is not simply: what did Jesus do or say? Jesus said: Love God and love neighbor. But to say that his mission was to teach love is not accurate. Jesus said: learn of me for I am meek and humble of heart. But it is incorrect to say that he came down to earth to teach us how to be humble, how to live. Jesus wished that his disciples and his Father be one. But he did not say that his mission was to bring disciples into union with the Father. We are not here discussing simply the words and deeds of Jesus, as some theological books might do.

Rather, in all that he did and said we are looking for the overarching purpose of his life.

THE MISSION OF JESUS ACCORDING TO THE FIRST AND THIRD LOOKS: THE REIGN-KINGDOM OF GOD

Wanted: Mission Statements. In our effort to get an insight into the mission of Jesus, what should we look for? Naturally, we should look for those statements whose unmistakable intention is to tell the reader about the mission of Jesus, about his life-purpose. Let us call these '*mission texts*.' Are there such? Yes.

Mission in Summary Form. We have some roadsigns from three different gospel writers. In these roadsigns, Jesus' mission is expressed in general and summary form:

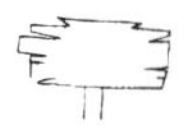

> Now after John was arrested, *Jesus came to Galilee, proclaiming the good news [gospel] of God*, and saying, 'The time is fulfilled, *and the kingdom of God has come near*; repent, and believe in the good news.' (Mk 1:14-15)
>
> Jesus *went throughout Galilee*, teaching in their synagogues *and proclaiming the good news of the kingdom* and curing every disease and every sickness among the people.... (Mt 4:23)
>
> Soon afterwards he went on through cities and villages, *proclaiming and bringing the good news of the kingdom of God*. (Lk 8:1)

Mission Statements: Reign-Kingdom of God. First, we must recognize these to be 'mission texts.' How so? Read well, but especially, listen well: Jesus went about the length and breadth of his land, absorbed, fixated almost, in one enterprise, that of proclaiming the Kingdom of God. Let us try a parallel once more Mother Teresa went about the streets and sidewalks of Pakistan, India and the world, picking up the dying poor of our planet. From the *tone* of such passages, it is obvious that the intention is to make plain to the reader the mission of Jesus and Mother Teresa.They are programmatic statements, telling the reader something about a basic charism and a program of action.

In fact, they are more than programmatic statements. The Mark and the Matthew statements are inaugural statements. They each, in their respective gospels, initiate the public career of Jesus.

What do these signposts say about Jesus' mission? They say that Jesus' mission was the proclamation of the *Reign-Kingdom of God*. All three evangelists are in one accord. The good news about the *Reign-Kingdom of God* was what Jesus broadcast to the fishing villages and elsewhere. This was his mission before he died on the cross.

Kingdom of God: Strand in Jesus' Career. Furthermore, these are not isolated statements in the New Testament. Re-read then the gospels some time. You will discover that the Kingdom of God is the single strand that runs through and binds the whole fabric of Jesus' career. By 'career,' I mean not only his earthly life, but as we will see, the whole range that will close with the 'second coming.'

And with what élan Jesus plunged into his life's work! With a certain irrepressible passion and heightened consciousness, Jesus says to Peter who wants Jesus to return to a certain town: 'Let us go on to the neighbouring towns, so that I may proclaim the message there also; for that is what I came out to do' (Mk 1:38).

And again:

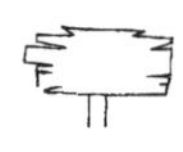

At daybreak he departed and went into a deserted place. And the crowds were looking for him; and when they reached him, they wanted to prevent him from leaving them. But he said to them, *'I must proclaim the good news of the kingdom of God to the other cities also; for I was sent for this purpose.'*

Mt 3:2; 4:17; (5:3,10); (6:10); 9:35; 10:7; 24:14; Mk 1:38-39; Lk. 9:2,11. See also Acts 8:12; 19:8; 20:25; 28:23; 28:31.

Jesus Enters the Stage of Human History. As Jesus enters history, his initial task is to proclaim the coming of final and definitive salvation, which, in his culture, is called Reign of God or Kingdom of God. The synagogues may already at this time have rung out with the plaintive plea: 'May your Reign-Kingdom be established soon and in our day!' This plea was lodged in the hearts of first-century Jews. To this plea Jesus responds: The Reign-Kingdom is at hand! It is drawing near!

Salvation = Kingdom of God. Incidentally, it is good to begin taking note of the following equivalence: salvation = Kingdom of God. For the rest of the journey, keep in mind that for Jesus and his culture, *final and definitive salvation meant the coming of the Kingdom of God.*

The Rest Is Commentary. The whole life and mission of Jesus hinges on this one sentence: "Jesus came into Galilee, proclaiming the gospel of God, and saying, 'The time is fulfilled, and the kingdom of God has come near ...'" (Mk 1:14-15). The brevity of this sentence is totally disproportionate to its importance. It is one of the weightiest sentences in the New Testament. The rest is commentary. In this sentence is expressed the whole historical message of Jesus and his original and initial mission. The one single focus was the Kingdom of God, present in the first coming of Jesus ... and consummated in his coming again in glory.

Succinctly, the life-purpose of Jesus, as it unfolded on our planet is this: on the cross his mission was to die in expiation for sin; before that, originally and initially, his mission was the proclamation of the Kingdom of God.

One Sure Historical Fact. As we take our first steps, it is encouraging to know that, from a scholarly point of view, we start on safe and secure ground. Jesus' proclamation of the Kingdom of God is the one sure historical fact about Jesus. Such is a virtual consensus among biblical scholars today. This safe and secure ground supplies an excellent take-off point for the rest of our quest.

Kingdom of God: Tentative Picture. If the pre-crucifixion mission of Jesus was centered on the Kingdom of God, our inquisitiveness should now be focused on: what is this Kingdom of God? Surprisingly perhaps, Kingdom of God, as Jesus spoke about it, is poorly understood by most Christians. Certainly, it is not enough to look up the dictionary under 'Kingdom' and 'God.' When shall we encounter a full discussion of the Kingdom of God? In the next stopovers, whose purpose, in fact, is a formal enquiry into the Kingdom of God.

For the time being, I offer a workable characterization of it: the Kingdom of God is a *new world on earth, to be consummated at the end of history.* It is *not* heaven.[7] According to our fisher-hosts, their catechism lessons always talk about heaven. We assure them that their pastor or catechist is not wrong in talking about heaven, but we add that that heaven, whatever meaning one attaches to it, is not the Kingdom of God.

The Kingdom of God, which is our ultimate destiny in the future will be a new earth here below. Furthermore, this new earth is filled with *life-blessings.* I intend to contrast '*life*-blessings' with 'spiritual grace.' Life-blessings are rice, fishing grounds, fish, education, good health and spiritual well-being—in short, any and every boon that gives any form of life. Life-blessings include, but are not limited to, spiritual grace, divine life, sanctifying grace or beatific vision.

Furthermore, these blessings come to *human beings, not to disembodied souls.*

For Jesus, there is indeed a heaven, Yahweh's abode in the firmament 'above,' but the Kingdom of God is *not* that heaven. Our fisherfolk, for whom land for vegetables and water for fish are precious, rejoice that the Kingdom of God is a new earth replete with life-blessings.

[7] I am aware that nowadays, especially under the influence of contemporary philosophy, 'heaven' has come to have many different meanings and non-meanings, such as the biblical meaning, the philosophical meaning, the popular meaning, the catechetical meaning, etc. which need not be gone into now. In any event, we should sedulously dissociate 'heaven' and 'Kingdom of God' from each other. For instance, the following is, at best, a faulty statement: 'The Kingdom of God is heaven on earth.' My insistence on keeping these two apart will, I hope, become gradually clear in our journey. Hopefully by mid-journey, we can differentiate between these two, just as we can tell sailboats apart from airplanes, bananas from mangoes.

A Note on Terminology: Reign-Kingdom. The Hebrew word *malkuth* – which is the basis for the New Testament Greek *basileia*—has two aspects: (1) 'reign,' 'rule,' 'sovereignty' (*paghahari*) and (2) 'kingdom' (*kaharian*). Hebrew has only one word for both these aspects. Each aspect complements and implies the other. Some of our modern translations render 'Reign of God,' with 'Kingdom' implied; others render 'Kingdom of God,' with 'Reign' implied. I prefer 'Kingdom of God,' because it is less abstract and, in its concreteness, conveys more satisfactorily the original biblical meaning.

Sharpening the Focus

The Proclaimed Is Not the Proclaimer. By this time, anyone of us can say in our sleep: Jesus' mission before the cross was to proclaim the Kingdom of God. But before we sit back and relax, let us take note. The proclaimer is not the proclaimed. The proclaimed is the Kingdom of God, the new earth. The proclaimer is Jesus. The two are not the same. The Kingdom is not Jesus. Jesus is not the Kingdom. This is so notwithstanding the inexact assertions of some theologians.

It will not do to make the *philosophical* statement that where Jesus is, there the Kingdom also is. Historically and biblically, it is inaccurate and misleading. Pastorally, it is dangerous. It allows one to say: 'The Kingdom is where Jesus is. Well, Jesus is in the chapel, in the Holy Scriptures, in my heart. So I need not be on the lookout for the Kingdom of God elsewhere ... and get involved.' A convenient escape hatch indeed. So syllogisms are a poor substitute for reality.

While on the subject of philosophy and syllogisms, we take note in passing of our penchant for abstract, philosophical language. For example, I used to think that the more abstract I was, the more profound. I liked to hear myself talk about 'the dignity of man'—until I heard Jesus talk simply about food for the hungry, sight to the blind, land to the meek. Jesus was not a philosopher. He was closer to the earth and therefore to the heart ... and to the truth.

Kingdom of God Not Identified With the Cross. One more lingering issue: is not the Kingdom of God identical with the cross? Was not the Kingdom of God realized precisely when Jesus gained salvation on the cross? The answer is no. According to a claim made by Jesus, the Kingdom of God was already present *long before* his saving death on the cross. Referring evidently to healings and saving deeds during his lifetime and *before* his death, Jesus pointedly told the pharisees that the Kingdom of God was already present. Similarly, Jesus pointed to his exorcising activity during his lifetime and *before his death*. Look, he said, the Kingdom of God has come upon you!

Once Jesus was asked by the pharisees when the kingdom of God was coming, and he answered, "The kingdom of God is not coming with things that can be observed; nor will they say, 'Look, here it is!' or 'There it is!' For, in fact, *the kingdom of God is among you.*" (Lk 17:20-21)

> If it is by the finger of God that I cast out demons, then the *Kingdom of God has come upon you.* (Lk 11:20 = Mt 12:28)

No, the arrival of the Kingdom of God is not identical or contemporaneous with the saving death on the cross. It preceded his death on the cross.

More Specific Mission Statements: Lk 4:16-21; Mt 11:2-6

More Mission Statements: Lk 4:16-21; Mt 11:2-6. Are there other mission texts, texts whose intent is to convey the life-purpose of Jesus? There are, and they give a more graphic and concrete picture. Here are our next roadsigns:

Luke 4:16-21

> When he came to Nazareth, where he had been brought up, he went to the synagogue on the sabbath day, as was his custom. He stood up to read, and the scroll of the prophet Isaiah was given to him. He unrolled the scroll and found the place where it was written:
>
> 'The Spirit of the Lord is upon me,
> because he has anointed me
> to bring good news to the poor.
> He has sent me to proclaim release to the captives
> and recovery of sight to the blind,
> to let the oppressed go free,
> to proclaim the year of the Lord's favor.'
>
> And he rolled up the scroll, gave it back to the attendant, and sat down. The eyes of all in the synagogue were fixed on him. Then he began to say to them, '*Today this scripture has been fulfilled in your hearing.*' (Lk 4:16-21; cf. Isa 61:1-2)

In the Luke 4 statement, we have the very first words uttered by Jesus in his public ministry. Like our previous signposts, it is clearly a mission statement. In fact, it is more than that. In the gospel of Luke, too, it is an inaugural address. It is like the discourse given by nation leaders as they begin their term of office. Luke 4 inaugurates the public life of Jesus. All the episodes that precede—the infancy stories, the Jordan baptism, the temptation in the desert in chapters 1 to 4:13—are all introductory.

Luke 4:16-21 opens the curtain to the drama of Jesus' public ministry. The place is solemn: the synagogue, the place designated for prayer and studies. The time is solemn: the sabbath day. Jesus gets up before the people and makes a public disclosure of his agenda. He reads a portion from the scroll of Isaiah and, at the end, intones: 'Today this scripture has been fulfilled in your hearing.' He solemnly enunciates his life-purpose. He articulates his 'platform.' Although this episode is found only in the gospel of Luke and not in the other evangelists, it reflects features that belong to the life-purpose of the pre-crucifixion Jesus, since it harmonizes well with the core picture of Jesus that can still be pieced together. This will gradually become clear as we proceed.

Matthew 11:5-6

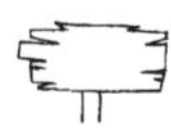

> When John heard in prison what the Messiah was doing, he sent word by his disciples and said to him, *'Are you the one who is to come,* or are we to wait for another?' Jesus answered them. *'Go and tell John what you hear and see*: the blind receive their sight, the lame walk, the lepers are cleansed, the deaf hear, the dead are raised, and the poor have good news brought to them. And blessed is anyone who takes no offense at me.' (Mt 11:2-6 = Lk 7:18-23)

This statement in Matthew 11 has even more chances of capturing those lineaments that belong to Jesus' pre-crucifixion life.[8] It is likewise a mission statement. John the Baptizer, while being detained behind bars, sends messengers to Jesus to ask about Jesus' identity. Who are you?—John wants to know. Are you the promised agent of salvation? John's question is equivalently an inquiry about Jesus' mission. What else would Jesus' response be but a declaration of mission?

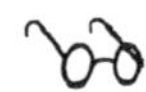

Pre-Crucifixion Mission: Well-Being for Humans. Matthew's and Luke's signposts that we have just looked at are declarations of Jesus' pre-crucifixion mission, that is, of his mission before he died on the cross. We shall be saying more about these two signposts later. For now, I ask you to make sure your Third Look glasses are on. Then, I ask you to take time out for a long critical look at the signposts.

Take note of a (pleasantly) startling discovery I once made. In these very foundational signposts, nowhere does Jesus say: 'The Spirit of the Lord is upon me so that I might die for the forgiveness[9] of sin.'[10] We do not hear him saying: 'Go and tell John that souls are being saved.' Why or why not? Were these particulars taken for granted by the evangelists? Or, did Matthew and Luke omit these through forgetfulness? No. Assumptions by the evangelists or their loss of memory are not viable explanations.

Rather Matthew 11 and Luke 4 are, thank God, happy remnants of a tradition regarding the pre-crucifixion mission of Jesus. And that mission is centered on salvation. But what form does salvation take? It takes the form of life-blessings such as health for the sick, life to the dead, liberation from poverty for the poor, freedom to the oppressed and prisoners.

Incidentally, let us not make light of Jesus by saying that he was referring to the 'spiritually sick,' those 'dead in mortal sin,' and so forth. The people that Jesus

---

8 This text, Mt 11:2-6 = Lk 7:18-23, is found in an old document, which ante-dates Matthew and Luke, and whose contents are considered to be close to what Jesus actually said.

9 The Greek word *aphesis*, which elsewhere is used for the release/forgiveness of sin, definitely does not refer to sin-forgiveness here in Lk 4, but to *release* of captives and *liberty* of the oppressed.

10 Note: we are not saying that Jesus did not forgive sins or that forgiveness of sins is not part of his mission. What we are pointing to is that it is not mentioned in key mission statements.

healed—the blind, the paralytic, the hemorrhaging woman, the dead Lazarus – are too real for such an interpretation. It is a form of overkill. Jesus is talking not about salvation of souls but about *well being for humans*. Small fisherfolk in our time, losing their traditional fishing grounds to high-tech trawlers, would warm up to this Jesus, wouldn't they?

The life-blessings cited in these signposts by Matthew and Luke—good news to the poor, sight to the blind, etc.—are, as we shall soon see, nothing less than concrete manifestations of the Kingdom of God. That is why these signposts are mission statements which spell out in detail what the previous mission statements about the Kingdom of God said in general terms.

Where Have All the Sinners Gone?

Sin and Sinners, Forgiveness. On the morrow, we continue our reflections. It has struck our fisher-hosts that so far very little has been said about sin and sinner. Yet press the Jesus button on a Second Look computer, like the one I used to have, and quite likely it will shower the screen with the words 'sin,' 'sinner,' 'forgiveness.' These are the almost mechanical associations I used to make with Jesus. Well, suspect a virus! That is what I have since learned. So then, let us examine the place of sin, sinners, conversion, forgiveness in Jesus' life and mission. It is helpful once more to use the framework 'Jesus on the cross' and 'Jesus before the cross.'

On the Cross. *On the cross*, Jesus died for all sinners. His sacrificial death gained forgiveness of sins for us. '... But God proves his love for us in that while we still were sinners Christ died for us' (Rom 5:8). There are many such attestations which deal with Jesus' act on the cross.[11]

During His Lifetime. How about *during his lifetime*? Did Jesus forgive sins and was this part of his mission? Yes, the gospel records testify that Jesus forgave sins, or rather more accurately, he forgave sins in the name of God. (The formula was 'Your sins are forgiven'; it was a roundabout way of referring to God while avoiding pronouncing his name.) And of course, conversion or forgiveness of sins is a life-blessing. And it belongs to the pre-crucifixion work (and mission) of Jesus.

---

[11] In such instances, there is no intention to deny or void Jesus' pre-crucifixion activity:
They *put him to death by hanging him on a tree*; but *God raised him on the third day* and made him manifest... And he commanded us to preach to the people, and to testify that he is the one *ordained by God to be judge of the living and the dead*. This is preceded by: You know the word which he sent to Israel, *preaching good news of peace by Jesus Christ* (he is Lord of all), the word which was *proclaimed throughout all Judea, beginning from Galilee* after the *baptism which John preached*: how *God anointed Jesus of Nazareth with the Holy Spirit and with power*; how *he went about doing good and healing all that were oppressed by the devil*, for God was with him. And we are witnesses to *all that he did both in the country of the Jews and in Jerusalem*. (Acts 10:36-42)

To a paralytic whom he cured, Jesus said 'Son, your sins are forgiven' (Mk 2:1; also Lk 7:48; 19:1-10).

Mk 2:17; Mt 9:13: Another Mission Statement (?) and Its Interpretation. In fact, there is a statement which has the tonality of a mission statement: 'I have come to call not the righteous but sinners' (Mk 2:17; Mt 9:13).

Here is our road-sign:

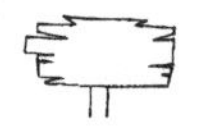

And as *he sat at dinner* in Levi's house, *many tax collectors and sinners were also sitting with Jesus* and his disciples—for there were many who followed him. When the scribes and the pharisees saw that *he was eating with sinners and tax collectors,* they said to his disciples, 'Why does he *eat with tax collectors and sinners*?' When Jesus heard this, he said to them, 'Those who are well have no need of a physician, but those who are sick; *I have come to call not the righteous but sinners.*' (Mk 2:15-17; Mt 9:10-13). Luke has an addition: 'I have come to call not the righteous but sinners to *repentance.*' (Lk 5:32; 15:1-32)

How do we assess such a statement? First, a preliminary observation: the 'I came (in order) to' type of statements, such as this, may not be original Jesus sayings but formulations of the later Christian community. Be that as it may, let us give it a chance. The most obvious interpretation of that statement is, of course, that Jesus' mission had to do with forgiveness of sins and sinners. But is this the only possible interpretation? Is it even the right one?

A Parallel: Social Not Moral Interaction. Let us see whether we can sensitize ourselves to still another possible reading of this statement. To help us, let us first take a parallel example of a social worker who is at the same time a priest. He interacts with the so-called dregs of society such as prostitutes, thieves, and drunks. One level of interaction – and the most significant – is to socialize with them. He eats, drinks and enjoys himself with these people, whom society self-righteously labels 'sinners.' It is farthest from his mind to administer sacramental confession or to forgive their sins. Whether they are moral transgressors or not is not the issue for him. His dealings with them are more social than religious or moral.

Different from Sacramental. This level of interaction is different from still another plane in which he exercises his priestly charism of forgiving sins. He hears the confession of those who ask and he bestows forgiveness on them. However, this is not his typical or usual way of relating with these unpretentious people.

Who Were the 'Sinners' in Jesus' Time? Our sources bid us see Jesus in the same light. Who were the 'sinners'? And what were Jesus' dealings with them? There were prostitutes, thieves and drunks in his society. Were they real sinners? Only God knows. In any case, that is beside the point. (Our fisherfolk concur.) In point of fact, however, many of these human beings were most likely not moral malefactors, just plain unsuspecting victims of poverty. Such were perhaps many of the prostitutes and thieves. Or, many of these so-called sinners were the illiterate poor who were untaught and uninitiated in their catechism (the Torah[12] and rabbinical teachings), and so they violated regulations of ritual purity. The self-righteous elite loved to stick the label 'sinners' on them.

With 'sinners' are paired off the tax-collectors. They collected more than they were supposed to (Lk 3:13) and they worked for the hated Romans. They were sinners in the eyes of people like the pharisees[13] who liked to think of themselves as enlightened and respectable.

Jesus' *Tuba* Ministry. What was Jesus' 'ministry' to these sinners, imagined or real? Was it a sanctimonious mission of whipping up his ever-ready stole to shrive and absolve every drunk or adulteress that came his way? Not quite —is the correct guess of our fisher-hosts, who, while some were roasting squid, others were opening the Scriptures where the records say: Jesus ate and drank with them. Can you imagine Jesus today having *tapsilog*[14] lunch with pickpockets and prostitutes at a *turo-turo*[15] joint? Or can you see him drinking *tuba* (coconut wine) with our unpretentious fisherfolk at a seaside village?

Lunch or Party? We said, 'having lunch.' In fact, that is perhaps too mild. He apparently had a great good time, resolutely overstepping the iron fences of respectability. Neither the ritual nor social etiquette of the pharisees seemed to be in Jesus' priority-list of correct behavior. For again, the records say he loved food and drink. Jesus was '... a glutton and a drunkard, a friend of tax collectors and sinners!" (Mt 11:19; Lk 7:34; Mt 21:31). Of course, these words are not Jesus' self-description; they are rather a censure from his enemies. Yet, it is remarkable that we do not find much trace of disavowal or self-defense on the part of Jesus or the evangelists.

Kasalo-salo Siya sa Hapag ng mga Anak Pawis.[16] Jesus encountered 'sinners' during his lifetime. But we must not rush to construct a Jesus, forgiving sins at the drop of a hat. And the so-called sinners were not always morally bad people. Many of them stole, sold their bodies, got drunk or just violated a rule of ritual purity – all because they were poor and knew no better. Jesus' typical life-style with them is to fraternize with them, dipping his whole being into the common eating bowl of the ostracized. *Kasalo-salo siya sa hapag ng mga anak pawis.* Our hosts chuckle approvingly.

---

[12] The books of Genesis through Deuteronomy. Although it is (inaccurately) translated "law," the word actually means 'instruction.' For all intents and purposes, the Torah was the religio-civil constitution and legal corpus of the people Israel. It consisted not only of legal material but also of history.

[13] Let me anticipate an observation which I will make later in our journey. In the interest of historical accuracy, we note (1) that in their origins the pharisees were a courageous and 'prophetic' group; (2) that our gospel records, as they stand, are colored by an antagonistic spirit of a time later than Jesus; (3) that not all of the pharisees and scribes were 'bad.' Compared to sadducees, the pharisees were liberal, progressive and populist.

[14] An inexpensive meal consisting of a handful of rice, a piece of dried meat, egg and a bottle of soft drink.

[15] An inexpensive roadside eatery where customers pick out food from a selection on display.

[16] He shares the table with the pariahs of society

Back to Mk 2:17; Mt 9:13: An Alternative Reading. Thus, although indeed Jesus forgave sins and sinners before he died on the cross, his more typical interaction with them had as much of a social as a religious tonality – in fact, more. So, now, after having had a feel of Jesus' life-context, let us go back to our roadsign. 'Those who are well have no need of a physician, but those who are sick; I have come to call not the righteous but sinners.' Even if this were considered a bona fide mission statement, how should it be understood?

The 'sick' and 'sinners' – in the lifetime of Jesus, these words *could*, of course, refer to moral transgressors.[17] The designation 'sick' and 'sinners' in this case would have a religio-moral significance. *But* 'sick' and 'sinners' could also refer to the bent and broken members of the human community, victims of the systemic dynamics of society.

'The righteous and those who are well' *could*, of course, refer to the morally upright. *But* more likely than not, it referred to people who *thought* they were and called themselves 'righteous.'

Could Jesus then be saying: 'I have come to call *not those who call themselves righteous* but *those whom they call* sinners. I, the physician, extend my Kingdom-call and life-blessings not to self-appointed saints but to the broken members of our human community—the tax-collectors, thieves, prostitutes.' (Remember that, as reported by the evangelists and as a likely enough setting, this saying of Jesus was pronounced in the company of tax-collectors, sinners, pharisees.) Dial to the right frequency to pick up the ironic banter in Jesus' words. Thus, this saying (Mk 2:15-17; Mt 9:10-13), need not be a grand manifesto of a mission to forgive sins and sinners. In fact, the opposite may be true: it is another version of 'good news to the poor.'

Inadequate and Adequate Résumés of Jesus' Mission. Forgiveness of sins in the pre-crucifixion stage of Jesus' life was part of his mission. But it is incorrect to think that 'sin and forgiveness of sin' is the adequate and complete résumé of Jesus' mission. Rather, health for the sick, life for the dead, liberation for the poor and similar blessings are also integral to the mission of Jesus.

Sin and Its Effects and Consequences? 'Way back in high school, I used to think that Jesus' mission could all be put under the grand rubric of 'sin,' an opinion buttressed by the following imprecise notion: "Sickness, death, injustice are all simply 'effects' and 'consequences' of sin. Thus, when he heals the sick, he is dealing with the effects of sin. When he forgives sin, he is dealing with the cause of sickness." Such a view is rather commonplace—which makes our hosts wonder whether their lung and gastric illnesses are a punishment for their sins or rather the byproducts of a social system.

---

[17] Among them, according to Luke (Lk 15:1-24; 18:9-14) were 'prodigal sons' whom Jesus found more ready for conversion than were the pharisees and scribes; and Jesus was happy when they repented.

What was Jesus' view? On one occasion, he seemingly subscribes to the theology that the cause of sickness is sin. In curing the paralytic, instead of saying, 'Stand up and take your mat and walk'? (Mk 2:9) he said, 'Your sins are forgiven.'

This would have been reason enough to peg Jesus immovably to a sickness-is-an-effect-of-sin theology, were it not for a bit of loose soil in the gospel of John. Jesus once passed by a man, blind from birth. His disciples asked him, 'Rabbi, who sinned, this man or his parents, that he was born blind?' Jesus answered, *'Neither this man nor his parents sinned*; he was born blind so that God's works might be revealed in him' (Jn 9:1-3). This saying of Jesus could help us to channel our energies less to moralizing speculation and more to making God's healing works manifest.

Sharpening the Focus Some More

Even If Jesus Did Not Die On the Cross. Let us make one more claim which may sound somewhat shocking : even if Jesus did not die on the cross, he already had a full-grown mission, namely, the pre-crucifixion mission of proclaiming the Kingdom of God! This is the way to read the biblical evidence. Archbishop Romero had his own 'pre-crucifixion' mission before he died on his cross! We must make this same claim about Jesus' mission clearly and strongly. We have at least two reasons. One is: in order to be faithful to the biblical data. The other is: Jesus' pre-crucifixion mission helps us to appreciate our own mission in the world today and its biblical foundations.

From Diapers to Loin-Cloth. To see Jesus passionately nurturing a death-wish from the start is to make of him a suicidal case. And such theology was and is not uncommon. Consider our Christmas carols, Christmas cards and Christmas poems. Some of them depict the unsuspecting Babe on the manger already fantasizing his cross! Only later did I realize that this view, which used to be a precious part of my piety, is pure heresy, distilled through centuries of mis-information.

For though Jesus was indeed divine, he was also truly human. But I did not allow him to grow, as Luke does. 'And Jesus increased in wisdom and in years, and in divine and human favor' (Lk 2:52). I was and am not alone. We make the Babe in diapers put on the loin-cloth of the Crucified! And ponder this: Christmas cards and carols are merely reflections of a still prevailing non-biblical catechism and theology! Let us not rush Jesus. Let us give him his space. Let us not make him a pathological misfit.

Anticipatory Statements. But, come to think of it, is it not Matthew who puts the loin-cloth on the Baby Jesus? Does not Matthew in narrating the infancy years – in fact, the pre-infancy years—of Jesus say: '... She [Mary] will bear a son, and you are to name him Jesus, for he will save his people from their sins' (Mt 1:21)? Let us try to clarify this matter by situating Matthew and this text. Any storyteller, living after the death and resurrection of Jesus and with a lively consciousness of Jesus' death and its paramount significance, could tell the Jesus-story as if his mission from the start were to die for sin.

To come back to Archbishop Romero. During his early years, Archbishop Romero's mission was certainly not to die for the sin of his assassin. And yet it is possible for his biographer, writing after his death, and writing about his infancy, to say: 'This baby's mission is to die for the sin of his assassin.' So too, Matthew's statement anticipates the cross without voiding the initial mission of Kingdom-proclamation.

Who Do They Say I Am. What about that classical text in which Jesus asks Peter, 'Who do people say that I am?'

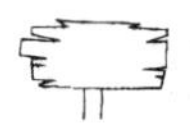

> Jesus went on with his disciples to the villages of Caesarea Philippi; and on the way he asked his disciples, '*Who do people say that I am*?' And they answered him, 'John the Baptist; and others, Elijah; and still others, one of the prophets.' He asked them, 'But who do you say that I am?' Peter answered him, '*You are the Messiah*.' And he sternly ordered them not to tell anyone about him. Then he began to teach them that the Son of Man must undergo great suffering, and be rejected by the elders, the chief priests, and the scribes, and *be killed*, and after three days rise again. He said all this quite openly. And Peter took him aside and began to rebuke him. (Mk 8:27-32; Mt 16:13-23; Lk 9:18-22)

This text is certainly a mission text. But it can be misread as follows: Jesus' mission is to be the redeemer who will die for sin and rise again. Rather, what we have in these texts is the following. Jesus who is perceived to be a prophet and confessed to be the Messiah is the Son of Man who *will be killed*. But *nothing* is said about dying *for sin*.

Take a close look at our roadsign and make an accurate reading: the text speaks of being killed, but there is nothing about 'dying to atone for sin'! Casuistry has again split hairs, you will say. But no. Since this point will become clear later, a provisional explanation will do for the moment.

The death of Jesus has two aspects: (a) his being killed, which was the result of his Kingdom practice and his conflict with the authorities; and (b) his dying for the expiation of sin; this was the theological significance given to his death. Our present roadsign does not say 'he would die for sin.' It simply reports that he would be killed, executed, put to death. We will look into this more fully in Stopover 15 (on conflict in Jesus' practice) and Stopover 16 (on the death of Jesus).

The Lamb of God in John's Gospel. But, again, in John's gospel, is not Jesus from his first adult day called the Lamb of God, who will die a sacrificial death (cf. Jn 1:29)? Yes. But on this issue, John's gospel is rather a theological meditation than a report of a historical fact. Actually, John's gospel, which, more than the other gospels, is more meditation than history, does not even report Jesus' mission of proclaiming the Kingdom of God.

At His Baptism Perhaps? It is also alleged—with only debatable proof—that at his baptism, Jesus was already aware of his mission of atoning death. The better and more pleasant time to discuss this will be later when we reflect on the death of Jesus in Stopover 16.

Conversion and Kingdom of God: The Odd Couple

Jesus: Moral Conversion Is Only Part of a Bigger Affirmation. Now, let us go back to our principal roadsigns – Mk 1:14-15; Mt 4:23; Lk 8:1—and discuss a certain uncritical reading of them. It runs something like this: "Did not Jesus go about all Galilee, saying, 'The kingdom of God has come near; *repent*, and believe in the good news' (Mk 1:14-15)? This shows that his mission was to go about asking people to repent and to have their sins forgiven."

Such a view is only partially correct. It also puts the stress on the wrong place. Yes, Jesus did call people to repentance, or better, conversion. However, this challenge to conversion is only part of a bigger affirmation, the first and main part of which is the proclamation of the Kingdom of God. The focal point of Jesus' message is the Kingdom of God and its proclamation. Then follows the call to conversion. The Kingdom of God remains the principal part. But alas for some of my earlier preaching—rich in moralisms, poor in the Kingdom of God.

Preaching in the Early Church: Ditto. In the Acts of the Apostles, we are in touch with Church-life as it developed soon after the death and resurrection of Jesus. Similarly, an uncritical reading of the preaching of the early Church as recorded in the Acts of the Apostles, seems to suggest that the mission of the Church and of Jesus has to do only with sin, conversion, forgiveness. And Peter said to them, '*Repent*, and be baptized every one of you in the name of Jesus Christ *so that your sins may be forgiven*; and you will receive the gift of the Holy Spirit. For the promise is for you, for your children, and for all who are far away, everyone whom the Lord our God calls to him.' And he testified with many other arguments and exhorted them, saying, '*Save yourselves* from this corrupt generation' (Acts 2:38-40).

Yes, in the early Church's preaching there is a call to repentance and forgiveness of sins. But that call does not stand alone. It is coupled with the Kingdom-proclamation to which it is attached. The main message in the Acts of the Apostles remains, as with Jesus, the proclamation of salvation or Kingdom of God. Paul 'entered the synagogue and for three months spoke out boldly, and argued persuasively about the *kingdom of God*' (Acts 19:8. See Acts 8:12; 14:22; 20:25; 28:23,28). Repentance and forgiveness of sins don't stand alone in glorious isolation but are spoken of in view of obtaining healing, salvation, the Kingdom of God.

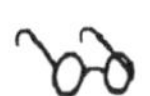

Conversion Not To Be Equated with Kingdom of God. Conversion and Kingdom thus go together. Yet, on the other hand, they are not identical. That brings us to another faulty understanding of conversion. We sometimes equate conversion with Kingdom of God. Kingdom of God is conversion of hearts. Conversion of hearts is Kingdom of God.

Again, a parallel may help. *Nanay* calls out to her children: 'I announce a super-special *adobo* for this coming week-end. Therefore, you have to be good during the week.' *Nanay's adobo* is one thing. The children's good behavior is another thing. Kingdom of God is one thing. Conversion is another thing. Kingdom of God and conversion are not to be equated. They are not the same.

The Kingdom of God is a new earth, announced by Jesus. Conversion, a change of life, is a moral act, a response by the disciple. Jesus proclaimed a new earth. In order to 'enter' it, the potential disciple had to input his moral act. Thus, while preparing a homily, deep into a Saturday night, it dawned on me that proclaiming the Kingdom of God is not the same as conversion or the call to conversion.

The Silent Treatment?

Omissions. Once we have put the pieces of the puzzle together, we can go on to pick up other interesting bits to enhance the picture. Remember the mission statements Lk 4:16-20 and Mt 11:2-5? They are mission statements par excellence. We have taken note of the striking fact that in these statements, forgiveness of sins, though it can be counted as part of Jesus' pre-crucifixion mission, is not one of the blessings mentioned. The blind see, the lame walk, captives are freed, etc. But there is no mention of sinners being forgiven!

Similarly, the beatitudes (Mt 5:3-10; Lk 6:20-21) offer something to tease the attentive mind. The beatitudes too are sources par excellence of Jesus' vision for the future of humankind and yet we do not have a beatitude which says: 'Blessed are sinners, for theirs is forgiveness of sins.' We have beatitudes for the hungry, the meek, the pure in heart, but not one for sinners.[18]

[18] Paul, quoting Ps 32:1-2, 'Blessed are those whose iniquities are forgiven, and whose sins are covered' has a beatitude on sin and sinner. But this makes it all the more striking. Paul does. Jesus does not.

Talking of omissions, it is ironic that our modern liturgy makes the inverse omission. Whereas the Scriptures omit mention of forgiving sins, our eucharistic liturgy extols only those Christ-events which are related to sin—'Christ has died, Christ has risen, Christ will come again' (to judge the living and dead) – and bypasses the Kingdom ministry of Jesus! Where is the Filipino church that reverberates with the acclamation 'Jesus went on through cities and villages, proclaiming and bringing the good news of the Kingdom of God!' before it celebrates his death, resurrection, and second coming?

PCP II and Jesus

PCP II is the work of the whole Philippine Church – lay, religious, clergy. It is an accomplishment which would warm the heart of the First Look Jesus. It asks, 'How to live as Christians? … The answer *cannot be abstract.* [19] For it leads us back to the person of Christ, Jesus *of Nazareth*.'

PCP II's Jesus is a First Look Jesus:

… Jesus who preached and worked miracles … He lived among us as our fellow human being, like us in all things, sin alone excepted. He underwent the process of human growth. He 'grew and became strong' and 'advanced in wisdom, and age and favor before God and man.' He lived the life of a carpenter, shared the life of the human community …

… In his own hometown he announced his mission solemnly, dramatically declaring. [It then quotes the mission statement of Lk 4:16-20].

The document continues in a disarmingly simple way: 'This is why we need to contemplate the face and the heart of Christ.'

PCP II is aware of the original mission of Jesus:

'Jesus proclaimed this Kingdom as a gift of God. It is a seed quietly sown…. God's Kingdom is the gift of salvation….

'But the Kingdom of God has already broken into our world. By the word and work of Jesus….' [20]

A Convenient Summary

John 10:10. 'I came that they may have life, and have it abundantly' (Jn 10:10). This sounds great. The First Look in a nutshell! However, a little caution is called for. In the context of John's gospel, 'life' carries the principal meaning of divine or eternal life. It approximates what the Second Look would call the 'life of grace.' It is narrower than the all-embracing scope of Jesus' mission. His mission encompasses

19 Italics in this section are mine.

20 See PCP II #35-40.

the totality of life-blessings. It includes, but is not limited to, the 'life of grace.' However, the statement of Jn 10:10, lifted momentarily out of the Johannine setting, is as radiant as a full moon on the surface of the fisherfolk's sea. For it glows with the soft brilliance and warmth of what Jesus' mission is all about—to bring life in all its fullness.

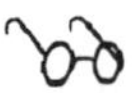

It has been a long day for us. It is getting to be evening. Our hosts invite us for a walk on the beach. After some conversation, we find ourselves naturally falling silent. We listen to the wavelets on the shore and feel their briny strokes on our feet. After these moments of stillness, we turn in for the night.

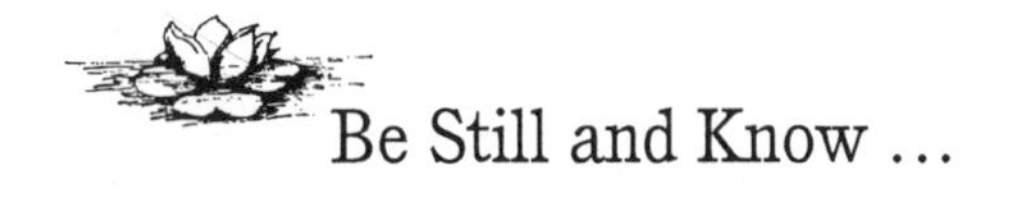

Be Still and Know ...

Stopover 3

Of Guavas and Golf Courses (The Kingdom of God According to Jesus Based on Isaiah)

OUR HOST: Peasants in a Vegetable Farm

Wanted: Meaning of Kingdom of God. Our sojourn at the fishing village acquainted us with the pre-crucifixion mission of Jesus, that of proclaiming the Kingdom of God. And now, what is this Kingdom of God? The roadsigns from this Stopover 3 to Stopover 12 will help us to find the answer to one question: *What* is the Kingdom of God according to the First Look? What was Jesus' understanding of the Kingdom of God?

Jesus and Isaiah. Jesus' vision of the Kingdom of God echoes the vision of Isaiah. Isaiah's writings could very well have been Jesus' favorite bedtime reading. Isaiah's words and images tend to reappear in Jesus' language.

ISAIAH: SALVATION AND KINGDOM OF GOD

Isaiah, A Rich Source. Isaiah will then provide us with our first set of signposts. Have you been to a vegetable farm bursting with a spectacular variety of vegetables and fruits? Isaiah's vision of the Kingdom of God can be compared to that. It is a rich harvest of vibrant details about the Kingdom of God. Accordingly, our roadmap now directs us to a community of fruit and vegetable growers.

The Book of Isaiah—according to the researches of modern scholarship—consists of two or three distinctive parts, authored by Isaiah and by two or three other people, living in different centuries (8th to 6th century B.C.E. [21]) In Jesus' time, no distinction was made among these parts. Neither do we make distinctions. For we are interested in Isaiah 'as Jesus read Isaiah.' Here is our signpost:

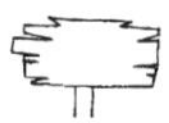

How beautiful upon the mountains
are the feet of the messenger who announces peace,
who brings *good news,*
who announces *salvation,*
who says to Zion, 'Your *God reigns.*' (Isa 52:7)

Get you up to a high mountain,
O Zion, herald of *good tidings;*
lift up your voice with strength,
O Jerusalem, herald of *good tidings,*
lift it up, do not fear;
say to the cities of Judah,
'*Here is your God!*' [or: 'The *Reign of God* is manifest.'] (Isa 40:9)

Then the *eyes of the blind shall be opened,*
and the *ears of the deaf unstopped;*
then the *lame shall leap like a deer,*
and the *tongue of the speechless sing for joy.*
For *waters shall break forth in the wilderness,*
and *streams in the desert.* (Isa 35: 5-6)

On that day the *deaf shall hear*
the words of a scroll,
and out of their gloom and darkness
the *eyes of the blind shall see.*
The *meek ['anawim] shall obtain fresh joy in the Lord,*
and the *neediest people shall exult in* the Holy One of Israel. (Isa 29:18-19)

The *spirit of the Lord GOD is upon me,*
because the LORD has anointed me;
he has sent me to bring *good news to the oppressed* ['*anawim*],
to *bind up the brokenhearted,*
to *proclaim liberty to the captives,*

[21] Before the Common Era.

and *release to the prisoners;*
to *proclaim the year of the Lord's favor.* (Isa 61:1-2)

Is not this the fast that I choose:
to loose the bonds of injustice,
to undo the thongs of the yoke,
to *let the oppressed go free,*
and *to break every yoke?* (Isa 58:6)

Here is *my servant,* whom I uphold,
my chosen, in whom my soul delights;
I have put *my spirit upon him;*
he will *bring forth justice to the nations.*
He will not cry or lift up his voice,
or make it heard in the street;
a bruised reed he will not break,
and a dimly burning wick he will not quench;
he will *faithfully bring forth justice.*
He will not grow faint or be crushed
until he has *established justice in the earth;*
and the coastlands wait for his teaching. (Isa 42:1-4)

Your *dead shall live, their corpses shall rise.*
O *dwellers in the dust, awake and sing for joy!*
For your dew is a radiant dew,
and the earth will give birth to those long dead. (Isa 26:19)

Also: Isa 52:7-10; 40:9-11; 35:1-10; 61:1-4; 29:17-21; 42:1-9; 26:19; 24:23; 51:4-5; 25:8

Isaiah: A Portrait of Salvation. Several centuries before Jesus, Isaiah was projecting his dream of a salvation to come.

The italicized words in our signpost are those that Isaiah used to draw his *portrait of future salvation*. Note that Isaiah's idea of salvation is not: souls going to heaven. Rather salvation is a bonanza of vivid human boons and blessings. Our hosts, fruit and vegetable farmers, are pleased.

But for a total appreciation of it, we must first take a closer look at one of the roadsigns, Isa 61:2 and get acquainted with the *'year of the Lord's favor.'*

Jubilee Year. There were two unique years in the biblical calendar. One was the sabbatical year, to be observed every 7 years. The other was the jubilee year, to be observed every 50 years. The *year of the Lord's favor* (Isa 61:2) of our signpost could refer to either or both. In our present text, it more likely referred to the jubilee year. Anyway, the provisions of the sabbatical year are incorporated in the jubilee year. The jubilee year is described in Leviticus 25. It is to be celebrated every 50th year.

The provisions of the jubilee year can truly warm the hearts of us in the Third World, with a particular appeal to peasants and farmers, such as our present hosts. For if you are a peasant, a favorite child of poverty for generations, Leviticus 25 tells you that (1) the land and house you were forced to sell due to poverty will all go back to you; (2) your 'pet' daughter who has had to serve as a housemaid in Manila or Athens will now be free and come home to you with sufficient economic security; (3) you will do well by letting your farm rest – rest from chemical fertilizers and rest from greed for excessive profit; (4) all the debts you have incurred from banks and usurers are wiped clean. Once more, our hosts, recalling perhaps a relative or two in overseas employment, smile with nostalgia.

Since the biblical jubilee year is hardly found in the pages of our Second Look catechism, I will lay it out a bit, by letting Leviticus 25 speak. It has the following provisions:

Restoration of property (fields, houses) to impoverished Israelites

> 'If anyone of your kin falls into difficulty and sells a piece of property (land or houses)' (v 25), a relative, or he himself, if his situation improves, may buy it back. But surely at the end of fifty years, he 'shall return to his property' (v 10,14,27). He 'returns to their ancestral property' (v 41).

Release of Israelite slaves

> 'If any who are dependent on you become so impoverished that they sell themselves ... they shall serve with you until the year of the jubilee. Then they and their children with them shall be free from your authority; they shall go back to their own family and return to their ancestral property' (39-41). As a slave 'you shall return every one of you to your family' (v 10). This is also a sabbatical year[22] provision.

Rest for the land

> 'You shall not sow, or reap the aftergrowth, or harvest the unpruned vines' (v 11). This is also a sabbatical year provision.

Cancellation of debts

> This is a sabbatical year provision, only implicitly part of the jubilee year. 'Every seventh year you shall grant a remission of debts. And this is the manner of the remission: every creditor shall remit the claim that is held against a neighbor, not exacting it of a neighbor who is a member of the community, because the Lord's remission has been proclaimed' (Dt 15:1-2).

Note: When unpaid debts are the reason for people going into slavery or giving up their lands, the release of slaves and restoration of land imply that the debt has automatically been cancelled. Thus, the slave release and land restoration of the jubilee year imply the cancellation of debts.

Towards a Humane Order. The biblical jubilee year is about a socio-economic program. It is about social transformation. It is about a humane order for the human community – social, political, economic. The biblical jubilee year is a move against the accumulation of wealth. It is a move towards the removal of poverty. It is aimed at the promotion of equal status in the human community. It is about the

[22] Every seven years.

restoration of freedom. And note, it is a religious happening! And for the Israelites it was a spiritual event!

There Shall Be No Poor. Why these very humanitarian provisions of the jubilee? The reason is distilled in one simple phrase: 'There will be no poor among you ...' (Dt 15:4, RSV). In that phrase you will find the spirit and motivation behind the sabbatical and jubilee prescriptions. Yahweh's desire and dream for the Israelite community is that there shall be no poor among them.

What God Wants. Our farmer hosts are curious. Did the Israelites get to practice the jubilee year? Scholars debate this. But whether the Israelites, human beings like us did or not, the jubilee year remains a testimony to what *God* wants.

Isaiah's Picture of Salvation Spelled Out. Let us go back to Isaiah's total picture of a future salvation – that windfall of vivid human boons and blessings. From our signposts, there emerges this picture of future salvation:

It is a time when God asserts *sovereignty* in people's history. God is king. *God's Kingdom will come*!

They shall see the glory of the Lord, the majesty of our God. Strengthen the weak hands, and make firm the feeble knees. Say to those who are of a fearful heart, 'Be strong, do not fear! Here is your God. He will come with vengeance, with terrible recompense. He will come and save you.' (Isa 35:2-4)

This is *good news*. *Together with* the coming of God's Kingdom, blessings such as these will be experienced:

Good news (of liberation and justice) will be announced *to the poor and the oppressed*.

They will *rejoice*.

The *blind will see, deaf hear, lame walk, the dead will live again*.

Captives will be freed.

The provisions of the *jubilee year —restoration of property, release of slaves, rest to the land, cancellation of debts*—will become reality. Justice will come to Israel and to the nations.

A spirit-filled servant of God will come to establish justice on the earth.

What a scenario! Note again that salvation for Isaiah is not a soul-going-to-heaven scenario. It is the coming of a new earth, experiencing a new and different history.

Isaiah: Kingdom of God. So far, we have reconstructed Isaiah's picture of *salvation*. With just one more blink of the eye, we will see *Kingdom of God* as understood by Isaiah. We do this by noticing that in this scenario of salvation, the (assertion of the) sovereignty or Kingdom of God is one of the details of salvation. It takes only one glance to see that, for Isaiah, Kingdom of God consists in all the other features with which it is associated.[23] The Kingdom of God comes, and in its train is a procession of salvific blessings: health to the sick, etc. Fresh from Isaiah's own consciousness and pen, good news of God's kingship then means:

eyes of the blind shall be opened
ears of the deaf unstopped
the lame leap like a hart
deaf shall hear
eyes of the blind shall see
'*anawim* find joy
poor rejoice
good news to the poor
liberty to the captives
opening of the prison
year of the Lord's favor
oppressed go free
justice to the nations
justice on the earth
dead will live, their bodies shall rise

This plenteous crop of raw data can be inventoried with the following labels: health for the sick (Our hosts speculate about the presence of organic farming in Isaiah's Kingdom of God), joy for the poor, good news (of liberation) for the poor, liberty for prisoners, freedom to the oppressed, redistribution of land, release of slaves, rest for the land, cancellation of debts, justice to the nations, the vanquishing of physical death. The over-all label for all these life-blessings would be 'Isaiah's Kingdom of God.'

Jesus: Kingdom of God

Jesus Re-Contextualizes Isaiah. These Isaianic pronouncements, though composed centuries earlier, were read, studied and meditated on in synagogues and schools in Jesus' time. Judging from Jesus' liberal use of them, these Isaianic passages we have just examined must have been the subject of Jesus' meditations. At the same time they were re-interpreted by him in the context of his own time. For example, these prophecies originally spoke of the good news of God's kingly power liberating the oppressed Jews from the Babylonian exile (around 586-530 B.C.E.). Now, in the gospels, it is good news of the Kingdom of God for the people of Jesus' time.

Jesus Echoes Isaiah. What were Jesus' 'sources' for his understanding of the Kingdom of God? One principal source is the book of Isaiah. The next roadsigns

23 In fact, Kingdom of God (new earth) is a practical synonym for salvation. I pointed this out earlier on page 12. At this juncture of our journey, we should begin to gradually see why this is so.

are important statements of Jesus. Compared to Isaiah, Jesus is a man of relatively few words. We note, with all the more care how Jesus echoes the ideas, images and words of Isaiah. Still, after an attentive scrutiny of the Isaiah signposts, deciphering the Jesus signposts should be child's play. Here are the signposts with a brief commentary after each. Each of them reflects Jesus' understanding of the Kingdom of God based on Isaiah:

Matthew 11:2-6.

'Go and tell John what you hear and see:
the *blind receive their sight,*
the *lame walk,*
the lepers are cleansed,
the *deaf hear,*
the *dead are raised,*
and the *poor have good news brought to them.*
And blessed is anyone who takes no offense at me.' (Mt 11:2-6 = Lk 7:18-23)

We have been introduced to Matthew 11:2-6 as a mission statement.[24] This time we see it again as an answer to our question, 'What is the Kingdom of God?' Clearly, what this Matthew signpost contains are features or blessings of the Kingdom of God, taken right out of Isaiah's scroll.

Luke 4:16-21.

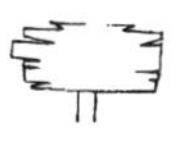

When he came to Nazareth, where he had been brought up, he went to the synagogue on the sabbath day, as was his custom. He stood up to read, and the scroll of the prophet Isaiah was given to him. He unrolled the scroll and found the place where it was written:

'The *Spirit of the Lord is upon me,*
because he has *anointed me*
to *bring good news to the poor.*
He has sent me to *proclaim release to the captives*
and *recovery of sight to the blind,*
to *let the oppressed go free,*
to *proclaim the year of the Lord's favor.*'
And he rolled up the scroll, gave it back to the attendant, and sat down. The eyes of all in the synagogue were fixed on him. Then he began to say to them, 'Today this scripture has been fulfilled in your hearing.' (Lk 4:16-21; cf. Isa 61:1-2)

Likewise Luke 4:16-21 is familiar to us as a mission statement.[25] This time we meet it as depicting different aspects of the Kingdom of God. It is again evidently lifted right out of Isaiah 61, with some significant modifications.

---

24 page 16.
25 page 15.

One such alteration is this: 'to bind up the brokenhearted' (Isa 61:1), a psychological state, is omitted, and 'let the oppressed go free,' a social program, is brought in from Isa 58:6. This substitution indicates that Jesus and/or Luke want to address themselves to social, rather than psychological, conditions of people. Religion is not just the gentle touch of psychological consolation. It is also the strong advocacy of social liberation. Religion and salvation are concerned not just about the private introspective drama of my soul. They are also about people enmeshed in the socio-economic-political (dis)order.

The 'the year of the Lord's favor' is of course the jubilee year of Leviticus 25. Your bible translation may give any of the following translations: 'the acceptable year of the Lord,' 'the favorable year of the Lord,' 'the year when the Lord will save his people.' These translations all refer to the jubilee year. Our peasant hosts get a special thrill from the jubilee legislation and ask if a Christian society today can be serious about it.

Matthew 12:18-21.

This was to fulfill what had been spoken through the prophet Isaiah:

'Here is my *servant*, whom I have chosen,
my beloved, with whom my soul is well pleased.
I will put my *Spirit upon him*,
and he will *proclaim justice to the Gentiles.*
He will not wrangle or cry aloud,
nor will anyone hear his voice in the streets.
He will not break a bruised reed
or quench a smoldering wick
until he *brings justice to victory.*
And in his name the Gentiles will hope.' (Mt 12:17-21)

In this signpost, Mt 12:18-21, we find a much overlooked biblical text. And yet Matthew does no less than use it as a main summary and conclusion to one of the sections of his gospel. It is another extract from Isaiah's portrait of salvation and Kingdom of God. Remarkable in this signpost and largely unremarked in the Second Look is a certain individual handpicked by God to proclaim and execute justice in the world, or as Matthew puts it, to bring justice to victory.

Note that even if our three just cited signposts, Mt 11:2-6, Luke 4:16-21 and Mt 12:18-21, do not explicitly contain the term 'Kingdom of God,' we know that they refer to blessings of the Kingdom, drawn from Isaiah, and proclaimed by Jesus.

Mk 1:14-15. The reverse situation obtains in our next signpost, Mk 1:14-15. The term 'Kingdom of God' is present, but no description of the blessings is given.

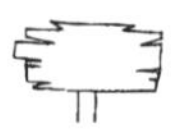

Now after John was arrested, *Jesus came to Galilee, proclaiming the good news [gospel] of God*, and saying, 'The time is fulfilled, and *the kingdom of God* has come near; repent, and believe in the good news.' (Mk 1:14-15)

Yet, there is no mistaking the language. It is Isaianic (proclaiming the *good news* of God ... the *Kingdom of God* has come near ... believe in the *good news*). Thus, even if Mark 1:14-15 does not spell out the specifics, we know from the Isaianic backdrop, that 'good news of the Kingdom of God' points to the bounteous variety of life-blessings that abound in Isaiah.

Lk 6:20. And listen to the last signpost, Lk 6:20. It has a familiar ring, the Isaianic ring.

'*Blessed* are you who are *poor*, for yours is the *kingdom of God*.' (Lk 6:20)

Our hosts, the peasant community, hear reverberations of Isaiah's 'Kingdom of God' and 'rejoicing of the poor.' Do you hear it too? Listen: '*Blessed* are you who are *poor*, for yours is the *Kingdom of God*!' Isaiah's salvation and Kingdom of God break through that simply worded beatitude of Jesus.

Other possible signposts: Lk 16:16=Mt 11:12-13; Mt 11:2-6=Lk 7:18-23; Lk 11:2=Mt 6:10; Lk 10:9; Mt 10:7-8; Mt 4:23; Lk 4:44; Lk 12:31=Mt 6:33; Mk 1:14-15; Mk 1:38-39; Mk 3:14-15; Mk 1:32-34; Mk 3:7-12; Mk 6:54-56; Mk 9:1; 9:47; 10:14-15; 10:23-25; 12:34; 14:25; 15:43

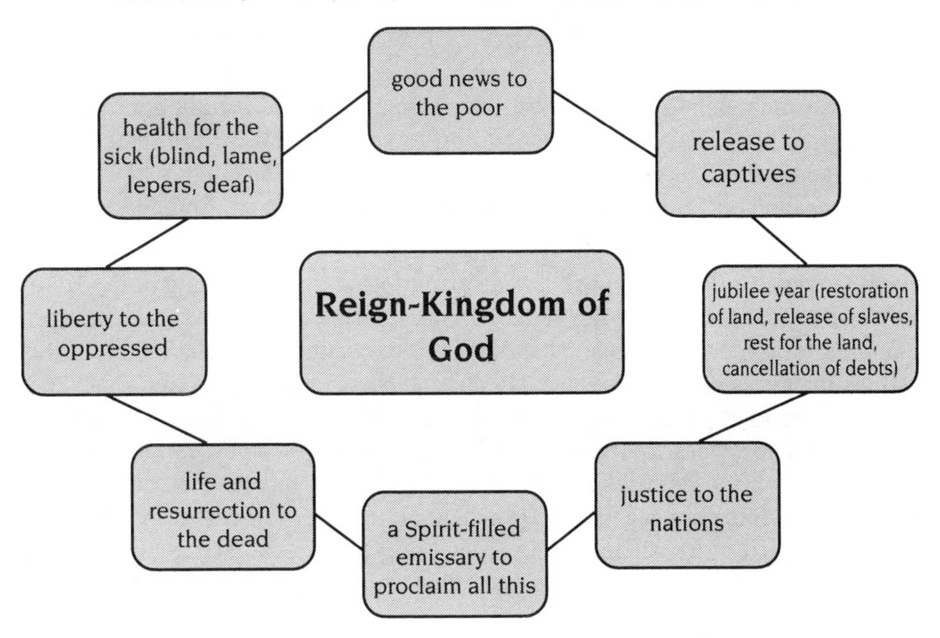

Kingdom of God According to Jesus Based on Isaiah. In short, Kingdom of God for Jesus is a *new world*. One gathers that that new world is *on earth*. In it humankind will experience various life-blessings.

Kingdom Is a New Earth, Not Heaven. For Isaiah and Jesus the Kingdom of God is not to be identified with heaven, although for both of them there is indeed a heaven, Yahweh's abode. For the First Look then, odd as it appeared to me as a Second Looker, Kingdom of God is not to be equated with heaven. One possible reason for the mistaken equation is the mix-up of the following three terms:

'heaven'
'Kingdom of God'
'Kingdom of heaven'

As we shall see more clearly later, for the biblical people, 'heaven' is the firmament above. It is not earth below.[26] 'Kingdom of God' is earth, a new earth. In the phrase 'Kingdom of heaven,' the *word 'heaven,'* is used to *substitute* for the *word 'God.'* 'Kingdom of heaven' then is not heaven! 'Kingdom of heaven' is a new earth! It is identical with 'Kingdom of God.'

We are presently partaking of some boiled *kamote* which our hosts are serving us. Did you just now feel like a big hot piece is burning in your mouth or stuck in your throat? This may sound too bizarre or too confusing to you. Well, if so, you are not the first nor the last to experience that discomfort. And in fact, others have felt a knot in their gut. One possible reason? Intellectuals have a sophisticated term for it: paradigm shift. However, with some forebearance and a gulp of fresh coconut drink, you should eventually see that it is a shift back to the original Jesus rather than a maneuver to be clever or innovative. Our hosts seem to take a liking to this shift. They say that our catechesis will have nothing to lose and much to gain by taking a cue from Jesus and Isaiah: the Kingdom of God, that final and definitive salvation towards which we are headed and which has been initially experienced in the ministry of Jesus, is not heaven but a new world on earth. But more of this hot *kamote* in the next stop-overs, hopefully, more agreeable and palatable as we advance.

From Guavas to Golf Courses? Isaiah's and Jesus' understanding of the Kingdom of God is as rich and colorful as the small farms we are currently visiting. Bananas, avocados, mangoes, papayas, kaimitos, kamote, patola, eggplant, tomatoes, string beans, lettuce, pechay abound there. But we are told that soon big commercial and industrial 'developers' are coming in to change the face of the earth. The colors and shapes will change into golf courses, commercial complexes, tourist facilities for the rich. Our hosts tell us that this change represents a false concept of development. It is a movement away from the vision and spirit of Isaiah and Jesus. They are getting organized in anticipation of bulldozers and graders. They ask whether we are with them. We pledge solidarity, advocacy and prayers.

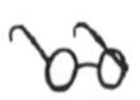

[26] In the pre-scientific cosmology, heaven is above, and earth is below. Examples: '*Lift up your eyes to the heavens*, and *look at the earth beneath*; for the heavens will vanish like smoke, the earth will wear out like a garment. (Isa 51:6)'; 'You shall not make for yourself an idol, whether in the form of anything that is in *heaven above*, or that is on the *earth beneath*... (Ex 20:4)'

It is time to take leave of our hosts. But before we do, we feast our eyes on this remarkable spread of vegetables and fruits, rich with all the colors of the rainbow and with shapes more extravagant than a jigsaw puzzle. No philosophizing. No theologizing. Just watching, appreciating, gazing. We feel connected and we move on.

Stopover 4

At a Goldmine (The Kingdom of God in the Beatitudes)

OUR HOST: Indigenous People in Mines

The Beatitudes: a Goldmine. We continue our search for the meaning of the Kingdom of God. Our present stop is a community of indigenous people living atop a goldmine!

Are you looking for a compact concentration of data about the Kingdom of God, deposited in one single place? You will find it in the beatitudes (Mt 5:3-10; Lk 6:20-21).[27] These beatitudes are a goldmine. A mine for its wealth. Gold for its inspiration.

Dirt or Gold? Unfortunately, our usual theological technology brings up more dirt than gold. This happens, for example, when we treat the beatitudes as moral imperatives rather than as proclamations of good news. The litany of 'blessed are you who ...' seems to be endorsements of virtue or imperatives for meritorious

[27] The beatitudes are part of but are not the whole Sermon on the Mount or the Sermon on the Plain.

moral behavior. 'Blessed are the hungry....' Hey, the hungry are being blessed! That sounds great. It sounds like hunger is a recommended Christian way of life! Alas, such a reading is antipodes apart from Jesus' mind. While some of us might start to be a bit fidgety, our indigenous hosts smile as if they knew this intuitively.

Well, strange as it may sound, the beatitudes do not tell us how to live or how to be. In fact, some of them tell us what Jesus does *not* want us to be! When he pronounced the beatitude on the hungry, he did not mean that he was recommending hunger as a virtue. On the contrary, he was proclaiming liberation from hunger.

There are elegant pitfalls in the study of the beatitudes. We proceed with care, as we resume our search for other meanings of the Kingdom of God, buried in the beatitudes.

A Key: The Second Part. For Isaiah and Jesus, the Kingdom of God, as we have seen in the last stopover, is not to be identified with heaven. It is a new earth. We now pick up the same nugget of wisdom from our next signpost, the beatitudes (Mt 5:3-10; Lk 6:20-21). And the clue to that wisdom is simple: the meaning of Kingdom of God is *embedded in the second part* of each beatitude (and not in the first).

'Blessed are the meek (first part), for they shall inherit the earth (second part).' The Kingdom of God is a new earth! – and indeed based not only on this beatitude but on the others too. Our guileless hosts let out a chortle of agreement. Look for the Kingdom of God in the second part of the beatitude. That is a simple key. Easy to use. But beware, it is also easy to lose.

Guidelines for Digging

But let us put some system into our excavation. We need to hold on firmly to the following pointers:

Proclamations. First, the beatitudes are *proclamations or announcements of salvation*. For example: 'Blessed are you that hunger, for you shall be satisfied' is a proclamation of salvation to people who are hungry. And the salvation being proclaimed is satisfaction of hunger – food, in plain words. The different beatitudes proclaim different forms of salvation to different groups of people.

Salvation Is Synonymous with Kingdom of God. Second, for Jesus and his contemporaries, 'salvation' and 'Kingdom of God' are interchangeable. In expectation of salvation, the Jew did not say: 'I pray to go to heaven.' Rather he would say: 'I pray that the Kingdom of God may come.' *This is a fundamental and pivotal insight to hold on to*. Salvation did not mean 'going to heaven.' It meant the coming of the Kingdom of God. *Kingdom of God and salvation are equivalents*. They are one and the same thing.

The beatitudes are therefore proclamations of salvation or Kingdom of God.

Second Part of the Beatitude. Thirdly then, where or how do we find salvation or Kingdom of God expressed in the beatitudes? *'Kingdom of God' and 'salvation' are to be found*, as I have said, *in the second part of each beatitude*. The second part represents a biblical term for salvation and Kingdom of God. If you want to know what Kingdom of God and salvation meant for Jesus, look for it in the second part of each beatitude. There you will find the different faces of Kingdom of God, its different aspects, its different descriptions. The assertions in the second portion of each beatitude are nothing but different ways of talking about the Kingdom and its salvific blessings.

Spotlight on the Second Part

First Part	Second Part
Blessed are you who are poor,	for yours is the kingdom of God. (Lk)
Blessed are the poor in spirit,	for theirs is the kingdom of heaven. (Mt)
Blessed are you who are hungry now,	for you will be filled. (Lk)
Blessed are those who hunger and thirst for righteousness,	for they will be filled (Mt)
Blessed are you who weep now,	for you will laugh. (Lk)
Blessed are those who mourn,	for they will be comforted. (Mt)
Blessed are the meek,	for they will inherit the earth. (Mt)
Blessed are the merciful,	for they will receive mercy. (Mt)
Blessed are the pure in heart,	for they will see God. (Mt)
Blessed are the peacemakers,	for they will be called children of God. (Mt)
Blessed are those who are persecuted for righteousness' sake	for theirs is the Kingdom of heaven (Mt)

Focus on Second Part: A World of Blessings. Let us now train our focus on the second part. In our present search, it will be misleading to look at the first part, which contains the recipients of salvation. We are not in search of the recipients but of the blessings of salvation. I repeat: ignore the first part; focus on the second part. As you thus let your eye settle kindly on each of the beatitudes, you will discover a remarkable world of blessings. And that is what the Kingdom of God is.

The Kingdom of God, in the Scriptures' own words, is satisfaction of hunger, laughter, comfort, inheriting the earth, obtaining mercy, seeing God, becoming children of God. It is a place under the sun where all of us, together with our hosts, the indigenous community, would want to live.

This Kingdom of God has both a present and a future aspect. As present, it took the form of Kingdom-blessings that Jesus imparted during his ministry. As future, it is our final destiny; it is the biblical equivalent of the longed for Utopia, of Shangri-la, of Nirvana. It is this future aspect, or some aspects of it, that is sketched in the second part of each beatitude. Let us now look more closely into each of the beatitudes. We begin towards the bottom of the list.

THEY SHALL BE CALLED CHILDREN OF GOD

Kingdom of God As Divine Filiation.

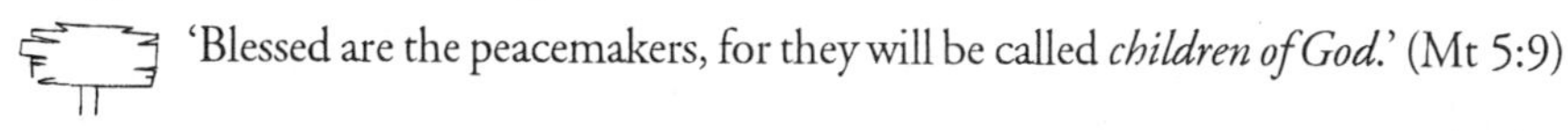

'Blessed are the peacemakers, for they will be called *children of God.*' (Mt 5:9)

Divine sonship or daughtership has several levels of meaning in biblical culture, but the bottom line – 'you shall become God's children' – is a special relationship to God.

In Jesus' beatitude, we savor the quality of this blessing when we recall how special children were to Jesus. "Then little children were being brought to him in order that he might lay his hands on them and pray. The disciples spoke sternly to those who brought them; but Jesus said, 'Let the little children come to me, and do not stop them; for it is to such as these that the kingdom of heaven belongs.' And he laid his hands on them and went on his way" (Mt 19:14-15).

Feel too the heartbeat of this 'our father,' 'my father,' 'your father' whose parenthood we will relish as a Kingdom-blessing. 'If you then, who are evil, know how to give good gifts to your children, how much more will your Father who is in heaven give good things to those who ask him!' (Mt 7:11; 6:7-8; 6:26)

It is a parent who has the traits of a mother: 'Your Father knows what you need before you ask him' (Mt 6:8). 'Look at the birds of the air: they neither sow nor reap nor gather into barns, and yet your heavenly Father feeds them. Are you not of more value than they?' (Mt 6:26. Cf. Mt 23:37) It is of such a Father-Mother that we shall become children when we come into possession of divine daughtership and sonship in the Kingdom—in the fullest, most exhaustive, most absolute way.

THEY SHALL SEE GOD

Kingdom of God As the Vision of God.

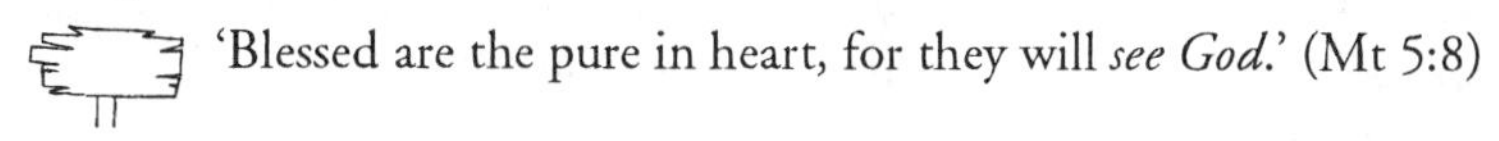

'Blessed are the pure in heart, for they will *see God.*' (Mt 5:8)

In Jesus' time, to see God's face brought death (Gen 32:30; Ex 33:20; Isa 6:5). But in this beatitude, human life reaches its absolute fulfillment when human beings with bare eyes gaze at the nakedness of the Divine! St Paul formulates it thus: 'For now we see in a mirror, dimly, but then we will see face to face. Now I know only in part; then I will know fully, even as I have been fully known' (1 Cor 13:12). In fact, it is most likely more than an eyeball-to-God happening. It is perhaps, so to speak, an essence-to-Essence experience.

One can indeed say that this vision of God represents the pinnacle of any experience, other than which there is nothing more sublime.

'Seeing God' in this beatitude could be roughly equivalent to the Second Look's 'beatific vision,' meaning a direct experience of the divine essence. But note: whereas in the Second Look this vision is practically the only blessing, in the First Look it is one of several. Another difference is that in the Second, it is the disembodied soul that will see God; in the First, it is the risen body-person.

As I look at the cloudless eyes of our hosts, I sense that it is people like them who can have a better appreciation of this Kingdom-blessing. Indigenous peoples are more in touch with primordials: not only with the song and discourse of the rocks and trees but also with the luminous silence of the outer and inner worlds. There are fewer lowering clouds in their spiritual worlds. More openings to the clear blue sky. Thus, more knowing-without-knowing is a (fore-)taste of the essence-to-Essence experience.

They Will Obtain Mercy

Kingdom of God As the Compassion of Social Justice.

'Blessed are the merciful, for they will receive *mercy*.' (Mt 5:7)

'Mercy' in this beatitude does not refer indiscriminately to any kind of compassionate act. The underlying Hebrew word is *checed.* In contexts that have a prophetic ring, it has a more pointed significance. It refers to the compassion that goes hand in hand with justice. It is the '*feeling* partner' of justice (*mishpat*). Together, *cheched* and *mishpat* forge a fellowship which can be called 'social justice with a heart.'

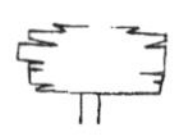

But as for you, return to your God,
hold fast to love (*checed*) and justice (*mishpat*),
and wait continually for your God. (Hos 12:6)

He has told you, O mortal, what is good;
and what does the Lord require of you
but to do justice (*mishpat*), and to love kindness (*checed*),
and to walk humbly with your God? (Mic 6:8)

The sense of our beatitude then is: 'Blessed are those whose compassionate heart does the works of social justice, for the Kingdom of God for them will likewise be the experience of justice and compassion.' Our indigenous hosts exchange knowing looks. Living atop a gold-mine does not mean they own it. The transnationals do. O, for a pinch of the Kingdom in their lives!

They Shall Inherit the Earth

Land in Biblical Consciousness.

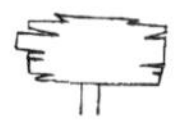
'Blessed are the meek, for they will inherit the *earth*.' (Mt 5:5)

Land! Inheriting land! Possessing it! That is the Kingdom of God! As for our indigenous hosts, this message had powerful overtones for Jesus' hearers. For it more than evoked oft-repeated lines that reverberate in their Scriptures. Less reverently, one could say the refrain 'possess the land' sounded like a broken, but welcome, record in Israelite ears. Yahweh promised and gave land to their ancestors and to them as a people. They remembered that Yahweh said to their ancestors: 'all the land that you see I will give to you and to your offspring forever.... Rise up, walk through the length and the breadth of the land, for I will give it to you' (Gen 13:15-17; 15:7; Ex 6:8).

They remembered that Moses, in his Deuteronomic homilies, constantly reminded them of the gift of the land (Dt 8:1;12:1; 19:14; 30:5; Num 33:53; Lev 20:24, etc.). They endearingly called it a land 'broad and good, flowing with milk and honey.' At this point, let us adjust our Third Look glasses well and pause long enough to ingest this piece of truth: Land was salvation for the Israelites. Our hosts are wrapped in appreciative silence.

Real Not Symbolic Earth. Is the land for real?—our hosts wonder in their hearts. In the minds of Jesus' Jewish hearers this land was real land, not metaphorical. 'For the Lord your God is bringing you into a good land, a land with flowing streams, with springs and underground waters welling up in valleys and hills, a land of wheat and barley, of vines and fig trees and pomegranates, a land of olive trees and honey, a land where you may eat bread without scarcity, where you will lack nothing, a land whose stones are iron and from whose hills you may mine copper. You shall eat your fill and bless the Lord your God for the good land that he has given you' (Dt 8:7-10).

What was in the mind of Jesus when he spoke of a land to be inherited? Did he find the Jewish hope too earthy? No. He also meant a real earth. In the absence of contrary evidence, we must take Jesus' words at face value, and not automate him and his words into a program assembled for him by a later theology. Did you hear our hosts, particularly the elders, breathe a sigh of relief?

Kingdom of God As Land or New Earth. What is the Kingdom of God in this beatitude? A First and Third Look tells us that it is land. It is earth. This could be one of our most startling discoveries. *Salvation – final salvation – is not heaven, but earth!* This beatitude has a message for my childhood Second Look theology. Let us be exceedingly clear and thoroughly familiar with the following statement. 'There *is* a heaven, BUT....' Although there is indeed a heaven to go to after death, *final* salvation is not 'going to heaven,' but 'inheriting the earth.' Our ultimate destiny is a new earth.

This beatitude now begins to open the window of our mind. We begin to get a glimpse of that biblical vista of 'a new heaven and a new *earth*' which will become a reality at the end of our present history (Rev 21:1-5). It is not a symbolic earth. It is not an ethereal earth for bodiless souls. It is as real as the ancestral lands of the indigenous peoples which they are in danger of losing, or have already lost, to the big mining enterprises and their talon-like bulldozers.

Meek = *'anawim*. To whom does Jesus' beatitude assign the earth? By way of exception to our way of proceeding, we look briefly to the first part for our answer, to the meek. Who are these? The 'humbled poor and oppressed' would be the best designation. Actually, this beatitude is a quotation of Psalm 37:11. It reads: 'The *'anawim* shall inherit the land, and delight themselves in abundant prosperity.' Read the whole psalm. You will see that the *'anawim* is counterpoised with 'the wicked,' *r^{e}shaim*. *R^{e}shaim* in certain contexts, such as Psalm 37, refers to oppressors who possess wealth and power.

In any case, seldom does *'anaw* have a positive meaning (Num 12:3 'the meek or humble Moses'). Most of the time it refers to the afflicted, humbled, subjugated, lowly, and the frequent application is to the poor (e.g. Ps 9:12,18; 10:12,17; Pr 14:21; Isa 11:4; Am 2:7). Moreover, the root stem here is *'anah'*, which, as we shall soon see, has the basic meaning of 'oppressed.' Consequently, the people who are referred to as 'meek' in this beatitude are actually the 'oppressed poor who are humbled and afflicted.' Our hosts understand little of this philological excursus, but they tune in very well.

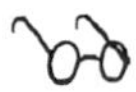

What, Not How or Who. Before we move on to the next beatitude, a word of caution. The beatitude tells us that one of the blessings of the Kingdom is a new earth. It tells us *what* Jesus and his God want for humankind. It stops there. It does *not* say *how* this will be brought about or *who* is to bring it about. However, just the 'what' – namely, that salvation or Kingdom means a new earth – is already one giant step away from the Second Look for which *final* salvation is heaven.

You Shall Laugh. They Shall Be Comforted

Kingdom of God As Laughter and Comfort.

'Blessed are you who weep now, for you will *laugh*.' (Lk 6:21)

'Blessed are those who mourn, for they will be *comforted*.' (Mt 5:4)

The Kingdom of God means joy, comfort, laughter. No place for tears of sadness in the Kingdom of God. What is envisioned here is not the 'eternal happiness of the soul,' but the full-throated bliss of flesh and blood people. The unrehearsed smiles and laughter of our open-hearted hosts are perhaps anticipation of this bliss. For indeed unburdened by wealth and worries, they can wear a smile, not of resignation but of hope in struggle.

They Shall Be Satisfied

Kingdom of God As Food.

'Blessed are you who are *hungry* now, for you will be *filled*.' (Lk 6:21)

'Blessed are those who hunger and thirst for *righteousness*, for they will be *filled*.' (Mt 5:6)

Luke and Matthew Differ. Again, for a change we look briefly at the first part of the beatitude(s) and notice that, although both Luke and Matthew are inspired texts, they differ from one another. Luke refers to people with empty stomachs whose hunger is for rice and bread. I notice, among our hosts, the thin frames of some undernourished children. Matthew refers to people who hunger for moral uprightness and holiness and receive it.

Matthew's Moralizing Tendency. Here and elsewhere, Matthew has the tendency to shift from the concrete-sociological ('no food in one's stomach') to the religious-moral ('hungry for righteousness'), as can be observed also below (from 'poor' to 'poor in spirit'). This moralizing tendency, a Matthean characteristic, is due to the social circumstances in which Matthew wrote. He was ministering to a community where the matter of contention was righteousness or uprightness. Who was upright? The Jew of the mother religion? Or the break-away Jesus-follower? Matthew's concern was to show that Christian righteousness was as good as, if not better than, Jewish uprightness (Mt 5:20). Thus, the reformulation of the present beatitude. When this moralizing tendency is present, we have Matthew's adaptation and modification of the original statement of Jesus.

Luke: Closer to Jesus. It is Luke that more accurately reports what Jesus actually said. On the lips of Jesus, the beatitude referred to bodily hunger and to physical food. The Kingdom of God means rice, fish, vegetables, meat for hungry people. Bodily food for bodily hunger. But – goes my Second Look rejoinder — how can that be when food is 'material'? This is a stumbling block for the Second Look for which only things 'spiritual' are to be catalogued for eternal salvation. Can something 'material'[28] then be part of eternal salvation? A simple response for the moment is: it *can* be and *is* so for Jesus. Here is a bit of learning I picked up along the way: when tempted to be more Catholic than Jesus, resist. It is one temptation worth resisting.

Nourishing Meal. As we ponder this, we share a sparse meal of root crops and salt with our hosts. But they and we hope that one day their and our continuing education and common struggle will bring more nourishing meals to their tables. That will indeed be a nutritive bit of Kingdom of God in palpable form.

For the Hungry. Take note that the blessing is not food as such. It is food *for the hungry.* The beatitude does not bestow the blessing of more food for the (over)

---

[28] I am using 'material' and 'spiritual,' as the Second Look would. The division of matter and spirit is not biblical, as we will see in Stopover 6.

satiated. Certain people in the world overproduce grain, are overfed and dump the leftovers of their national economy into the sea. That is not the sort of situation to which Jesus refers in his beatitude. In fact, the opposite is true. Some of the harshest words of Luke, and perhaps of Jesus himself, are found in the value judgment pronounced on the overfed. 'Woe to you who are full now, for you will be hungry' (Lk 6:25).

Yours Is the Kingdom of God

Differences Between Matthew and Luke.

'Blessed are you who are poor, for yours is the *kingdom of God.*' (Lk 6:20)

'Blessed are the poor in spirit, for theirs is the *kingdom of heaven.*' (Mt 5:3)

I bring your attention to two significant differences between Matthew and Luke.

First Difference. Luke has 'Kingdom of *God*' whereas Matthew has 'Kingdom of *heaven*.' We are sufficiently familiar by now with the Kingdom of God. But what is this Kingdom of heaven? We have touched on this earlier. But now is the time for a fuller explanation. At the outset, it must be said emphatically that 'Kingdom of heaven' and 'heaven' are two very different things. Why so? The matter is simple, if one holds on to the elementary biblical fact that sometimes the word 'heaven' substitutes for the word 'God.'

Heaven: Entity, Word. Heaven, in biblical culture is an entity, commonly understood as a 'place' up above where God ordinarily resides. Thus, in the Lord's Prayer we find: 'Our Father who are in heaven.' There too, according to our Faith, is where good people go after death.

Now, *normally* the *word* 'heaven' designates the *entity* heaven. But there are times when the *word* 'heaven' does not refer to the *entity* 'heaven.' This happens when the word 'heaven' substitutes for the word 'God.' To show reverence for the sacred name of God, the Jews avoided pronouncing it and, instead of the word 'God,' they used other words, such as 'the Glory,' 'the Power' (Mk 14:62), 'the Almighty' (2 Cor 6:18), 'Heaven.' For example: "I will get up and go to my father, and I will say to him, 'Father, I have sinned against heaven [=against *God*] and before you'" (Lk 15:18)—are the words of the so-called prodigal son to his earthly father.

'Kingdom of Heaven' and 'Kingdom of God.' In the phrase 'Kingdom of heaven,' the word 'heaven' substitutes for the word 'God.' For example, consider the same statement of Jesus in the two parallel versions of Luke and Matthew:

'Let the little children come to me ... for it is to such as these that the kingdom of *God* belongs' (Lk 18:16)

Let the little children come to me ... for it is to such as these that the kingdom of *heaven* belongs' (Mt 19:14)

'Kingdom of heaven' and 'Kingdom of God' mean exactly one and the same thing, and neither of them refer to the entity, heaven. Each of them refers to a new earth where there is food and laughter.

Second Difference. Luke speaks of the 'poor,' while Matthew speaks of the 'poor in spirit.' Luke refers to the really —economically, materially—poor. Matthew, on the other hand, refers to the 'poor in spirit' or the spiritually poor.

Matthew's Poor in Spirit. Who are Matthew's 'poor in spirit'? Here are two possible meanings:

(a) Matthew is referring to people who are inwardly poor, i.e., humble. In this meaning, anyone, economically rich or poor, can be poor in spirit. Matthew has the tendency to shift from the concrete-sociological ('poor') to the religious-moral ('poor in spirit'), as we have observed above. Again, we have Matthew's adaptation and modification of an original statement of Jesus, which is still found in Luke.

(b) Matthew is talking about the concrete-sociological poor who, in their economic poverty, are religiously (='in spirit') humble and open to God's salvation. In this meaning, the 'poor in spirit' are still the economically poor but the religious dimension is given emphasis.

Real Poor. It is Luke and Matthew's (b) that more accurately report what Jesus actually said. Originally, then, on the lips of Jesus, poor referred to the really poor, such as beggars (Mk 10:46), casual workers (Mt 20:1-9), tenants (cf. Mt 21:33), slaves (Mt 8:6), debtors (Lk 16:5), the poor of the land (Jn 7:49). In our day, the reference would be to people like our hosts. They have little food in their stomachs, no money in their pockets, no 'titles' to communal ancestral lands which they stand to lose.

Poor and Oppressed. In fact 'poor *and oppressed*' is the most accurate expression. Why? Because—our hosts submit with good grace to more philology—the underlying Hebrew word *'anawim'* or *'aniyim* in the Hebrew Scriptures frequently referred to (a) people who were oppressed (b) due to economic poverty. (See Ps 37:11; Ex 22:25; Lev 23:22, etc.)

The root word is *'anah* which has some or all of the following connotations: look down, browbeat, afflict, humble, force, trouble, weaken, oppress, put down, become low, humiliate, stoop, mishandle. As you can see, *'anah* conveys the meaning of oppression or violence being done to someone of a low status.

The violence or oppression can be political (Gen 15:13), personal-psychological (Gen 16:6), cultural (Gen 16:9), social (Ex 22:22), sexual (Gen 34:2; 2 Sam 13:12-32), economic (Isa 11:4). *'Anawim* in actual life, then, are people who suffer some form of oppression; frequently the oppression is due to economic poverty (Ex 22:25; Lev 19:10; Dt 15:11; Job 24:4; Ps 10:12,17, 72:12; Isa 3:14; Jer 22:16; Ezek 18:12; Am 8:4).

Kingdom of God As Justice and Liberation for the Poor. We return to our original quest. What is the meaning of Kingdom of God in this beatitude: 'Blessed are you poor, for yours is the Kingdom of God'? According to our key, we should look at the second part. The second part already explicitly speaks about the Kingdom of God. But can we explore further? What is implied? Recall that a beatitude is a proclamation of salvation. What then is a proclamation of salvation to the poor and oppressed? The answer to that question will lead us to discover one underlying meaning of the Kingdom of God.

That underlying meaning of Kingdom of God in this beatitude is: justice and liberation. The salvation which this beatitude proclaims to the poor and oppressed should *at least include* their deliverance from poverty and oppression. In other words, salvation in this particular beatitude, whatever else it is, must include what we call today liberation and justice.

Therefore, the *first beatitude makes sense only if it means: Blessed are the poor and oppressed because the biblical God wants liberation and justice for them*. The words 'justice and liberation' are contemporary words of our time. They are not Jesus' words. Yet, they are the sum and substance of the very first beatitude that falls from the lips of Jesus! And they make supreme sense to our hosts. Try your glasses, if they don't to you.

Humane Life, Not Wealth. Note, however, that Jesus does not say 'Blessed are you *'anawim*, for you will become wealthy.' Jesus does not proffer wealth as the antithesis of poverty. Wealth has a minus valuation in Jesus' books (Lk 6:24; 12:16-21; 33-34; 16:19-23; Mk 10:23-25). If we may read the mind of Jesus, a life worthy of a human being is what he wants for the poor. To be able to own and run a transnational mining enterprise would not be Jesus' idea of liberation for our hosts, the indigenous peoples. Neither should we be miserly, however, and allow the poor, as we sometimes patronizingly do, only 'the basic necessities.'

At the Heart of Jesus' Message. When I was a theology student, we were made to identify and memorize the most important tenets of the Faith. To the best of my recollection, social justice and liberation was not one of them. In fact, a few years later, Christians who proclaimed and worked for social justice were called communists and were arrested, tortured, and killed. And Church people were deathly afraid of the word 'liberation.'

And yet there it is, at the very heart of Jesus' message. Why have we missed out? Because it is merely implicit in the Kingdom of God? Hardly, I think. One reason for missing out is the greater emphasis given to abstract dogmatic truths and less to Jesus' simple, down-to-earth commentaries about real life. In any case, as a Second Looker I would find it difficult to extract justice and liberation from a Second Look *concept* of the Kingdom of God.

Economic, Not Moral, Standing. Another thing to note: the poor are blessed not because they are upright or virtuous. 'Poor' or 'poverty' here does not refer to a moral standing. It refers to an economic condition. Whether the poor are simple, open, pious or gifted with any other noble quality is beside the point. Jesus is referring to their situation of privation, want, and oppression. His words are a pronouncement of reversal, issuing a manifesto for humane living, justice, liberation.

Equivalents. Note that this beatitude on the poor is just another way of saying 'Good news to the poor.' 'Good news to the poor' and 'Blessed are the poor ...' are equivalents. We have repetition and variety – an indication of the weight of this all-important datum.

Some More Cartloads

Three Kinds of Poverty. In the New Testament, we can discern three different kinds of poverty. It is good to keep them apart. Otherwise, we fall into no-sense statements such as, 'God loves the poor. He wants us to be like the poor.' This makes no sense. The first sentence is correct. The second is wrong.

One is the poverty of *destitution*. It is dehumanizing. This is what Jesus' original beatitude was about. It is not a blessing. It is an evil which the God of the Bible wants liberation from.[29] This is the poverty that the majority of the world's population, including most indigenous peoples, experience.

The other one is *poverty of spirit*. This is what Matthew speaks about. It most likely meant humility. In later times, it got to mean detachment from possessions. This poverty of spirit is good and is a high form of spirituality.

There is a third kind, which, in religious circles is referred to as '*evangelical poverty*.' This is the practice of leaving home, family, possessions in the following of Jesus. Thus the first followers of Jesus left their boats, nets, parents, servants and followed Jesus (Mk 1:16-20). Levi left his tax collection office (Mk 2:14; cf. Lk 8:2; See also Mk 10:17-20). This form of poverty is, of course, commendable.

If we mix up these three types of poverty, we are bound to make confusing and ambiguous statements, such as: 'Poverty is good.' 'God calls us to be poor.' Which poor? Which poverty?

Both poverty of spirit and evangelical poverty are praiseworthy. Men and women in religious life have, in the course of centuries, taken vows of poverty. Being candid about it, we must admit that often on the stage of real life, we religious vow evangelical poverty while the lay people practice it. And the poor, like our hosts, practice the poverty of destitution.

The ideal would be that those who practice poverty of spirit and evangelical poverty would band with the poor and uproot dehumanizing poverty from our earth.

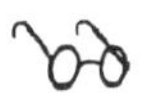

The Poor, the Hungry, the Weeping, the Meek. The first three or four beatitudes are about the poor, the hungry, the sorrowing and the afflicted. These beatitudes refer to one group of people, the *'anawim*, the poor and oppressed. They are

[29] This poverty acquires a positive and praiseworthy significance when freely embraced to accompany the poor *in* their poverty, and, we should add, *out of* their poverty.

not therefore three different sets of people. They are the *'anawim* who are poor, hungry and weeping, afflicted. And the salvation that Jesus wants for them is liberation, food, laughter and land. People like our hosts are the addressees of these beatitudes.

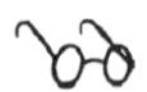

'Spiritual Gifts?' There could, however, be a lingering question: does not Jesus wish more than just liberation, justice, food, land for the poor? Does he not want also spiritual gifts for them? The response is: of course, he does. He wishes gifts of the spirit to all of us, poor or non-poor alike. But let us be clear on this: in the face of the *'anawim* and poverty, his unequivocal wish is liberation; in the face of the hungry and hunger, his unequivocal response is food. And this is what he unequivocably states in the beatitudes. There is no side-stepping the issue for Jesus. There is no stealthy retreat into irrelevant sermonizing which skirts around the summons of the moment.

In my younger days, my idea of a retreat for workers was to teach them prayers, to remind them of the commandments, especially sobriety, obedience to authority, fidelity to their spouses and dedication to their family, to make them sorry for their sins, to talk to them about God's love, to bring them to the sacraments – but nary a word about their human right to food, land, health, decent wages, participation and organization. I am grateful to people like our hosts who have given me several jolts. They have given me a re-education in the University of Life.

How to Avoid Pitfall 1

Correct Method. With simple pick and shovel, we have just quarried a goldmine. The gold nuggets have been the data and insights about the true nature of the Kingdom of God and salvation. Since there are many pitfalls, one cannot be sufficiently forewarned about the correct method for digging.

Focus on Second, Ignore First Part of Beatitudes. In quarrying the beatitudes for Jesus' understanding of the Kingdom of God, one must focus on the second part and ignore the first part.

For, the question is: *What* is salvation or Kingdom of God? And this is answered in the second part of each beatitude.

It is the second part which contains the blessings of salvation.

The first part tells us about *who* is to take possession of the Kingdom of God or what human situation is entitled to salvation. The first part merely indicates the recipients or the human situation for whom salvation is envisioned.

For example: Blessed are the pure in heart (=recipient) for they shall see God (=salvation or Kingdom of God).

Another important company secret: the first part does not contain virtues. Or, more accurately, it does not intend to propose virtues to be practiced. More of this in the next section. Nor does it contain blessings to be enjoyed.

First Part	Second Part
Blessed are you who are poor,	for yours is the kingdom of God. (Lk)
... poor in spirit,	... the kingdom of heaven. (Mt)
... you who are hungry now,	... you will be filled. (Lk)
... those who hunger for righteousness,	... they will be filled (Mt)
... you who weep now,	... you will laugh. (Lk)
... those who mourn,	... they will be comforted. (Mt)
... the meek,	... they will inherit the earth. (Mt)
... the merciful,	... will receive mercy. (Mt)
... the pure in heart,	... they will see God. (Mt)
... the peacemakers,	... they will be called children of God. (Mt)

Try constructing your understanding of the Kingdom of God, using the first part, which speaks of the poor, hungry, mournful, and you come up with a Kingdom of God which consists of (a community of) the poor, the hungry, the mournful, the weeping, who practice the virtues or enjoy the blessings of hunger, grief, etc. No. That is an atrocious notion. That is digging for dirt. Rather, conduct the search in the second part and you will find gold.

How to Avoid Pitfall 2

Proclamation, Not Exhortation. Second, we must insist that the beatitudes are proclamations or announcements. They are *not* exhortations. There is a big difference between a proclamation and an exhortation. 'I announce an exemption from exams' is a proclamation. 'Work hard on your studies' is an exhortation. 'There is plenty of gold in this mountain' is an announcement. 'Let us put in our best efforts' is an exhortation.

You treat the beatitudes as exhortations when you hold views such as: 'The beatitudes give us a blueprint for living.' 'The beatitudes are a list of virtues to be practiced.' 'God blesses poverty.' 'Poverty is a virtue.' 'The beatitudes teach us to be poor.' 'Poverty is the will of God.' 'Let us be poor.' 'In order to enter heaven, you must be poor.' 'Let us practice poverty.' 'God wants us to be like the poor whom he loves.' These and similar statements are exhortative in nature. That is *not* the way to treat the beatitudes.

Why is it easy to slip and stumble? Because the *language* of the beatitudes is slippery ground. 'Blessed are the poor, etc.' seems to have a positive ring. It seems to applaud the poor and poverty, etc. That is the slippery part. The beatitudes announce various blessings; it is important to know why. Is it because it is good to be poor, because poverty is a virtue, because God wants people to practice poverty? No. People are declared blessed or fortunate in that a form of salvation is being announced to them. 'Blessed are you poor, yours is the Kingdom of God' does not mean, 'Fortunate are you, because poverty is good, and God will reward you with the Kingdom.' On the contrary, it means, 'God wants you to be liberated from your poverty. Fortunate are you, because to you is announced your liberation from poverty.'

When you say to a ward of cancer patients: 'Blessed are you, cancer patients, because yours is a new miracle drug against cancer,' you do not mean that cancer is good, a virtue to be practiced, a condition to be desired. You mean the opposite. Cancer is a non-blessing and you are announcing liberation from cancer. That is why they are fortunate.

Kerygmatic; Declarative. It pays to know what kind of language is used in the beatitudes. It is declarative, not imperative. Although the tone begins to change with Matthew, the beatitudes were originally *kerygma* (announcement of good news) and not *paraenesis* (exhortation to virtue and good moral acts). They were joyful indicatives, not imperatives. They announce, they do not offer counsel or advice or command. Originally, that is, on the lips of Jesus, the beatitudes were intended to be announcements of salvation: 'I am proclaiming such-and-such salvation to you who are (already) poor, pure in heart, hungry. And so, blessed, happy, graced, fortunate are you.'

Not Virtues. The beatitudes then are not recommendations to certain virtues as in statements such as 'Poverty is a virtue.' 'Hunger is a virtue.' 'Purity of heart is a virtue.' Does this mean that a positive quality, such as purity of heart, is not a virtue and that Jesus does not exhort us to it? Purity of heart *is* indeed a virtue and Jesus strongly exhorts his followers to it, but *not in and through the beatitudes*. The exhortation is found at great length, for example, in the whole chapter 7 of Mark's gospel. Mark 7 is exhortative. The beatitudes are announcements.

Not Blueprint for Living. They do not offer advice towards a certain way of living. 'Be poor!' 'Be pure in heart!' 'Be a peacemaker.' 'Be hungry!' 'Strive to be hungry; salvation will be yours.' The beatitudes take for granted that the hearers are already poor or pure in heart or a peacemaker or hungry.

Missalettes and Songbooks. All this needs to be explained and stressed. Many preachers, even theologians, need to be alerted to this elementary aspect of the beatitudes. I once came across a missalette that said something to this effect: 'This Sunday's gospel is about the beatitudes. Jesus here teaches us how to live. He gives us a plan of life. He gives us a blueprint for living.' Thus, unwittingly, we make poverty, hunger, sorrow a Christian way of living! No wonder that without our intending it, we preach a pie-in-the-sky religion. *Mag-antus aron masantos.*[30] Some of our religious songs, too, inadvertently treat the beatitudes as exhorta-

[30] Accept suffering and become a saint.

tions when they sing about poverty as a Jesus-virtue to be imitated. *Mapapalad kayong mahihirap … mapapalad ang mga katulad ni Hesus.*[31]

Not a Moral Code. Not Conditions for Entry. The beatitudes do not offer precepts to follow. They are not a moral code. They do not list rules of conduct. The moral code is *another* aspect of Jesus' message, the ethical aspect, which will be taken up later in Stopover 14.

They are not conditions for entry into the Kingdom of God. 'In order to enter the Kingdom of God, you must be poor or pure or hungry.'

Some Samples:

For the sake of our pastoral concerns in the Third World, I risk being repetitive. Let us take some samples.

Not: 'It is good to be poor and oppressed, for yours is the Kingdom of God. God loves you. Suffer your poverty for the sake of the Kingdom.'
Rather: 'God wants you to be free from poverty. Therefore, rejoice. You are blessed.' From this understanding today's *'Anawim* can rightly draw the unspoken truth: 'Therefore God is in solidarity with us in our struggle to be free.'

Not: 'Be resigned to your family's hunger, for you shall be satisfied in heaven.'
Rather: 'You are hungry. God wants your hunger to be satisfied.'

Not: 'God wants you to weep, mourn and be sad. We live in a valley of tears.'
Rather: 'You are weeping now. God wants joy and laughter for you.'

Not: 'Be pure in heart, for then you will see God' (at least not in the beatitude).
Rather: 'I take for granted that you are pure in heart. And to you who are (already) pure in heart I proclaim the salvation of seeing God.'

Criterion for Interpretation: The Practice of Jesus. The beatitudes do pose a problem of interpretation. They may look blissfully simple. But the way they are expressed is, in fact, ambivalent. We must recognize this fact. They can be taken to be declarative. They can also be imperative. In fact, at first blush, they sound imperative. And this is why we, even pastors and theologians, are misled.

How to choose the correct reading? Happily, there is a deciding factor—the practice and actions of Jesus. Interpret Jesus' words through his practice and actions. When Jesus encountered the hungry, the sick, the sorrowing, what was his practice? What did he *do*? Did he counsel hunger, sickness, sorrow as virtues to be practiced? Did he not rather have the people fed, healed, and consoled? It is in that spirit that we must interpret the beatitudes of Jesus.

When in doubt about anything theological, avoid speculation; go back to Jesus and his practice. Interpret what Jesus says through what he does. This is a safe and sure criterion.

---

[31] Blessed are you who are poor … who are like Jesus.

Additional Cartloads

Promised Future Only?

Let us consider one possible objection. The salvation proclaimed in the beatitudes is still for the future. What good is that for people who are suffering now? It is true that in the beatitudes the blessings of salvation are mostly future. Later in our journey we will encounter signposts that talk about the present aspect of the Kingdom. These blessings which Jesus proclaimed in the beatitudes were not just future blessings but also blessings for the here-and-now. But even in the first beatitude, one can find a hint in the use of the present tense of the verb: 'Blessed are you who are poor, for yours *is* the kingdom of God' (Lk 6:20).

Moreover, it is shown by Jesus' practice. It was a practice which was undoubtedly exercised in favor of the oppressed poor of his own here-and-now. In fact, the beatitudes and their promises must have derived their credibility from the tangible here-and-now blessings which Jesus wrought. But more of the present aspect later in our journey ....

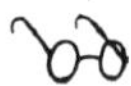

The What, Not the By Whom, When, How. We have explored the beatitudes for the meaning of the Kingdom of God and in the course of it, we have discovered only *what* the Kingdom of God is. What I had said earlier bears repeating: we have not yet dealt with the *by whom,* the *when,* the *how.* The beatitudes convey information about what the Kingdom of God is and what the God of the First Look wants for humankind.

But the beatitudes do not tell us by whom this Kingdom of God is to be brought about, nor when and how it will come about. There will be other signposts for this. I underscore this in order to avoid expecting too much from the beatitudes or reading too much into them. The beatitudes tell us what blessings the God of the Bible wants for us and especially for people like our indigenous hosts. Impatient as we might understandably be, we cannot yet derive answers about 'who' are to bring about these blessings and 'how' they will come about.

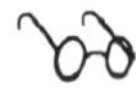

Why No Explicit Beatitude on Women? We cannot expect Jesus to be a twenty-first century person like us. Our feminist consciousness has been awakened and raised. However, Jesus was one who began to depart from customary ways of treating women. One of the more obvious examples is his formulation of the divorce prohibition, where the woman, not just the man, is seen as a possible litigant (Mk 10:12).

In the Christian tradition, Jesus can be considered as having initiated the movement towards women's equality and liberation ... or pointed our steps toward it. It has taken twenty centuries and we are still far from home. We are still exiles in a land of patriarchy and hardness of heart. But women, and men too, have begun to lead us home where gender is a way of being human, not a weapon for the ego.

Beatitudes, Not Parables. Much treasure, one spot—that is what the beatitudes have been for us in our search for the meaning of the Kingdom of God. Others have tapped the parables. We have not and we will not. The theme of most of the parables is indeed the Kingdom of God. However, while the parables give us some *aspects* of the Kingdom of God, they say little about its basic nature and substance. They exhibit its characteristics rather than 'it.'

The parables assume that the Kingdom of God is a new world of blessings and merely give us some of its features. The Mustard Seed (Mk 4:30-32; Mt 13:31, 32; Lk 13:18-19) is about small beginnings. The Sower (Mk 4:3-8; Mt 13:3-8; Lk 8:5-8) is about various responses to the proclamation. The Lost Sheep Story (Mt 18:12-13; Lk 15:4-6) is about God's care for the lost. The Pearl (Mt 13:45-46) is about the great value of the Kingdom. The ten Bridesmaids (Mt 25:1-12) is about watchful waiting for the Kingdom.

The Beatitudes: Original Words of Jesus? Before we conclude this visit, we would like to address a scholarly concern of one of our co-travelers. Are each of the beatitudes an original utterance of Jesus? Well, perhaps not letter by letter, word for word. But the general thrust and spirit is certainly Jesus. All of the beatitudes are of the same color-scheme as the core of the Jesus-story. And what have we so far seen of this core? Well, we have seen the Jesus of the Kingdom proclamation, of the mission statements. We have more to see as we proceed.

And how do we proceed? Not by major premise to minor premise to conclusion. Rather as we proceed, our roadsigns reveal various vignettes of Jesus. A vignette, according to a dictionary, is 'a picture, photograph, film image, etc. with no definite border, shading off gradually at the edges into the background' and (I would like to add) into one another. I might also add, that our vignettes are like living cells, reciprocally interacting with another and growing together to eventually take the shape and form of the biblical Jesus.

The Aggregate

New World, New History. Working hard, avoiding pitfalls we and our genial indigenous hosts have found some precious ore: The Kingdom of God which emerges from the study of the beatitudes, is a *new world and a new history*. What does this new world look like? How does this new history look? It is a world and history where the oppressed poor of our present human history will have justice, liberation, joy; will inherit the earth; will be satisfied; and where people in general will experience compassion; will have a direct experience of God and will be called children of God.

This new world is far from the ethereal heaven I once thought our ultimate destiny to be! We will see that we, like Jesus, are called to fashion something of this new world—an alternative economic, social, political, religio-cultural order—in our here-and-now. And, as in the case of Jesus, people will believe that the future new world can and will come only if they see samples and anticipations of it now.

We have been so pre-occupied with prospecting, that until now we have failed to notice the trees, so tall, so sturdy; the brooks, the ancient boulders, the brown mud, the wild vegetation, the earthworm. All together they put on a symphony of stillness. We join them.

Be Still and Know...

Stopover 5

At a Barrio Fiesta (The Kingdom of God As Rice)

OUR HOST: Barrio Fiesta Folks

Barrio Fiesta. We hear the peal of church bells. People are in the streets in their Sunday best. The town band, with the inevitable majorettes, is parading around the streets. It is the feast of Señor San Isidro. It's the town fiesta! We come just in time for the *handa*, the fiesta meal: *Lechon, kare-kare, panga, potsero, kinilaw, imbutido, leche flan, matamis na makapuno, ube, suman sa latik, beer, tuba* – all elbow for space atop the banana leaves on the fiesta table. The folks will be in debt for the rest of the year. But tomorrow will take care of tomorrow. Who will hinder music today?

No need for invitations. We walk in ...

One of Jesus' table companions would have enjoyed our fiesta. For his idea of the Kingdom of God – and that of many other Jews – is a banquet. "One of the dinner guests, on hearing this, said to him [Jesus], 'Blessed is anyone who will eat bread in the kingdom of God!'" (Lk 14:15)

Striking Way of Speaking. In our last stop, we rejoiced with the hungry people of this world. Food, according to one of the beatitudes, was what God wants to see on their tables. The New Testament gives us an impetus to follow this through. In the New Testament, one of the most significant images of the Kingdom and its blessings is 'sitting at table, eating and drinking.' It is significant, of course, because it overturns some of Second Look's cherished axioms. The Second Look tends to rule out of court anything 'material.'

But what truly makes it significant and striking is the frequency with which food-and-Kingdom is mentioned in the New Testament documents. The New Testament writers generally take for granted the meaning of the Kingdom of God. After all, they were addressing first generation readers. They therefore scarcely provide an explanation or description. And yet in that scarcity, the most frequent blessing associated with the Kingdom of God is food. So it is not amiss that our roadmap directs us to a barrio fiesta and to take part in it.

Here is one of the happy surprises of my biblical search: the Kingdom means sitting at table, food, drinking, absence of hunger, meal, feast, banquet!

Check your eyeglasses....

The Kingdom of God As Food

The Kingdom of God Is Rice! Look at our signposts carefully. Originally these texts were not intended to give a theological exposition of the Kingdom of God. Yet they happen to contain refreshing information:

> Blessed are you who are *hungry* now, for you will be *filled*. (Lk 6:21)

The future definitive salvation or the Kingdom of God means food. The hungry are satisfied – an old insight from the beatitudes.

> One of the dinner guests, on hearing this, said to him [Jesus], 'Blessed is anyone who will *eat bread in the kingdom of God*!' (Lk 14:15)

A typical, expected and normal activity in the future Kingdom of God is 'to eat bread'!

> Give us this day our [daily] *bread*. (Mt 6:11)

One of the main petitions of the Lord's Prayer is for our '*epiousion* bread.' The original Greek '*epiousion*' can have several possible meanings.

(a) It can refer to the usual food we ordinarily eat from day to day. One meaning of *epiousion* is 'daily,' 'from day to day.' Thus it refers to the fish, rice, and *pan de sal* we usually and regularly need from day to day. This is the meaning we have in mind when we pray the Lord's prayer in our day.

(b) There is, however, another and different meaning. Pay close attention to it because it is the original meaning on Jesus' lips. *Epiousion* refers to the *food of the coming Kingdom of God at the end of time.* For *epiousion* can also mean *'for the future.'* This refers to the banquet which peoples will enjoy in the new earth at the final and definitive Kingdom at the end of our present history. This, according to contemporary scholarship, was the *original meaning as Jesus first taught the prayer.* In the original Lord's Prayer, Jesus' disciples prayed not for the day-to-day meal but for the barrio fiesta of the final Kingdom of God! 'Give us today our *epiousion* bread' is the exact parallel and equivalent of: 'May your Kingdom come.'

We Filipinos and Asians would say: 'The Kingdom of God is rice!' In doing so, we are in the good company of Jesus and the First Look. Our hosts chime in: 'The Kingdom of God is a barrio fiesta!'

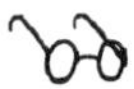

Frequent. The frequency with which the New Testament writings associate bread/food with the Kingdom of God is striking. Give yourself a treat.

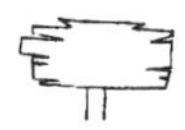

> Then people will come from east and west, from north and south, and *will eat in the kingdom of God.* (Lk 13:29; Mt 8:11)
>
> And I confer on you, just as my Father has conferred on me, a kingdom, so that you may *eat and drink at my table in my kingdom,* and you will sit on thrones judging the twelve tribes of Israel. (Lk 22:29-30)
>
> Someone gave a great *dinner* and invited many. At the time for the *dinner* he sent his slave to say to those who had been invited, 'Come; for everything is ready now.' But they all alike began to make excuses.... Then the owner of the house became angry and said to his slave, 'Go out at once into the streets and lanes of the town and bring in the poor, the crippled, the blind, and the lame.' And the slave said, 'Sir, what you ordered has been done, and there is still room.' Then the master said to the slave, 'Go out into the roads and lanes, and compel people to come in, so that my house may be filled. For I tell you, none of those who were invited will taste my *dinner.*' (Lk 14:16-24; Mt 22:2-10)
>
> ... The bridegroom came, and those who were ready went with him into the *wedding banquet;* and the door was shut.... (Mt 25:10)
>
> Blessed are those slaves whom the master finds alert when he comes; truly I tell you, he will fasten his belt and have them *sit down to eat,* and he will come and serve them. (Lk 12:37)
>
> Truly I tell you, I will never again drink of the fruit of the vine until that day when I *drink it new in the kingdom of God.* (Mk 14:25; Lk 22:15-16)

Real or Symbolic? *Our hosts* evidently appreciate our signposts. But sheepishly they go on to ask: 'The food of the Kingdom—is it real?' This is now our problem. For indeed the Scriptures might be speaking figuratively. Was Jesus not using metaphorical language? Might banquet not be a symbol merely for communion with God and community fellowship?

Real. We assure our hosts, Jesus was not using merely figurative or symbolic language. Real food is the more obvious reference of our texts—unless from the start, without reflection and under the influence of a theology later than Jesus, one has opted for a symbolic interpretation. As isolated statements, our signposts, many of which are parables, may not carry a realistic meaning. But all the references taken together forbid us from imposing a purely symbolic meaning.

Best Evidence: The Lord's Prayer. Our best piece of evidence, however, is found in the Lord's prayer, 'Give us today our *epiousion* bread.' Again, listen carefully. Listen to the tone of the prayer. Are you praying for symbolic bread or real food? No one, I think, will say that in the Lord's Prayer we are asking for symbolic bread. We are asking for real food. Such is the *tone and obvious significance* of the prayer. Well, then if you recall that *epiousion* bread originally referred to the bread of the Kingdom, there is little doubt that the bread of the Kingdom of God appears to be real!

Concretist Thought-Mode. Of course, what we have here is not a newspaper report, and we do not exactly know what the reality will be; but we will do violence to the concretist thought-modes of Jesus and his culture by attempting to rob the bread-language of all realism.

The Risen Body and Food. Our hosts who, presently are in the twilight zone between the Third and Second Looks, ask for clarification. We respond: help could come from the realization that, at the Kingdom of God in the end-time, we will be resurrected people. The resurrected person is a real, physical self (Cf. 1Cor 15:35, 42b-45; Lk 24:6-43; Mk 9:2-3; Dan 12:2-3). Although of course we will no longer be a this-worldly body, we will *not cease to be a real* body. We will be a transformed body, but a body nonetheless. Therefore why, pray, may it not eat real food? It could be 'transformed food' for a transformed body, if you will, but real nonetheless. Our hosts feel their bodies, as if to assure themselves that they are indeed bodies.

The Risen Christ and Broiled Fish. We continue: Watch Jesus. The fact that a risen body is not averse to food is illustrated by that delicious little incident of the risen Jesus asking for, getting and eating broiled fish with his dumbfounded disciples.

> Jesus himself stood among them … They were startled and terrified, and *thought that they were seeing a ghost.* He said to them, 'Why are you frightened, and why do doubts arise in your hearts? *Look at my hands and my feet; see that it is I myself. Touch me and see; for a ghost does not have flesh and bones* as you see that I have….' While in their joy they were disbelieving and still wondering, he said to them, Have you *anything here to eat*?' They gave him *a piece of broiled fish, and he took it and ate in their presence.* (Lk 24:36-43)

A risen person, like Jesus, according to the First Look mentality, may eat real food. We may want it baked or fried, but Jesus had it broiled. His was as real as ours. Just now a fresh platter of *relyenong bangus*[32] is being passed around by our hosts ...

Salvation and Food in Biblical Tradition

Roots in the Hebrew Scriptures. Jesus and the First Look had strong bonds with Semitic[33] culture and the Hebrew Scriptures which tend to be concrete and earthy. We have been cut off from much of that. Instead we have bonded well with a non-Semitic tradition which inclines towards abstractions. This is one possible block for us today.

Total Well-Being and Food. The Hebrew Scriptures, particularly the prophets, envisioned future salvation in terms of a renewed earth. In that renewed earth one finds total well being, justice ... and *food*. These prophetic statements are not just background, they are the roots of First Look ways of seeing. Isaiah pictures final salvation as real, not symbolic, feasting. Statements such as these are the historical and cultural antecedents of the tradition about final salvation as food and fiesta. Notice Ezechiel's total and integral salvation, involving both the religio-moral renewal of heart-and-spirit *and* grain-and-fruit. Some signposts:

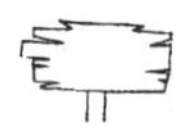

On this mountain the LORD of hosts will make for all peoples
a *feast of rich food, a feast of well-aged wines,*
of *rich food filled with marrow, of well-aged wines strained clear.* (Isa 25:6)

They shall come and sing aloud on the height of Zion,
and they shall be radiant over the goodness of the LORD,
over the *grain, the wine, and the oil,*
and over the *young of the flock and the herd;*
their life shall become like a watered garden,
and they shall never languish again. (Jer 31:12)

A *new heart* I will give you, and a *new spirit* I will put within you; and I will *remove from your body the heart of stone and give you a heart of flesh.* I will *put my spirit within you,* and make you follow my statutes and be careful to observe my ordinances. Then you shall live in the land that I gave to your ancestors; and you shall be my people, and I will be your God. I will save you from all your uncleannesses, and I will *summon the grain and make it abundant and lay no famine upon you.* I will *make the fruit of the tree and the produce of the field abundant, so that you may never again suffer the disgrace of famine* among the nations. (Ez 36:26-30)

---

[32] Milkfish.

[33] 'Semite' or 'Semitic' refer to Afro-Asiatic peoples such as the Hebrews, Arabs, Phoenicians, Akkadians. This is the culture of Jesus.

> Then the LORD became jealous for his land, and had pity on his people. In response to his people the LORD said: I am sending you *grain, wine, and oil, and you will be satisfied*; and I will no more make you a mockery among the nations.
>
> Similar texts: Isa 1:19; 7:21-22; 30:23-24; 33:16; 51:14; 62:8-9; 65:13; 65:21; Jer 31:10-14; Hos 2:21-22; Jl 2:18-27; 3:18; Am 9:13; Zech 9:17.

Who said Filipinos had a monopoly on barrio fiestas?

A Casual, Spontaneous Remark. 'Who is the luckiest person in the world?' As a young boy in catechism class, I would shoot back with this answer: 'Blessed is the soul that will see God face to face in heaven.' A prize-winning answer.

Ah, the price of growing up! The cost of re-education. I later learned that the First Look would replace each word in that sentence.

Blessed ... the soul	that will see God face to face in heaven.
Blessed ... the person	who will eat bread in the Kingdom of God.

I now enjoy that cheerful little sentence in Luke. It is a matter-of-fact sentence as Luke has it, but to the attentive reader it is quite striking. Out of nowhere, somebody makes the casual and unguarded remark: 'Blessed is anyone who will *eat bread in the kingdom of God*!' (Lk 14:15). It is quite revealing in its casualness. It is taken for granted that the Kingdom is not a disembodied world. Rather it is a world where people will eat bread!

That's how things stand in the biblical tradition. We Asians would conjure up varieties of rice! The translation of the New English Bible can all but suppress its enthusiasm: 'Happy the man who shall sit at the feast in the Kingdom of God!' Food for thought! Our hosts reach higher levels of appreciation.

Cautious Conclusion and Problems.

But Wait ... Our cautious conclusion at this point is: We cannot exclude the possibility of real food in the Kingdom of God. But there are problems ... and answers.

Problem: The risen person in the final Kingdom of God is pictured as not marrying; some would infer from this that the risen person does not take in food either.

> For when they rise from the dead, they neither marry nor are given in marriage, but are like angels in heaven (Mk 12:25).

Response: False reasoning. There is no marriage or sex being in the state of resurrection? Well, whatever that means, it does not follow that food is excluded as well.

Problem: Our hosts, honest and truthful people, somehow remember the following 'problematic' words of St. Paul who says that Kingdom of God has nothing to do with food and drink!

'Food is meant for the stomach and the stomach for food,' and God will destroy both one and the other. (1 Cor 6:13)

For the Kingdom of God does not mean food and drink but righteousness and peace and joy in the Holy Spirit. (Rom 14:17)

Response: There are several possible ways of taking up this question. One: we should not try to harmonize all biblical texts, that is, we cannot expect all texts to have a uniform theology. If indeed Paul did exclude food/drink from the Kingdom (and this is not the only possible interpretation of Paul), all that amounts to is that, regarding Kingdom and food, Paul's theology is different from Jesus'.

Another possible response: more generally, some rabbinic teachers in Jesus' time said the Kingdom-banquet was real; others, symbolic. In Jesus' case, as we have seen, the Kingdom-bread cannot be reduced to something purely symbolic.

Still another possible response: in Paul's Christian communities, there was intense debate about whether or not to eat meat offered to idols in the pagan temples. It is possible that in a pique, Paul exclaims: 'Look, the Kingdom of God is not (a debate about) food and drink ...'

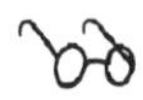

Problem:

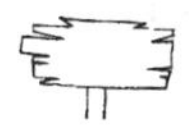

The tempter came and said to him, "If you are the Son of God, command these stones to become loaves of bread." But he answered, "It is written, 'One does not live by bread alone, but by every word that comes from the mouth of God.'" (Mt 4:3)

According to a Second Look view, this is the devil's approach: 'I am tempting you to make your messiahship and your Kingdom one that is concerned for material things, like bread.' Jesus allegedly responds: 'My Kingdom is not about bread and material things. It is about spiritual things.'

Response:

(1) What is the issue here? About whether Jesus' salvation is concerned with bread or not? That Jesus rejected bread and opted for spiritual things? That is highly doubtful. Such a view goes against the very core of the Lord's prayer, in which one of the principal petitions is for real bread! It also jars with one of Jesus' great messianic acts, the feeding of the crowd of hungry thousands (Mt 14:13-21; Mk 6:30-44; Lk 8:10-17).

Rather, the situation is that Jesus is hungry (Mt 4:2; Lk 4:2) after 40 days of fasting, and the most natural thing is to put Jesus to the test, hitting him where he was weakest at that moment, his hunger. 'You are hungry? Show your power! Work a miracle! Change stones into bread!'[34]

Actually a simple parallel is being made here. Just as Israel, Yahweh's son in the Old Testament, was tested about manna and failed, so Jesus is being tested about bread and emerges victor. But, I repeat, the issue is not about the nature of the Kingdom of God.

(2) But, so the objection persists, does not Jesus say that to live we need not just bread, but the will of God? Response: to a tempter who is using bread to test a hungry Jesus, Jesus simply reminds Satan that life is not all about food; it is also about God's word, quoting Dt 8:3. But in saying that, Jesus does not thereby mean to exclude bread from human life nor from the Kingdom of God.

An Aside. And while we are on the subject of God's will, let us feel the full weight of the following statement: *God's will or God's word need not be identified with 'spiritual things' only. God's will can be for such 'material things'*[35] as manna, land, wheat, fig trees, etc. Listen to Deuteronomy 8:

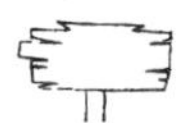

> He humbled you by letting you hunger, then by feeding you with *manna*, with which neither you nor your ancestors were acquainted, in order to make you understand that one does *not live by bread alone*, but by *every word that comes from the mouth of the LORD.* (v 3)

Deuteronomy continues, and notice how 'material' Yahweh's will is for his people who heed his commandments:

> Therefore keep the commandments of the LORD your God, by walking in his ways and by fearing him. (v 6)
>
> For the LORD your God is bringing you into a good land, a land with flowing streams, with springs and underground waters welling up in valleys and hills, a land of *wheat and barley, of vines and fig trees and pomegranates, a land of olive trees and honey*, a land where you may *eat bread without scarcity*, where you will lack nothing, a land whose stones are iron and from whose hills you may mine copper. You shall *eat your fill* and bless the LORD your God for the good land that he has given you. (vv 7-10)
>
> Take care that you do not forget the LORD your God, by failing to keep his commandments, his ordinances, and his statutes, which I am commanding you today. (v 11)

Another Aside. Finally, in order to get an insight into the 'will of God,' nothing can be more educational than the so-called 'last judgment' (Mt 25:31-46). The will of God—by which we will be judged and upon which our final destiny de-

---

[34] There are two other 'tests' that Jesus underwent: to throw himself down from the temple pinnacle and to worship the devil in exchange for the kingdoms of the world. It is doubtful whether the Second Look is justified in interpreting these three temptations beyond simply conventional challenges to perform standard miraculous acts of power.

[35] As in most of the occurrences thus far, I am using 'spiritual' here in the conventional sense of 'pertaining to the soul,' and 'material' as 'pertaining to the body.'

pends—is about 'material' things such as, *food* for the hungry, *drink* to the thirsty, *clothing* to the naked, etc. (See also Mt 12:1; 15:32, etc.).

Problem:

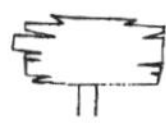

Jesus answered them, 'Very truly, I tell you, you are looking for me, not because you saw signs, but because you ate your fill of the loaves. Do not work for the food that perishes, but for the food that endures for eternal life, which the Son of Man will give you. For it is on him that God the Father has set his seal....'

Jesus said to them, 'I am the bread of life. Whoever comes to me will never be hungry, and whoever believes in me will never be thirsty....'

Very truly, I tell you, unless you eat the flesh of the Son of Man and drink his blood, you have no life in you. Those who eat my flesh and drink my blood have eternal life, and I will raise them up on the last day.' (Jn 6:26-54)

Response: The 'food which endures for eternal life' refers either to the eucharistic bread or Jesus' revelation. When compared to natural bread, it is indeed superior but again Jesus is not here discussing the Kingdom of God and its nature. The same response may be given for Heb 13:9.

Some of us would ban food from the Kingdom because it is 'material.' We saw this as an attempt or temptation to be more Catholic than the Scriptures, a temptation worth 'resisting,' if one wishes to think and talk Jesus.

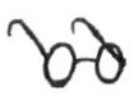

Problem:

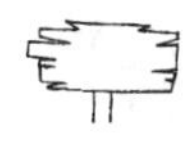

... Therefore I tell you, do not worry about your life, what you will eat or what you will drink, or about your body, what you will wear. Is not life more than food, and the body more than clothing? Look at the birds of the air ... But strive first for the kingdom of God and his righteousness, and all these things will be given to you as well. (Mt 6:25ff; Lk 12:22ff)

This Jesus-saying seems to say that one should not be concerned for food and such things and that one should concentrate on (what is conventionally understood as) spiritual things.

Response: This appears to be a difficult passage, until you note the following:

(1) Jesus counsels against *over*-anxiety (this is the meaning of the original Greek word) about food, drink and clothing. He is *not criticizing a legitimate concern for food and clothing*. The Greek word means 'to be unduly concerned,' 'be over-anxious' (Mt 10:19; Lk 10:41; Phil 4:6). Exaggerated – we could almost say, consumerist—concern for food, not food itself, is the issue here.

(2) A contrast seems to be made between God's Kingdom and food/clothing. Yet in the context of the whole passage, the contrast is rather between God's Kingdom and an *exaggerated concern* about food/clothing, typical of the spirit of the wealthy.

(3) Lastly and importantly, a closer look will reveal that, in this passage, Jesus is not juxtaposing 'spiritual things' with 'material' things. A Second Looker might expect Jesus to say:

Are not SPIRITUAL things (e.g., sanctifying grace)	more than	MATERIAL things? (body, life, food and clothing)

Rather, Jesus' statement is:

Is not something MATERIAL (body)	more than	something MATERIAL? (clothing)

Is not something MATERIAL (life)	more than	something MATERIAL? (food)

'Body' is a value for Jesus. 'Life' is a value for Jesus. Jesus did *not* say: 'Seek first the Kingdom of God, meaning, things of the soul, and all these things, clothing and food, will be added unto you!'

He loved 'body.' He loved 'life.' Addressing the over-anxiety of the wealth-ethos for fine(r) clothes and fine(r) food, he said: 'Body and life' are of more worth! Sometime in my growing up, I had to say goodbye to sermons which put other words in Jesus' mouth. Barrio fiestas or not, my homilies have had to change. We notice that our hosts are suprisingly somewhat pensive. We enquire. They have come upon a certain realization. Their problem is not over-anxiety. Their problem is over-spending!—as they cast a mortified glance on the fiesta table.

A Note. One might think that these words about over-anxiety are addressed to the poor, advising them not to be concerned for food and other 'material' things. No. These words, rather, are against what we would call today the 'consumerist' spirit, typical of the wealth-ethos. This saying of Jesus is in a cluster together with other sayings against the (typical wealth-ethos of the) rich. In Matthew it follows the saying to the rich: 'No one can serve two masters ... You cannot serve God and wealth' (Mt 6:24). In Luke it follows the parable on the rich fool, who said to himself, 'Relax, eat, drink, be merry.' But God said to him, 'You fool!' (Lk 12:15ff)

For Whom and When

An Aspect of Kingdom of God As Food: For the Hungry. Very well, the Kingdom of God is rice or bread. Take note, however, that Jesus is not talking about food in general. He is in particular talking about food and feasting for the hungry of the earth. Recall that the beatitude about food was addressed to the hungry. (Lk 6:21)

A whole parable, reported in slightly different ways in Mt 22:1-10 and Lk 14:16-24, describes the Kingdom in terms of a banquet or a marriage feast. Moreover, for Luke, it is a banquet for the poor. Many were invited, but they gave excuses. 'I have bought a field,' said one. 'I have bought five yoke of oxen,' 'I have just married, and therefore I cannot come,' said the other two. So, from out of the streets and alleys were invited the poor, the crippled, the blind, and the lame. The Kingdom is a banquet; some are too busy with their businesses and affairs. For whom is the banquet, then? It is for the malnourished poor of the land, therefore, the lame, blind, crippled.

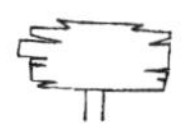

Blessed are you who are *hungry* now, for you will be *filled.* (Lk 6:21)

Someone gave a great dinner and invited many. At the time for the dinner he sent his slave to say to those who had been invited, 'Come; for everything is ready now.' But they all alike began to make excuses. The first said to him, 'I have bought a piece of land, and I must go out and see it; please accept my regrets.' Another said, 'I have bought five yoke of oxen, and I am going to try them out; please accept my regrets.' Another said, 'I have just been married, and therefore I cannot come.' So the slave returned and reported this to his master. Then the owner of the house became angry and said to his slave, 'Go out at once into the streets and lanes of the town and *bring in the poor, the crippled, the blind, and the lame.*' And the slave said, 'Sir, what you ordered has been done, and there is still room.' Then the master said to the slave, 'Go out into the roads and lanes, and compel people to come in, so that my house may be filled. For I tell you, none of those who were invited will taste my dinner.' (Lk 14:16-24)

Clarification. Let us add a remark to prevent misunderstanding of the parable (Lk 14:16-24). Understand the parable well. (1) Is the parable a prediction of what was to happen, i.e., Jesus foresaw that the non-poor would decline and the poor would accept? No. It is rather a summing up of Jesus' experience. It is Jesus' reflection, in timeless parable form, of what actually had happened and was happening in his ministry. (2) The parable does *not* intend to say that the poor were invited *only after* the non-poor had refused. The 'who,' not the 'when,' is what the parable speaks about.

Food for the Future Only? So far, our texts speak of Kingdom and banquet for the future. How about the present? Is food for the hungry limited to the future salvation of the definitive Kingdom? No. This biblical concern that the hungry be fed is, of course, not confined to the future world. Thus, it is in the *now* that the God of the Bible wants us to feed the hungry and give drink to the thirsty as the yardstick for our salvation at the last judgment (Mt 25:35, 37, 40). The Bible is concerned for the satiation of hunger both in the definitive future and in the provisional present, both at the point of arrival and in the journey day to day.

Corporal and Spiritual: A Non-Biblical Classification

Corporal Work of Mercy? As a Second Looker, I used to look down on food-for-the hungry as merely a 'corporal work of mercy.' It is of secondary importance only. It was not a 'spiritual work of mercy.' Corporal works benefit the material body. Spiritual works benefit the spiritual soul. I have since disabused myself of this non-biblical and Western distinctions.

In the biblical tradition, the human person is not made up of two components, material and non-material, linked into one. There are no two components that God, so to speak, put together and death puts asunder. No, for the Bible, as we will see in Stopover 6, the human being is one, indivisible person, made alive and made sacred by the puff of God's breath. Accordingly, in the Bible, there is no talk of corporal blessings for the body and spiritual works for the soul.

Life-Giving or Death-Dealing. And so, the Bible does not categorize works as 'corporal' or 'spiritual.' Works are only either 'life-giving' or 'death-dealing.' So it is at least for Jesus:

> Again he entered the synagogue, and a man was there who had a withered hand. They watched him to see whether he would cure him on the sabbath, so that they might accuse him. And he said to the man who had the withered hand, 'Come forward.' Then he said to them, 'Is it *lawful to do good or to do harm on the sabbath, to save life or to kill*?' (Mk 3:1-4)

'Spiritual' in the Bible = Under the Sway of God's Spirit. Incidentally, the word 'spiritual' is a perfectly biblical word. However, in a culture that does not divide reality into body and soul, it does not mean 'for or pertaining to the soul.' Rather it means any being that is suffused and transfused by, or at least, under the sway of, the Spirit of God (See 1Cor 15:44-45; Rom 12:1). Food for the hungry is a spiritual work!

Notes for Today

Food for the Hungry Today. While we celebrate with the barrio folk, we are acutely aware that poverty and hunger will mar their tomorrows. Our minds expand then to the millions of others who can do no more than just hallucinate about barrio fiestas. Many coax their sustenance out of garbage heaps and restaurant left-overs.

How do we deal with 'food for the hungry' today? Love that puts a ganta of rice onto the cupped hands of a beggar remains a way of feeding the hungry. But we know that this is a band-aid solution and will not do in the long run. Precise diagnosis and surgery are needed.

What causes massive hunger? No, not sloth. No, not the will of God. It is the social system. With the barrio-folk we will have to band together to dismantle social structures and rebuild.

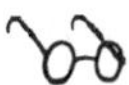

Catechesis Today. The biblical statements about food for the poor of the earth are summons to our conventional catechesis, theology, and pastoral practice. In the concern for the 'higher things,' less importance is given to the so-called 'corporal works of mercy'— which, as we have seen, is a very unbiblical way of thinking and speaking. Salvation in terms of food and drink is not part of traditional religious vocabulary. In fact, in the understanding of the blessing of salvation (soul seeing God face to face or 'beatific vision'), anything 'material' is scrupulously excluded.

The First Look, by contrast, in depicting the new world, speaks of bread and satisfaction, not of intellectual contemplation, for the once-hungry of the earth (cf. also Lk 1:53). For the Bible, definitive salvation itself has to do with food and drink!

It might perhaps be doubted that Matthew, Paul, and John spoke about the satiation of hunger for the poor. It cannot be doubted that Jesus did. In a saying best preserved in the gospel of Luke, Jesus proclaims, in ringing tones, that the hungry will be satisfied with real food (Lk 6:21).

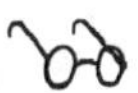

A Practical Daily Reminder. It is time to take leave of our hosts, celebrating their barrio fiesta. We say grace after meals and pray the Lord's Prayer once more. The 'Our Father' can be a practical daily reminder of this food-aspect of the Kingdom. In the 'Our Father,' we pray: 'Give us this day our daily bread' (Mt 6:11). The petition asks for either (1) 'our day to day food' or (2) 'food for the morrow' [=bread of the Kingdom]. This latter meaning would refer to the feast or banquet of the future and definitive Kingdom.

The combination of both meanings would make for the best pastoral practice today. We would be asking for the arrival of the final feast of the Kingdom, while we pray for the food that we need for our sustenance today.

Living as we do at a time when massive hunger is caused by the unjust organization of the global society, our prayer for rice acquires real meaning only when it is accompanied by action to create a just society where rice will be equitably shared by all.

It is the end of another day once more. We find ourselves in … a dance-hall! Well, it is not *really* a dance hall. But it is good enough for the barrio folk … and for us. It is a spacious enough patch of earth, a clearing between trees and houses. The young people are 'dancing' and having fun. But what is usually remarkable about events such as this is the noise … I mean, the music. Instantly, we have a problem in our hands. God, how can we be still and silent here? And it slowly dawns on us that we *can*, that silence is of the depths. Then we notice something else. There were some dancers rocking away, apparently beyond themselves, so to speak. They seem to be meditating. But no, you usually meditate *on* something. They seem to be thinking of nothing. They just seem to be *in* meditation.

Well, we got more than a few free meals at this fiesta….

Stopover 6

A Newborn Child
(Resurrection—a Feature of the Kingdom of God)

OUR HOST: Mother & Child

We move on now to another feature of the future Kingdom of God—resurrection.

A Newborn Child. Maria is the mother of a one-month old child. In her arms she cradles her first-born. She is a girl, 7.5 pounds of ruddy humanity, glowing with energy and life. After the barrio fiesta, our next stop is at the side of this mother and child. With them we learn another feature of the Kingdom of God: resurrection. We contemplate this newborn child. With the psalmist, we can exclaim: How splendid is the human being! You have made the human a little less than divine (cf. Ps 8)!

What is the ultimate fate of a newborn child? Shriveled old age and death? Our Faith says: no. A newborn is so beautiful that the Maker will not want to see her go to waste. A mother like Maria knows this in her heart of hearts. We will vanquish death. The radiant flesh and blood that this newborn child is now will explode into another dimension of infinite brilliance. Our signposts:

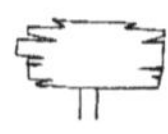

For since death came through a human being, the *resurrection of the dead* has also come through a human being; for as all die in Adam, so *all will be made alive in Christ.* But each in his own order: Christ the first fruits, then at his coming those who belong to Christ. Then *comes the end, when he hands over the kingdom to God the Father*, after he has destroyed every ruler and every authority and power. For he must reign until he has *put all his enemies under his feet. The last enemy to be destroyed is death.* (1 Cor 15:21-26)

This is indeed the will of my Father, that all who see the Son and believe in him may have eternal life; and *I will raise them up on the last day.* (Jn 6:40)

Jesus said to them, "Those who belong to this age marry and are given in marriage; but those who are considered worthy of a place *in that age and in the resurrection from the dead* neither marry nor are given in marriage. Indeed *they cannot die anymore*, because they are like angels and are children of God, being *children of the resurrection.*" (Lk 20:34-36)

Kingdom of God: The Human Being Will Live Again

Victory over Death. The New Testament paints the Kingdom of God at the close of history as victory over death. Biblical religion makes the claim that all enemies will be defeated: hunger, sickness, oppression, tears, pain, sin. And on the last day, the last enemy, death, will be destroyed. Those who have been vanquished by death will one day vanquish death itself. Those who have died will live again.

The *ultimate* destiny of our newborn child who will sleep in death will be to reawaken unto life. In the new world (Kingdom of God), life, not death, will triumph. Those who have died will rise to new life.

Resurrection of the Person, Not the Survival of the Soul. In what manner will this happen? Through a bodily resurrection.[36] The body-self will live again. This body-self that we are now will experience resurrection. First Look religion is a religion which is not afraid to be physical. Individually and collectively, all of us who were once a newborn child, will experience a physical resurrection.

The human being—that one, indivisible person (not just the soul)—will live again.

This is not the survival of the immortal soul, as in the Greek tradition, but the triumph of the body-self.

Look at our newborn child. The Second Look wants the salvation of her soul. The First Look has a different wish. The First Look wishes that the Lord 'will transform the body of our humiliation that it may be conformed to the body of his glory' (Phil 3:21). 'Body,' as we shall soon see, refers to the total person, not just to one part of the person. Thus, Jesus and his culture envisage a 'resurrection of the body' or better, a 'resurrection of the person.'

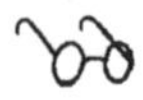

[36] The belief in the resurrection began to emerge clearly in Jewish tradition from 200 B.C.E. onwards (See 2 Mac 7:9, 14, 23; Dan 12:2-3).

Salvation of Souls: A Mistranslation. At once we encounter a problem. We find 'souls' and 'salvation of souls' in our Bible translations! The problem should be momentary. We have a simple case of mistranslation. 'Soul' (*psyche* in Greek), if understood to be the non-material part of the person, is a mistranslation. The underlying Hebrew *nephesh*, means life, person, being, self. It refers to the total person. The practical solution is to mentally substitute 'self,' 'person,' 'life' in place of 'soul.' In doing so, we get to the biblical meaning. For 'salvation of soul,' read 'salvation of person.' Get this insight by distinguishing the more accurate from the faulty translations of the same verse in the following:

1 Pet 1:9

As the outcome of your faith you obtain the *salvation of your souls.* – Revised Standard Version.

... because you are achieving faith's goal, *your salvation* – The New American Bible

James 1:21

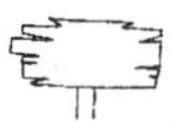

Therefore put away all filthiness and rank growth of wickedness and receive with meekness the implanted word, which is able to *save your souls.*— Revised Standard Version.

Strip away all that is filthy, every vicious excess. Humbly welcome the word that has taken root in you, with its power to *save you.* – The New American Bible

Away then with all that is sordid, and the malice that hurries to excess, and quietly accept the message planted in your hearts, which can *bring you salvation.* – The New English Bible

Mk 8:36

For what does it profit a man, to gain the whole world and suffer the *loss of his soul?* – Popular version

For what does it profit a man, to gain the whole world and *forfeit his life?*—Revised Standard Version.

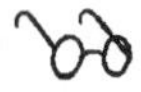

The Risen Person. What is the form and shape of the risen person? No one has had empirical experience of it. But the following signposts give us an idea of the biblical intuitions about it:

But some one will ask, 'How are the dead raised? With what kind of body do they come...?' What is sown is perishable, what is raised is *imperishable.* It is sown in dishonor, it is raised in *glory.* It is sown in weakness, it is raised in *power.* It is sown a physical body, it is raised a *spiritual body.* If there is a physical body, there is also a *spiritual body.* (1 Cor 15:35; 42b-45)

> Six days later, Jesus took with him Peter and James and John, and led them up a high mountain apart, by themselves. And he *was transfigured before them, and his clothes became dazzling white, such as no one on earth could bleach them.* (Mk 9:2-3)

See also: Dan 12:2-3; Lk 24:6-43, and, generally the resurrection appearances of Jesus.

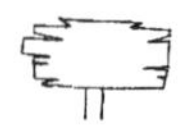

> He will *transform the body* of our humiliation that it may *be conformed to the body of his glory, by the power* that also enables him to make all things subject to himself. (Phil 3:21)

It is a body-self. It is not the soul. It is the human being in its undivided and indivisible unity. It is not the *soul* of Maria's child. It is the *child* – cheeks, arms, limbs, torso and all.

It is totally transformed. It is the same person, but having gone through a complete transmutation. It is the same person but having crossed over to an entirely different and elevated manner of existence.

The total transformation is due to the life-power of God. The risen person is so saturated with the divine Energy, the Spirit of God, that he/she is a 'spiritual body.' Can a body be spiritual? Difficult for the Second Look. Possible and desirable for the First Look. Our once beautiful newborn child, now a risen person, is animated and vibrates with the life and beauty of the Divine.

And so the risen person is radiant in glory and power. Peter, James and John get a preview of the dazzling but gracious demeanor of the risen person. It is modeled and anticipated by the transfigured Jesus on the mountain top:

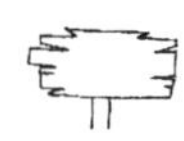

> And he said to them, 'Truly I tell you, there are some standing here who will not taste death until they see that the kingdom of God has come with power.' Six days later, Jesus took with him Peter and James and John, and led them up a high mountain apart, by themselves. And he *was transfigured before them, and his clothes became dazzling white, such as no one on earth could bleach them.* (Mk 9:1-3)

The Human Being Seen Through the Eyes of the Greek and the Hebrew

Two Cultures. Our Christian Faith has lived, moved and had its being in two major cultures, the Semitic and the Greek. The Semitic is the culture of Jesus and the biblical people. The Greek quickly followed; it is the culture of Europe and the West. Each of these cultures had its own way of answering questions about the human being.

What is the human being?

Greek:	soul (spiritual) and body (material)
Semitic:	one living being

What gives life to the human being?

Greek:	the soul
Semitic:	the breath infused in us by God the blood that courses through our veins the energy or strength that a living person experiences

What happens at death?

Greek:	the soul separates from the body
Semitic:	the person gives up his breath; the person sleeps

What is life after death?

Greek:	the soul survives; the body corrupts.
Semitic:	*Initially*, in the Old Testament, there was no belief in life after death. After death, one is a shadow in Sheol or Hades, the underworld. *Later*, 150 years before Christ, the belief was that the person awakes from sleep at the resurrection (Dan 12:2); this happens 'on the last day,' that is, at the end of time. *Meanwhile,* right after death, the person (not the soul) is somehow with God until he/she is raised from the dead 'on the last day.'

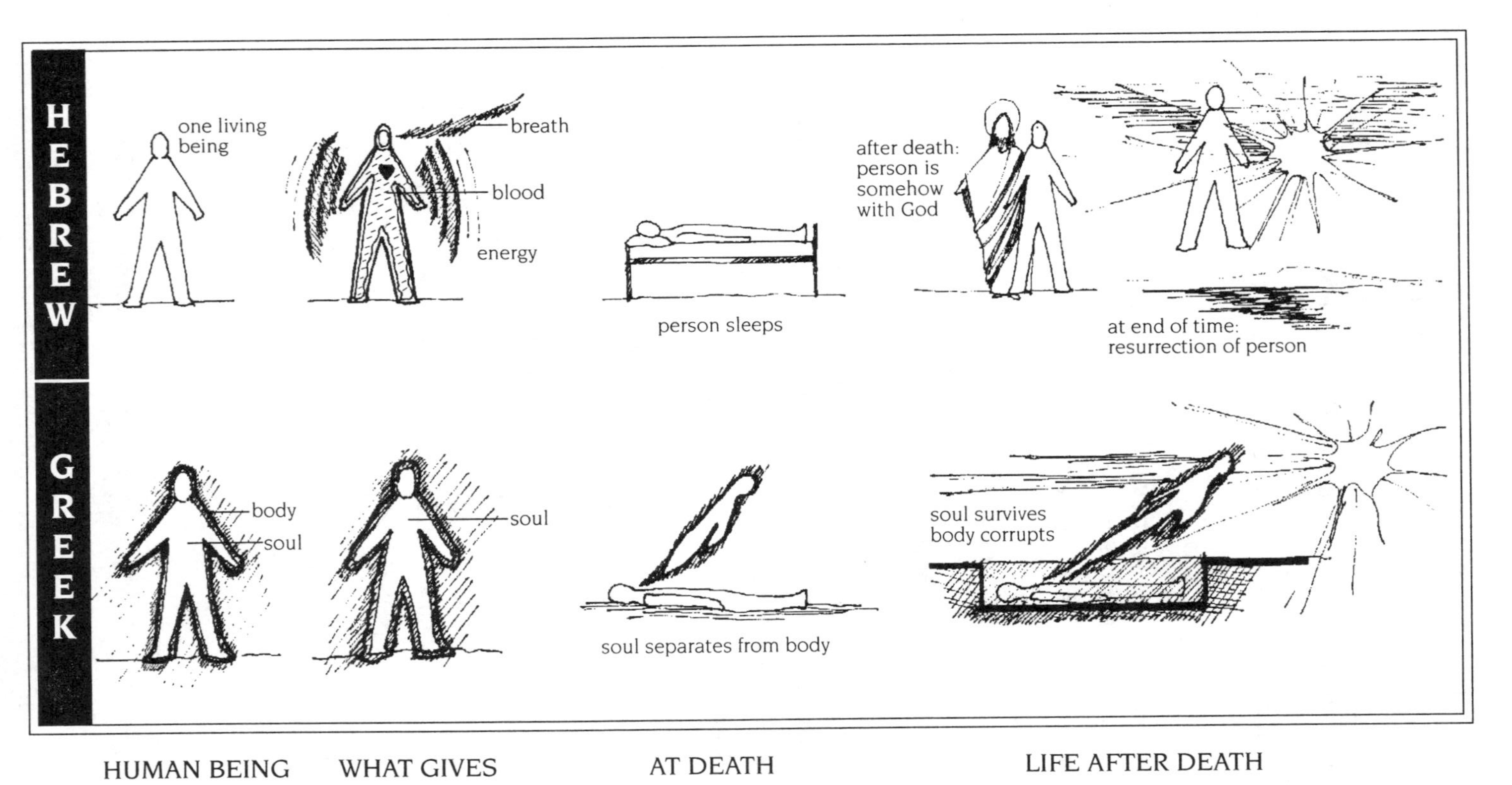
THE HUMAN BEING SEEN THROUGH THE EYES OF THE GREEK AND THE HEBREW
HEBREW
one living being
breath
blood
energy
person sleeps
after death: person is somehow with God
at end of time: resurrection of person
GREEK
body
soul
soul
soul separates from body
soul survives body corrupts
HUMAN BEING
WHAT GIVES LIFE
AT DEATH
LIFE AFTER DEATH

The Human Person: a Unity of One. In the Semitic view then, the human person is always a *unity of one*, so to speak, a *mono-entity.* The human person is not a composite, not an aggregate, not a compound—no matter how blended the elements are. In every stage of existence, our newborn child, the human being is one: in life, after death, at the resurrection.

To 'conceive' or imagine the after-death state in this Semitic view, may be difficult. One can certainly see the remains, the corpse, in the coffin. What survives? In the Greek view, the matter seems simpler: the soul-component survives. In the Semitic, it is still the whole person. How? Jesus' culture does not give an explanation. But it views the person after death as one and whole entity in 'an other mode' of existing, 'an other mode' of being.

In life, the human person is one. After death, the human person is one. At the resurrection the human person is one.

Two Languages. Jesus' view of the human person was, of course, *Semitic.* And we should look for the Semitic meaning when we read the Scripture. Now, this is not so easily done. This is because our New Testament Scripture is not written in a Semitic language but in Greek. In turn, our modern translations are mostly based on the Greek! So, in reading the biblical text, one should remember that the New Testament is written in the *Greek language* and translated into our modern languages *but the underlying culture and meaning are, for the most part, Semitic.* (There are, of course, exceptions. They occur when a Greek word has a Greek meaning.) Normally, a Greek word and its modern translation carry, or should carry, a Semitic meaning. When, therefore, the following words refer to the human being, we should look out for the underlying Semitic meaning. Here is a good rule of thumb: when you encounter any of the following English or Pilipino words, mentally read a Semitic meaning:

English Word and *Pilipino*	Semitic Meaning
'soul' or *kaluluwa* (*psyche* in Greek)	= the human being, sometimes connoting his/her *interiority*
'spirit' or *espiritu* (*pneuma* in Greek)	= the human being, sometimes connoting his/her *interiority*
'body' or *katawan* (*soma* in Greek)	= the human being, connoting his/her *exteriority*—observable, perceptible, sensory
'flesh' or *laman* (*sarx* in Greek)	= the human being, connoting his/her *exteriority*—observable, perceptible, sensory

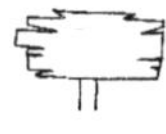

> We were in all two hundred seventy-six *persons* [*psyche*] in the ship. After they had satisfied their hunger, they lightened the ship by throwing the wheat into the sea. (Acts 27:38)
>
> And Mary said, 'My soul [*psyche*] magnifies the Lord, and my *spirit* [*pneuma*] rejoices in God my Savior.' (Lk 1:46-7)
>
> Therefore, do not let sin exercise dominion in your mortal *bodies* [*soma*] to make you obey their passions. No longer present your members to sin as instruments of wickedness, but present *yourselves* to God as those who have been brought from death to life, and present your members to God as instruments of righteousness. (Rom 6:12-13)

Note that 'bodies' of verse 12 is the same as 'yourselves' of verse 13.

> For no *human being* [*sarx*] will be justified in his sight by works of the law, since through the law comes knowledge of sin. (Rom 3:20)

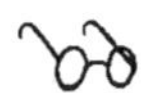

A Thorough Going-Over. We have come to another significant crossroad. It is time for a more thoroughgoing look:

English or Pilipino Word ...	... should have the following Semitic meaning:
'soul' (*psyche* in Greek) (*nephesh* is underlying Hebrew)	concrete person, self, being, 'I' (1 Cor 15:45; 1 Pet 3:20; Rev 16:3) self in its interiority or self as center of feelings, emotions, thoughts ('heart'), 'I' (Mt 26:38; Col 3:23) life (Mk 10:45; Mt. 2:20; Mt 6:25; Lk 6:9; Acts 27:22; Jn 10:11; Phil 2:30) Usually not 'soul' in the Greek sense!
'kaluluwa'	*Tao, ang sarili, buhay.*
Some problematic passages: Mt 10:28; 1 Thes 5:23; Heb 4:12; 1 Pet 2:11. Solution: (1) to be treated as exceptions to the general rule, or (2) still to be explained semitically.	

English or Pilipino Word ...	... should have the following Semitic meaning:
'spirit' (*pneuma* in Greek) (*ruah* is underlying Hebrew)	wind (Jn 3:8a) breath (Mt 27:50; Acts 7:59; Lk 8:55) self inwardly or self as center of feelings, emotions, thoughts ('heart'), 'I,' courage, temper (Mk 2:8; 8:12; Lk 1:47; Acts 17:16; 1 Cor 16:17-18; Mt 5:3; Phil 4:23; Gal 6:18; Phlm 25; Mk 14:38 (self as courageous is contrasted with same self as weak/afraid). The following may offer initial problems: 2 Cor 7:1; 1 Cor 7:34; 1 Thess 5:23; 1 Cor 5:3-5a; Col 2:5 ghost, shade of the dead (Lk 24:37,39; Acts 23:8-9) (This is not the Greek soul.) God's life, energy and power (Acts 1:8; Rom 5:5, 8:26; 1 Cor 6:19, 12:13; Gal 3:2). Important note: This divine life and power, like the wind, is invisible but need not be immaterial in the Greek sense. The same is true of the 'evil spirit' (e.g., Mk 1:23, 26). God's life and power itself, or, the human person possessing it (Rom 8:1-17; Gal 5:16-25, 6:8; Jn 3:6; 1 Cor 2:15) Usually not 'soul,' the non-material substance distinct from the body; not 'soul' in the Greek sense
'espiritu'	*hangin, hininga, kalooban, kaibuturan, multo, espiritu ng Dios.*
Some problematic exceptions: Heb 4:12, 12:23; James 2:26; Pet 3:19.	

English or Pilipino Word ...	... should have the following Semitic meaning:
'body' (*soma* in Greek) (*basar* is underlying Hebrew)	the human being the self the human person outwardly—observable, perceptible, sensory not the material component of the person, as opposed to the non-material component Generally has a positive connotation (e.g. Rom 12:1; Rom 6:12ff.) Examples: Mt 6:22,25; Rom 6:12; 8:23; 12:1; 1 Cor 6:13-15, 18-20; 7:4, 34, 9:27, 10:16-17, 11:24, 12:12, 13:3, 15:44; 2 Cor 4:10; Phil 3:21; Heb 10:10; 1 Pet 2:24; 1 Cor 7:34.
'katawan'	*tao, sarili*
Expect some problems with these passages. Many of them, though, may still carry a Semitic meaning. Or, they may be exceptions as in: Mt 10:28; Rom 8:10; 1 Cor 5:3, 7:34; 12:2; Heb 13:3; James 2:26.	

English or Pilipino Word …	… should have the following Semitic meaning:
'flesh' (*sarx* in Greek) (*basar* is underlying Hebrew)	human being (Mk 10:8, 13:20; 1 Pet 1:24, 3:20; Rom 3:20; 1 Cor 1:29; Gal 2:16; Jn 6:51-56) humankind (Lk 3:6; Acts 2:17) human (Eph 6:5; Heb 12:9a; Jn 1:13-14) human nature (Jn 8:15; Rom 1:3, 4:1; 8:3; 2 Cor 5:16; Jn 3:6) human condition (1 Tim 3:16; Phlm 16; Heb 5:7; Mt 16:17; 1 Cor 15:50) old self without God, weak, sin-prone, or sinful (Rom 8:3, 8:4-9, 8:12-13, 7:5; 18; 25; 8:3; 1 Cor 3:1, 3; Gal 3:3, 5:16-25; Mk 14:38 (perhaps) Generally *sarx* has a negative connotation in Paul. It refers to the human being or human nature minus the Spirit of God. human person outwardly—observable, perceptible, sensory (cf. above examples) not 'flesh' in the sense of one component of the person, as opposed to the non-material component Other examples 1 Cor 15:39; 1 Cor 5:5; 2 Cor 12:7
'laman'	*tao, sangkatauhan, buhay-tao, kalagayang-tao, karupukan ng tao*

Not Wrong; Different. We are not saying that the Greek anthropology is wrong. We are saying that it is different from the Semitic. The Semitic is concretist. The Greek is metaphysical. We are also saying that the Semitic is closer to our Third World perspective and concerns. The original biblical meanings and our pastoral commitments today mandate us to read the Semitic meaning behind many of our contemporary translations.

'Spiritual': The Aroma of God

'Spiritual'. In much of our journey, I am using the word 'spiritual' somewhat loosely. It is time to make some precisions. The meaning of 'spiritual' in the Greek culture is 'for or pertaining to the soul.' This is normally the meaning that the Second Look adopts. The sacraments, prayers, novenas, speaking in tongues, holy water, incense – are spiritual. Food, land, wages are—according to the Second Look—not spiritual matters.

For the First Look, on the other hand, any entity that is in God or with God or through God or from God is spiritual. Anything or anybody that has the aroma or the taste or the touch of God's Spirit is spiritual. The holy water blessed by the Holy Father is indeed spiritual. So is a cup of water given to a thirsty beggar. Treating your housemaid humanely or giving decent wages to your driver is generally spiritual whereas going to mass everyday need not be. The value of our mass is generally measured by what we do outside the church. A whiff of God's breath on any creature – that is the Spirit that makes our commonplace existence spiritual.

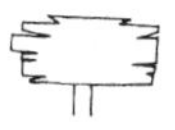

I appeal to you therefore, brothers and sisters, by the mercies of God, to present your *bodies* as a living sacrifice, holy and acceptable to God, which is your *spiritual* worship. (Rom 12:1)

It is sown a physical body, it is raised a *spiritual body*. If there is a physical body, there is also a *spiritual body*. (1 Cor 15:44)

The *fruit of the Spirit* is love, joy, peace, patience, kindness, generosity, faithfulness, gentleness, and self-control. (Gal 5:22-23)

The inaugural address in Nazareth (Lk 4:16-20) is instructive. The works or fruits of the Spirit are spiritual, are they not? Well, The *Spirit* of the Lord is upon Jesus. And what are the Spirit's fruits? What are the Spirit's works? *To proclaim good news (of liberation from poverty) to the poor; liberty to captives; health for the sick; freedom to the oppressed; the jubilee year blessings, that is, release of slaves, rest for the land, cancellation of debts, restoration to impoverished people of their ancestral land, property and homes.* All this is spiritual!

Today

Not Only for the End-Time. Is the biblical concern for the whole person only for the 'last day'? These signposts will help: Rom 12:1; 1 Cor 6:19-20; Gal 5:25; 2 Cor 3:18; Rom 8:11; 2 Cor 1:22; Mk 12:25. Even in the now, the Bible is concerned for the human person as a bodily self, not as a 'soul' struggling to escape from the 'body.' It speaks of presenting our bodies (read: whole person or living being) as a living sacrifice to God (Rom 12:1). The bodily self should be the temple of the Spirit (1 Cor 6:19-20); walk according to the Spirit (Gal 5:25); be transformed by the Spirit (2 Cor 3:18) and on the last day, in radiance and power, this same bodily self will be raised by the Spirit (Rom 8:11; 2 Cor 1:22; Mk 12:25).

Pastoral Work. Here in the biblical belief in the resurrection, I found some teasers for pastoral work. First Look salvation is oriented to a bodily resurrection, not to salvation of souls. If 'soul' refers to that non-material part of the person, distinct from, imprisoned in, and devoutly wishing to be liberated from, the body, then the New Testament never speaks of salvation of souls. One problem is that our preaching and catechism still do – if not always in word, often in thought and deed.

Social Causes. The New Testament inspires us today, as we help to remove the social causes of disease and death, to move a step forward to that transformed life where malnutrition, TB and death will have given way to health and life, and where God's life-giving breath will give splendor to our frames of clay.

From Beauty to Beauty. Before we depart we contemplate once more our newborn child. Maria, our mother-host, has shown us how frames of clay have their own beauty. The New Testament tells us that such beauty will not evaporate into a soul-salvation. Rather it will go from beauty to transcendent beauty. When that happens, we will have arrived. It is the Kingdom of God.

Be Still and Know ...

Stopover 7

At a Manufacturer of War Weapons (The Kingdom of God and the Casting Out of Devils)

OUR HOST: Protest Rally

We continue our search for the meaning of the Kingdom of God. From the irenic pair of mother and child, our roadmap takes us to three sets of protesters. They are waving flags and banners. One group is at the headquarters of the IMF-World Bank. The second group has formed a human barricade to stop trucks and chainsaws from hacking away at the few remaining forests of the world. The third group is massing outside the biggest manufacturer of war weapons in the world. Any of these three would be the next appropriate stop.

We opt for the third group, gathered outside a weapons assembly plant. It is relatively easy to see the obvious insanity that the arms industry is. In a planet inhabited by humans, there exists a business designed for humans to exterminate humans. And make a living in the process! We need to be exorcised from such madness.

A Militarized World. Centuries ago, Isaiah dreamt of a world in which the items of war—soldier's boots and clothing soaked in blood—would be thrown as fuel into the fire, to be erased from human memory and experience (Isa 9:5). How near is humanity to such a world after centuries of technological pole-vaulting? Goons and guns sow terror in otherwise quiet villages of peace-loving peasants. Superpowers and aspiring superpowers flex nuclear muscles. A highly militarized world is one of the materializations of the forces of darkness.

The Kingdom of God and the Defeat of Satanic Forces

Reign of God Defeats Reign of Satan. In Jesus' time, it was a belief that the earth was under the reign of Satan. This was the outlook of people who belonged to what is called the apocalyptic tradition. Evil was not just an impersonal force. It was a 'someone.' Satan was one of the names given to this personalized evil force in the world. He and his army worked evil in the world, causing sin, sickness, suffering, oppression, war, and death. The expected salvation would take the form of the destruction of the *reign of Satan* by the coming *Reign of God.* The coming of the Kingdom of God meant the defeat of the evil one and his rule.

Jesus Casts Out Satan. Our hosts have copies of the Bible. As we sit around in a circle, they open to these passages:

If it is by the finger of God that *I cast out demons*, then the *Kingdom of God* has come to you. (Lk 11:20 = Mt 12:28)

One of the more frequently reported works of Jesus was his casting out of evil spirits (Mk 1:25; 3:11; 5:8; 7:29; 9:25; 3:22-27). Statements that summarize his ministry mention this kind of activity.

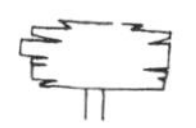

Whenever the *unclean spirits* saw him, they fell down before him and shouted, 'You are the Son of God!' (Mk 3:11)

That evening they brought to him many who were *possessed with demons; and he cast out the spirits* with a word, and cured all who were sick. This was to fulfill what had been spoken through the prophet Isaiah, 'He took our infirmities and bore our diseases.' (Mt 8:16-17)

Were these cases of epilepsy, mental illness, possession? In any case, Jesus saw his exorcisms as destruction of the reign of Satan and manifestations of the Kingdom of God.

Jesus Vanquishes Satan. Satan was thought to exercise his sway over individuals, causing physical or mental affliction; over nature, causing calamities; or over history and the world, engineering the inhumanity of the Roman Empire. In the gospels, Jesus is portrayed as vanquishing the power of Satan in individual people's lives.[37] Satan is the strong man who is now being bound and whose house is being plundered by Jesus (see Mk 3:22-26).

---

[37] An interesting suggestion has been made that the "legion" of spirits in the country of Gerasa that Jesus casts into the ravine (Mk 5:1ff) symbolizes the Roman legion.

Today

To Be Exorcised Today. We come back to our hosts, staging a protest outside an assembly plant. The Kingdom of God is far from our reach, our hosts say, as long as there exist people who produce guns, warplanes, tanks and chemical weapons of mass destruction. The production of these instruments of war is itself a big multi-billion business. It is in the service of other multi-billion dollar businesses that create the family of the super-rich existing in the same planet as their destitute brothers and sisters do. The mentality of war peddling is one of the evils that needs to be cast out of our system.

A Kingdom-Blessing. In the gospels, the destruction of satanic powers then is one of the Kingdom-blessings. It remains so today.

Outside the barricades and fences of this arms factory, we form a circle with our protesting friends. We move into silence. We meditate. These friends of ours are old hands at activism. They have realized for some time that the price of non-silence is burn-out. They also have realized that energy comes, yes, from the poor, but also from silence. So we sit now, silent shoulder to silent shoulder. We feel that we are receiving from, and sending healing energies to, the universe, similar to those that radiated from Jesus when he dethroned the forces of Satan.

Be Still and Know …

Stopover 8

Sorsogon
(The Kingdom of God As a New World, New Universe, New Creation)

OUR HOST: Nature and Family in Sorsogon

In this stopover we get acquainted with a synonym of the Kingdom of God, the 'new heaven and the new earth.'

HEAVEN-AND-EARTH = UNIVERSE

Not Looking Up but Looking Ahead to the Future. Our signposts have already pointed to salvation and Kingdom of God as being a new world. It is a new earth. This might be news for the Second Look. It is self-evident for the First Look. We look around and see the trees, birds, rocks, oceans, people. We look up and we see the sun, moon, and the galaxies. This is our universe. It is a beautiful universe. But our human hands have wrought wrongdoing, pain, death upon it. It is also a blighted universe. The prayer of the biblical people was not to flee from this valley of tears and go up to heaven; rather they looked forward to a *new* world, a new universe, a new creation. Notice, in addition, that they used a more picturesque language: a new heaven(s) and a new earth. It is a graphic way of talking about a new universe.

Blue Roof, Flat Surface. Before we talk about a *new* heaven and a *new* earth, let us first get acquainted with *heaven and earth.*

The pre-scientific person looks up and sees a blue roof above. It is the 'firmament' or 'sky' ... or 'heaven.' It is not empty space. Like a dome or an inverted bowl, it is solid. Sometimes this roof is seen as having not one but several layers, thus, 'heavens.' Onto the downside of this roof, as on a ceiling, are attached the ornaments. These are the stars, moon and sun, set like jewels on the firmament. Yahweh's dwelling place is in heaven or, more accurately, above the heaven(s). In the Lord's prayer, we say: 'Our Father who are in heaven.'

On the other hand, there is this flat surface on which we stand here below. It is called 'earth.' Modern science tells us that the earth is round. But for pre-scientific eyes, as in biblical culture, it is flat.

Heaven and Earth; Roof Plus Floor. Thus we have heaven above and earth below; the roof above, and the floor below. Add roof and floor together in simple arithmetic and what do you have? Add 'heaven' and 'earth' and what do you have? You have the universe. That is the pre-scientific architectural configuration of the universe. Heaven-and-earth or 'heaven and earth' (taken together as a composite unity) [38] is the pre-scientific way of talking about 'world,' 'universe,' 'creation.'

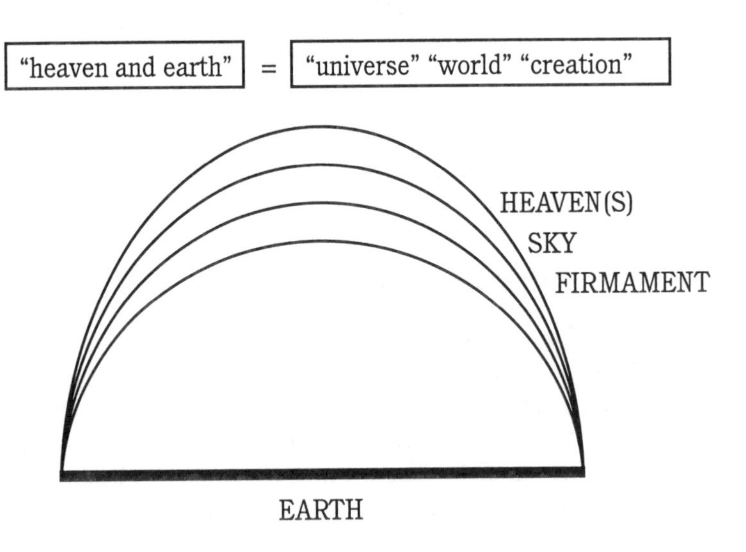

[38] Note that it is helpful to write the phrase with dashes or inverted commas.

NEW HEAVEN AND NEW EARTH = NEW UNIVERSE

New Heaven and New Earth. Accordingly, '*new* heaven(s) and *new* earth' means new universe, new world, new creation.

Semitic culture in Jesus' time envisaged the Kingdom of God as a new world. As our roadsigns will show, many New Testament writers held this view. How about Jesus himself? Since most of the roadsigns in our present stopover are not direct quotations of Jesus' own words, one may legitimately ask whether Kingdom of God as a new world was shared by Jesus. Our response to this is 'Yes.' Kingdom of God as a new world is so self-evident to Jesus' time and culture that, if he did not share their outlook, it would make Jesus an unintelligible cipher among his people.[39]

Sorsogon. Have you ever been to Sorsogon? It is a province in southern Luzon, Philippines. In the daytime you see the blue sea, throbbing with fish and adorned with fantastic corals. Move your line of sight onto the land, and your eyes meet the various healing shades of green and yellow. There before you are the riches of Asia: ricefields ready to harvest and coconut trees aiming for the sky.

Nestled peacefully and securely in this bucolic world is a rustic house. It is home for a family that lives in harmony with each other and with nature. Violence, oppression, injustice are a comfortable distance away.

Look further up. There are the narras, the molaves and their less rugged cousins—virile and tough, but from a distant perspective, looking every inch like the daintiest hand-woven embroidery. Let your eyes swing up to the pure, blue sky, with a garnishing of clouds here and there. Can you compare its beauty to anything but itself?

Stay till evening and watch the same sky put on its velvet *saya* and wear its jewels of the night. Complete the cycle. Look at the sea once more, now an eager mirror recording the tiniest glimmer of the farthest star. And when you are done looking, listen. Listen to the spiritual conversation of heaven-and-earth and the human family.

This household of humans and nature, forming one animate whole, are our hosts, for they can stimulate dreams of one possible way to be. They have nothing against development, but they tell us that the toxins we have injected into our living—chemical, noise, greed—are among the worst anticipations of the new heaven and the new earth.

---

[39] Here, I am enunciating a principle which is contrary to that of some scholars and to which evidently I do not subscribe. They say that any Jesus-saying which contains elements of his contemporary culture should be eliminated from authentic sayings of Jesus.

A NEW UNIVERSE WHERE THERE IS JUSTICE

What Did God Promise? According to this signpost, the salvation that God has promised is a new world where there is justice:

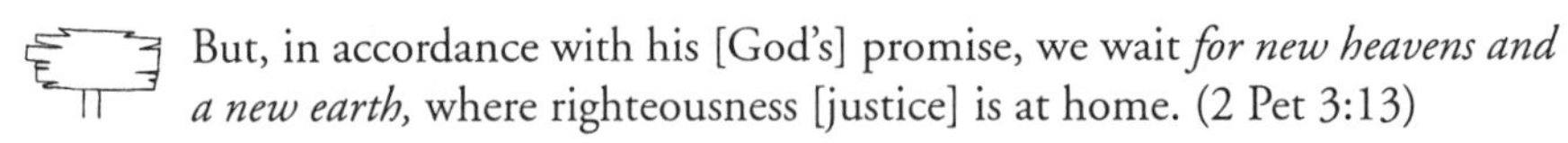

> But, in accordance with his [God's] promise, we wait *for new heavens and a new earth,* where righteousness [justice] is at home. (2 Pet 3:13)

Notice the casual, self-evident tone of that faith-statement. And with such economy of words!

In both First and Second Looks, God has made a promise and that promise is the basis of our hope. But pause to note the difference. To the Second Look, he promised heaven above. To the First Look he promised a new heaven *and a new earth.*

What do we find there? What will we experience? For the Second Look: intellectual contemplation. For the First Look: justice.

And for whom is this salvation? For the Second Look: for incorporeal souls or individual persons. For the First Look: for human beings, individually and collectively, and for creation itself.

This new world, according to the simple (or is it grandiose?) faith of biblical religion, is the ultimate destiny that God has promised.

Thus while the Second Look looks forward to a heaven in which souls see God face to face, the First Look looks forward to a new world where humankind and nature will experience God, justice and total well-being. The aspiration of the First and Third Looks is for a new Asia, a new Philippines. Our Sorsogon hosts feel they are living in anticipation of an even more beautiful new Sorsogon.

Justice or Righteousness? Some translations of our signpost, 2 Pet 3:13, read: '... new heavens and a new earth in which *righteousness* dwells.' In other words, in some translations, you will read 'righteousness' instead of 'justice.' 'Righteousness' is a generic term and means uprightness, saintliness, godliness, piety. A person who prays often may be called 'righteous.' 'Justice,' specifically social justice, is more pointed. It can refer to anything between fair wages for employees to agrarian reform for peasants. Both 'righteousness' and 'justice' are possible translations and in fact, the author of 2 Pet 3:13 most likely meant the former. However, Isaiah 65:17-25, which is the source and background, clearly meant a new world where there is *justice.*

Isa 65:17-25	Descriptive Comment
For I am about to create new heavens and a new earth; the former things shall not be remembered or come to mind. But be glad and rejoice forever in what I am creating; for I am about to create Jerusalem as a joy, and its people as a delight. I will rejoice in Jerusalem, and delight in my people;	JOY
no more shall the sound of weeping be heard in it, or the cry of distress (*za`aq* = cry of the oppressed).	JUSTICE
No more shall there be in it an infant that lives but a few days, or an old person who does not live out a lifetime; for one who dies at a hundred years will be considered accursed. (At this time there was as yet no belief in life-after death.)	LONG LIFE
They shall build houses and inhabit them; (In the old world, the worker builds without pay and the king inhabits. For example: Jer 22:13).	JUSTICE
they shall plant vineyards and eat their fruit. (In the old world, the poor plant and the princes devour the vineyard. For example: Isa 3:14.)	JUSTICE
They shall not build and another inhabit; (Note repetition, now in negative form)	JUSTICE
they shall not plant and another eat; (Note repetition, now in negative form)	JUSTICE
for like the days of a tree shall the days of my people be, and my chosen shall long enjoy the work of their hands.	JUSTICE
They shall not labor in vain,	JUSTICE
or bear children for calamity; for they shall be offspring blessed by the LORD— and their descendants as well.	CHILDREN OF GOD

Before they call I will answer, while they are yet speaking I will hear. (Contrast: Where there is no justice, there no prayer is answered. See Isa 1:12-17.)	JUSTICE and PRAYER
The wolf and the lamb shall feed together, The lion shall eat straw like the ox; but the serpent—its food shall be dust! They shall not hurt or destroy on all my holy mountain, says the Lord (Our host-family of Sorsogon loves this.)	JUSTICE and PEACE

Profiles of the New World

All Things New. Those who wish to have some detailed specifics about the new heaven and new earth will find it in Rev 21:1-5.

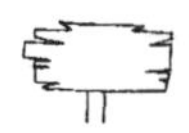

Then I saw *a new heaven and a new earth;* for the first heaven and the first earth had passed away, and the sea was no more. And I saw the *holy city, the new Jerusalem, coming down out of heaven* from God, prepared *as a bride* adorned for her husband. And I heard a loud voice from the throne saying,

'See, the *home of God is among mortals.*
He will dwell with them as their God;
they will be his people,
and God himself will be with them;
he will *wipe every tear* from their eyes.
Death will be no more;
mourning and crying and pain will be no more,
for the *first things have passed away.*'
And the one who was seated on the throne said, 'See, I am making *all things new.*' Also he said, 'Write this, for these words are trustworthy and true.' (Rev 21:1-5)

With the author, you have a vision of an old universe fading away and giving way to the new. People like myself who love water will be disappointed that 'the sea will be no more.' But we understand; in that culture, the sea was a place of tempests, shipwrecks, disasters. There will be a new capital city, radiant as a bride. One thing should not go unnoticed about this city: it is *coming down* to earth! [40] And *on this new earth* God will dwell. And God will have a special bonding with his people. [41] God

[40] Note that it is a new capital city, *not* heaven itself, that is coming down to earth. The Bible never envisions the coming down of heaven to earth.

[41] 'They shall be his people' is a formula used by prophets to express Yahweh's covenant with the people. Jer 24:7; 31:33; 32:38. Ez 14;11.

himself will wipe away every trace of suffering, pain and death. The already exalted declaration peaks: 'Behold, *I make all things new.*' The smog —chemical and moral— will dissipate and the galaxies will smile again. Our Sorsogon-hosts are trying to envision something more beautiful than their Sorsogon.

Before we proceed let us attempt to clear away a possible mental block. This text from the Book of Revelation and the ones to follow seem to speak in symbols, and so they do not mean to be taken at face value. As a response, I would say that the language is not purely symbolic. They are paintings. Although, therefore, they are not photographs, they mean to convey some life-reality. Thus 'new heaven and new earth' cannot point to anything other than a new world. Certainly, not heaven. The bride 'coming *down*' cannot suggest anything but that salvation is a descent to earth rather than an ascent to heaven.

Rebirth of the Universe. There are two other noteworthy passages, Mt 19:28 and Lk 22:29-30, which speak of a new world. Once more, justice is singled out as its attribute.

> And I confer on you, just as my Father has conferred on me, a *kingdom*, so that you may eat and drink at my table in my kingdom, and you will sit on *thrones judging the twelve tribes of Israel.* (Lk 22:29-30)
>
> Jesus said to them, 'Truly I tell you, *at the renewal of all things*, [in Greek: transformed creation] when the Son of Man is seated on the throne of his glory, you who have followed me will also sit on twelve *thrones, judging the twelve tribes of Israel.*' (Mt 19:28)

These two statements, one by Matthew and the other by Luke, are two slightly different versions of one and the same Jesus-saying. What Luke calls '*Kingdom*' is the same as Matthew's '*renewal of all things*' or transformed creation! Again, Kingdom of God is not heaven above but a transformed creation.

Justice Is Its Trait. And justice is the attribute of this new world.

This requires a little explanation. In certain biblical contexts, to 'sit on a throne' 'to reign' 'to be king' (*mlk*) mean doing justice for the poor and oppressed. 'To judge' (*shpht*) likewise means to vindicate or confer justice to the poor.

So goes a prayer for the king:

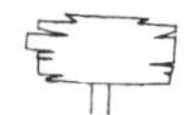

> Give the *king* [*mlk*] thy *justice*, O God,
> and your *righteousness* to a king's son.
> May he *judge* your people with righteousness,
> and your poor with *justice.*
> May the mountains yield prosperity for the people,
> and the hills, in righteousness.
> May he defend the cause [*shpht*] of the poor of the people,
> give deliverance to the needy,
> and crush the oppressor. (Ps 72:1-4)

> The language may not sit well with our anti-feudal sensibilities, but in biblical culture, 'to sit on throne,' 'to judge' means to execute justice in behalf of the poor and oppressed. Thus, quaint as the language may be, Matthew and Luke give us this picture of salvation: Jesus and his disciples will oversee a world where there is justice.

A Re-Born World Where There Is Justice. Matthew's 'new world' is *paliggenesia* in the original Greek. *Palin* means again, and *genesis* means birth. *Paliggenesia* is a colorful word, descriptive of re-birth, transformation, re-creation. The whole creation undergoes a re-birth. The whole created universe is transformed. The firmament and the earth, the whole nature and human beings, this world of hunger, disease and decay, all will be totally transformed into a new world and new history; there the king of justice will reign!

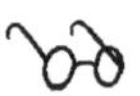

Universal Restoration of All Things. Let us move on to another roadsign. This is the scenario: Jesus 'ascends' into heaven. The apostles look up to heaven. They are told to go back to their normal lives. They are told that God will eventually send Jesus back to earth as the Christ. In the meantime, heaven will keep Jesus *until the 'universal restoration.'* All reality will be remade, rehabilitated, rejuvenated! It is a new universe at the end of history. And in it, an even lovelier Sorsogon! One can almost hear the dance and re-assembly of the planets in the sonorous Greek words, *apokatastasis panton*. Since purple-blue is a color close to the Divinity, our hosts wonder whether the universe will then take on much of the blue of their skies and seas.

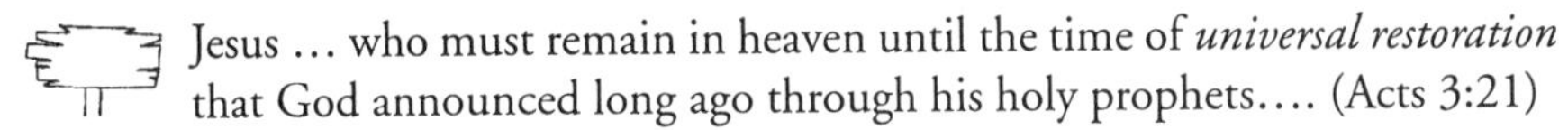

> Jesus ... who must remain in heaven until the time of *universal restoration* that God announced long ago through his holy prophets.... (Acts 3:21)

Unity of All Things in Heaven and on Earth. A similar panorama is presented by Eph 1:1-10. The plan and purpose of God, when history will have reached its culmination, is to draw *all things together into one unity, things in heaven and things on earth*! Roof and floor—everything in them will be swept together into one through the action of the Christ.

> He has made known to us the mystery of his will, according to his good pleasure that he set forth in Christ, as a plan for the fullness of time, *to gather up all things in him, things in heaven and things on earth.* (Eph 1:9-10)

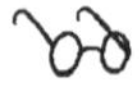

A Universe Soaked in God. Paul sees the climactic finale thus: the whole of the universe is permeated by the Divine Energy. (In somewhat roundabout language, Paul describes the work of Christ and the destiny of the universe. The Father has put all of reality, except of course himself, under the dominion of Christ. Christ reigns until he has subdued all his enemies, that is, all evil powers in the universe, the last enemy being death. Then comes the end of history.) At the end of history, Jesus delivers the Kingdom to his Father. The Son himself will then be subject to the Father. The peak of this drama is, in the words of Paul, 'that God may be all in all.' The *Divine Energy permeates all of existence, binds all of reality together.*

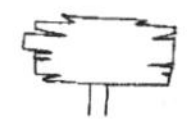

Then comes the *end*, when he hands over the *kingdom* to God the Father, after he has destroyed every ruler and every authority and power. For he must reign until he has put all his enemies under his feet. The last enemy to be destroyed is death. For 'God has put all things in subjection under his feet.' But when it says, 'All things are put in subjection,' it is plain that this does not include the one who put all things in subjection under him. When all things are subjected to him, then the Son himself will also be subjected to the one who put all things in subjection under him, so that *God may be all in all.* (1 Cor 15:24-28)

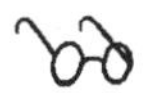

Kingdom Is an Earth Down Here. Next, we have two testimonies from the Book of Revelation. They inform us that the *Kingdom of God is down here on earth, not up in heaven.*

You have made them to be a kingdom and priests serving our God, and they will reign *on earth.* (Rev 5:10)

Then the seventh angel blew his trumpet, and there were loud voices in heaven, saying, 'The *kingdom of the world has become the kingdom of our Lord* and of his Messiah, and he will reign forever and ever.' (Rev 11:15)

Creation Itself Will Be Set Free From Its Bondage. Rom 8:19-23, though couched in language that needs to be deciphered, is precious. It not only says that we are heading towards a new creation. It also explicitates that *creation itself*—not only humans but also the mountains, forests, rivers, trees, birds—*will experience salvation.* Our hosts cast a dreamy glance at their mountains, skies and seas.

The whole of creation—both human and natural—long for full salvation. We humans, who already possess the first fruits of the Spirit, groan inwardly, longing for our bodily resurrection and thus become children of God.

But not just we humans. Nature too. Nature, according to Paul, has been subjected to meaninglessness, perhaps by God, but not without hope. The theological fact is that *creation itself will be set free from its enslavement to decay and it too will obtain the glorious liberty that we humans will enjoy as children of God.* Meanwhile, the *whole creation has been groaning* like a woman in the birth pangs of labor.

Nature and humans long for liberation; *we humans, from death; the rest of creation, from decay; we humans, for our resurrection; nature, for its transformation.*

For the creation waits with eager longing for the revealing of the children of God; for the creation was subjected to futility, not of its own will but by the will of the one who subjected it in hope that *the creation itself will be set free from its bondage to decay and will obtain the freedom of the glory* of the children of God. We know that *the whole creation has been groaning in labor pains until now*; and not only the creation, but we ourselves, who have the first fruits of the Spirit, groan inwardly while we wait for adoption, the redemption of our bodies. (Rom 8:19-23)

Ecological Theology. Here, in Rom 8:19-23, we find a firm foundation for our ecological concerns today. Nature and creation, forests, rivers, seas, environment—we are brothers and sisters all, longing for liberation.

Jesus and the New Testament: Simply and Splendidly

Jesus, Simple As Usual. Our roadsigns then point to the Kingdom of God as a new world, a new creation, a new universe. And Jesus said it quite simply:

Blessed are the meek, for they shall *inherit the earth.* (Mt 5:5)

Our hosts, the simple Sorsogon folks, resonate perfectly with these simple words of Jesus.

The Biblical Vision. 'New heaven and new earth' is another name for salvation or Kingdom of God.

My childhood theology hoped for beatific vision in heaven after death. The Bible hopes for a new earth where a new humanity and the rest of creation will experience and participate in a new history.

The biblical culture sees the new universe as creation totally transformed, where there will be a new and beautiful capital city. The people of this new world will be God's covenanted community. There, God will make his home and be at home. Pain, sorrow and even death will have been destroyed. After the destruction of all the powers of evil, all reality will finally be summed up in Christ, and God will be the Energy permeating the unity of all transformed reality.

Be Still and Know …

Stopover 9

Women and Carers of Nature (The Kingdom of God As a New and Different History)

OUR HOST: Women and Carers of Nature

This stopover introduces us to a little known synonym for the Kingdom of God, 'age-to-come.'

Alternative History. If there exist two groups of people whose ardent wish is to change the course of history, it would be women and carers of nature. They are our hosts at this juncture in our journey. They will help us to understand that salvation or Kingdom of God is an alternative history. Jesus and the First Look have a name for it, the 'age-to-come.'

In the story of humanity, so replete with wars, violence, disease, pain, sorrow, one longs for salvation. For the Second Look, it is to get out of this world and up into heaven. For the First Look, salvation is to experience another history for this world, an alternative history.

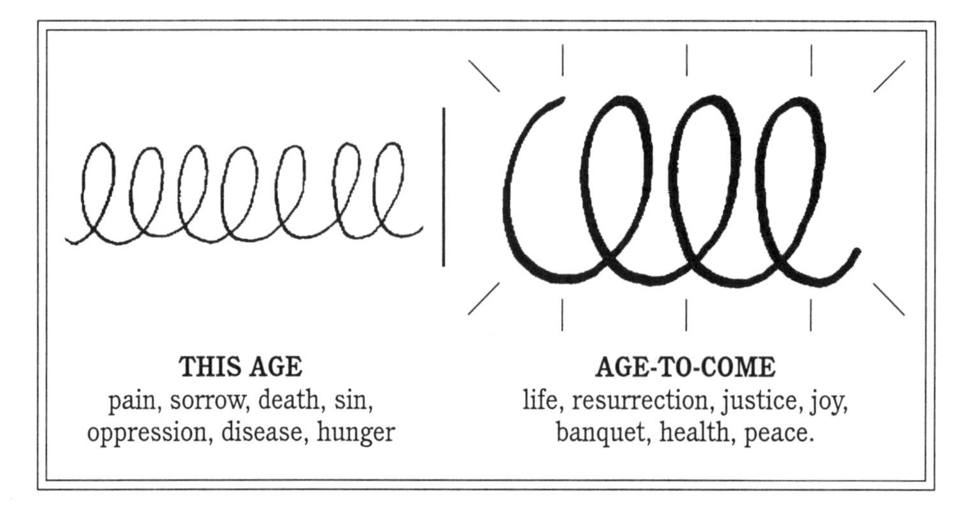

Jewish Background

Two Ages: 'This Age' and 'The Age-to-Come.' The Jews around the time of Jesus spoke of 'two ages.' This referred to two epochs, eras or histories.[42] There is 'this age,' the presently ongoing history of Israel and humanity. It is a history of pain, suffering, death, sin, oppression. Looking for salvation, they looked forward to the end of this presently ongoing history and to a different and new history in the future, an 'age-to-come,' where there would be justice, peace, life, health, joy. Salvation for the Jews meant experiencing a new history, a new era, a new epoch, a new age. Of course, it will be a history of or on this earth. The age-to-come is synonymous with Kingdom of God.

Jesus and the Age-to-Come

Jesus: Kingdom of God Is a New History. Did Jesus and the New Testament also speak of salvation and Kingdom of God as a new history? Yes. Since we are dealing with an unfamiliar, yet important, matter, it is good to have a visual image of the New Testament texts. Here are direct or indirect references to the age-to-come in the New Testament:

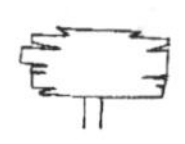

Jesus said, 'Truly I tell you, there is no one who has left house or brothers or sisters or mother or father or children or fields, for my sake and for the sake of the good news, who will not receive a hundredfold *now in this age*—houses, brothers and sisters, mothers and children, and fields, with persecutions—and *in the age to come* eternal life.' (Mk 10:29-30)

---

[42] Cf. 2 Baruch and 4 Ezra. These are writings outside our Bible.

> Whoever says a word against the Son of man will be forgiven; but whoever speaks against the Holy Spirit will not be forgiven, either *in this age or in the age to come.* (Mt 12:32)
>
> He raised him from the dead and seated him at his right hand in the heavenly places, far above all rule and authority and power and dominion, and above every name that is named, not only *in this age* but also *in the age to come.* (Eph 1:20-21)
>
> For it is impossible to restore again to repentance those who have once been enlightened, who have tasted the heavenly gift, and have shared in the Holy Spirit, and have tasted the goodness of the word of God and the powers of the *age to come....* (Heb 6:4-5)
>
> Jesus said to them, 'Those who belong to *this age* marry and are given in marriage; but those who are considered worthy of a place in *that age* and in the resurrection from the dead neither marry nor are given in marriage.' (Lk 20:34-35)
>
> Grace to you and peace from God our Father and our Lord Jesus Christ, who gave himself for our sins to set us free *from the present evil age*, according to the will of our God and Father; to whom be the glory for ever and ever. Amen. (Gal 1:3-5)
>
> The one who sows the good seed is the Son of Man; the field is the world, and the good seed are the children of the kingdom; the weeds are the children of the evil one, and the enemy who sowed them is the devil; the harvest is the *end of the age*, and the reapers are angels. Just as the weeds are collected and burned up with fire, so will it be at the *end of the age.* The Son of Man will send his angels, and they will collect out of his kingdom all causes of sin and all evildoers, and they will throw them into the furnace of fire, where there will be weeping and gnashing of teeth. Then the righteous will shine like the sun in the *kingdom of their Father.* (Mt 13:37-43)
>
> When he was sitting on the Mount of Olives, the disciples came to him privately, saying, 'Tell us, when will this be, and what will be the sign *of your coming and of the end of the age*?' (Mt 24:3)

Salvation = New History. Therefore, for Jesus and the New Testament, salvation was not about souls seeing God in heaven. Rather it was a new history for people, in possession of justice, peace, life, and other blessings for the human family. Typically, the movement is not from earth to heaven. It is not from down here to up there. Rather it is *from the old history to a new history on this earth.*

As anticipations of the age-to-come, women, like our hosts, today work to end millennia of patriarchy and to re-create a history of gender equality. Nature-carers work to end the rape of Mother Nature; and they help us to see the trees, birds, waters as our brothers and sisters ... and to rediscover our bondedness with them.

The Dimension of History

History-Consciousness and Christian Consciousness. This biblical idea of an age-to-come is one of the new and refreshing bits of learning I picked up in the course of my search through the scriptures. It provides a whole new dimension to the understanding of ultimate salvation. It provides the dimension of history. The big lesson that the age-to-come can teach us is that ultimate salvation is a new and different history for nature and for humankind, collectively *and* individually. Our hosts, women and people who want to correct and re-edit the story of our planet resonate with this.

My old catechism looked forward to a *'place'* called heaven; First Look theology looks forward to a *'place'* called the new world. But First Look theology provides a further sharpening: it looks forward to a new history, a new era, a new epoch, a new age.

This is in contrast to the Second Look's final salvation which is an a-historical private affair, that is, limited to souls seeing God in heaven. A good bit of concern for history—economic, social, political—has been felt in Church documents since Vatican II.

Our PCP II is outstanding in this regard. Would that there were more echoes in the everyday catechesis of schools and parishes. Then participation in ongoing history today will not be a matter for occasional rallies only but a part of habitual Christian consciousness and action. Shaping history toward the Kingdom of God becomes a normal chore in the household of God.

First Look and Second Look Vocabulary and Meanings

An Instructive Note. Let us play a little game. The text of Mk 10:17-30 offers a fascinating word study. It offers an opportunity to compare Second Look meanings with First Look ones. For the Second Look, 'to be saved,' 'eternal life,' 'Kingdom of God' mean 'going to heaven.' Not so for the First Look. Run your eye through the following; pay attention to the italicized words:

As he [Jesus] was setting out on a journey,
a man ran up and knelt before him,
and asked him, 'Good Teacher, what must I do to *inherit eternal life*?' (v 17)

... Jesus looking at him, loved him
and said, 'You lack one thing;
go, sell what you own,
and give the money to the poor,
and you will have treasure in heaven;
then come, follow me.' (v 21)

When he heard this, he was shocked,
And went away grieving,
For he had many possessions. (v 22)

Then Jesus looked around and said to his disciples,
'How hard it will be for those who have wealth
to *enter the kingdom of God*!' (v 23)

And the disciples were perplexed at these words.
But Jesus said to them again,
'Children, how hard it is
to *enter the kingdom of God*! (v 24)

It is easier for a camel
to go through the eye of a needle
than for someone who is rich
to *enter the kingdom of God*.' (v 25)

They were greatly astounded,
and said to one another, 'Then who can *be saved*?' (v 26)

Jesus looked at them and said,
'For mortals it is impossible, but not for God;
for God, all things are possible.' (v 27)

Peter began to say to him,
'Look, we have left everything and followed you.' (v 28)

Jesus said, 'Truly, I tell you,
there is no one who has left house or brothers or sisters
or mother or father or children or fields,
for my sake and for the sake of the good news, (v 29)
who will not receive a hundredfold
now *in this age*—
houses, brothers and sisters,
mothers and children, and fields
with persecutions—
and *in the age to come eternal life*. (v 30)
(Mk 10:17-30)

The pertinent words are:

(a) inherit eternal life (v. 17, 30)
(b) enter the Kingdom of God (vv. 23, 24, 25)
(c) to be saved (v. 26)
(d) age-to-come (v. 30)

Familiarity with the signposts we have encountered to date would tell us that none of these four expressions means going to heaven after death (Second Look). Rather, from the context, it is clear, first, that these four expressions are synonymous; second, that they carry a biblical—therefore, First Look—meaning.

	Second Look	First Look
inherit eternal life	= heaven	= Kingdom of God
enter the Kingdom of God	= heaven	= Kingdom of God
to be saved	= heaven	= Kingdom of God
age-to-come	[not used]	= Kingdom of God

Particularly:

Eternal Life. Biblically speaking, eternal life, a favorite Second Look expression, does not mean the life of beatific vision for the soul in heaven. Rather it is the fullness of life with resurrection, banquet, justice, joy, experiencing God in a new earth at the end-time.

Salvation. Biblically speaking, to be saved does not mean saving the soul for heaven but entering the Kingdom and the fullness of life.

Possible Problematic Sayings: Let us now take up two expressions which can be misleading:

> ... Go, sell what you own, and give the money to the poor, and you will have *treasure in heaven* ... (Mk 10:21)
>
> Rejoice and be glad, for *your reward is great in heaven*, for in the same way they persecuted the prophets who were before you. (Mt 5:12)

These sayings sound like: salvation means going to heaven after death and receiving one's reward. But the biblical meaning is: you now have a treasure/reward/ investment in heaven (and it will be yours when the Kingdom of God comes at the close of the age).

Note too, of course, that the word 'heaven' can function as a substitute for the word 'God.' Thus: your reward will be great in heaven (i.e. in the eyes of God) and you will have treasure in heaven (i.e., before God).

Biblical Salvation

Biblical Expressions for Ultimate Salvation. We have encountered the following biblical expressions:

Kingdom of God (highlighting the aspect of God's sovereignty)

New-heaven-and-new-earth (accent on 'world' or 'earth')

Age-to-come (accent on history)

Eternal life (dimension of life)

These are all practical synonyms for ultimate salvation. Of these the most frequent in the New Testament is Kingdom of God. Age-to-come and new-heaven-and-earth are relatively much rarer, but they are also used.

Biblical salvation refers to that fullness of life in the age-to-come, where I and every human being, having vanquished death, will participate in a new history of life-giving justice, joy, compassion, seeing God, being sons and daughters of God, and where God will be all in all.

Our hosts, the women and nature-carers help us to conclude with this thought: Today, working for eternal life is not just bringing souls to the everlasting life of heaven, as I used to think, but includes working towards that fullness of life for each human being, for all humanity and Sister Nature, as we journey towards the definitive age-to-come.

Be Still and Know …

Stopover 10

At the Deathbed of a Nationalist Heroine (The Kingdom of God As Future)

OUR HOST: Nationalist Heroine

The 'When' of the Kingdom. Very well, our signposts thus far have supplied a wealth of information about *what* the Kingdom of God is. We who have traveled this far are perhaps inquisitive and impatient about *when* all this will come about. Our signposts will show that the Kingdom of God has both a present and a future aspect. It is, as the dull formula goes, already here and not yet.

In this Stopover our signposts point to the Kingdom of God in its *future* aspect.

What Is It All About? In this Stopover, we find ourselves at the bedside of a human rights worker. She lies in critical condition, after being wounded by a military armalite.[43] After a lifetime of commitment, and facing possible death, she asks: is it all about going to heaven? Or is it accompanying humankind toward the final Kingdom of God?

[43] One such heroine is Liliosa Hilao. At 23, she was tortured, gang-raped and murdered. She was the first woman and first detainee murdered during the Marcos dictatorship in the 1970's in the Philippines.

A few years ago, if I had been asked, 'Which moment of our life is the most crucial?'—I would have had no second thought. I would answer, 'the moment of death of each individual person.' In my mind, that moment was associated with the soul's subsequent fate: eternal damnation or bliss. And it was my task to bring souls to heaven. But people like our dying host and, of course, the biblical Jesus, have taught me that it is not all about going to heaven at death. It is also about helping to move history towards the definitive Kingdom of God of the future.

KINGDOM OF GOD AS FUTURE.

Future ... These indicators talk about a Kingdom of God as something in the future:

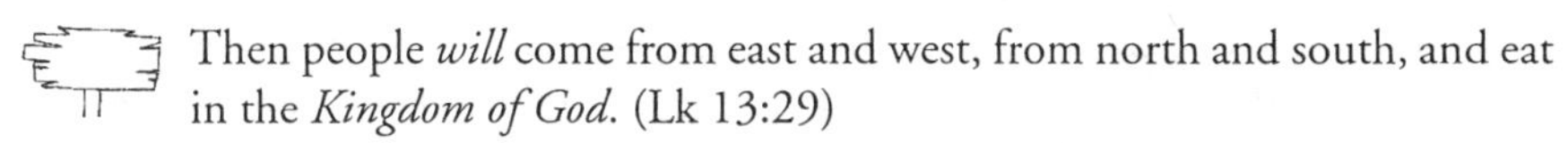

Then people *will* come from east and west, from north and south, and eat in the *Kingdom of God.* (Lk 13:29)

Jesus sees a vision of a future reality: it is a sight of men and women who *will* be streaming towards the banquet of the Kingdom from all parts of the globe.

Truly, I tell you, I will never again drink of the fruit of the *vine until that day when I drink it new in the Kingdom of God.* (Mk 14:25)

At the last supper, Jesus foresees that the next time he will share wine with his disciples will be in the *future* Kingdom of God.

[*May*] your Kingdom *come*! (Mt 6:10)

The principal petition in the Lord's prayer is for the Kingdom to come. It has *not yet come*. It is still in the future.

... End of Human History. Can we determine this future with more precision? When is this future moment of the coming of God's Kingdom? Is it the moment of a person's death? Or is it some other moment in the story of humankind? Our signposts:

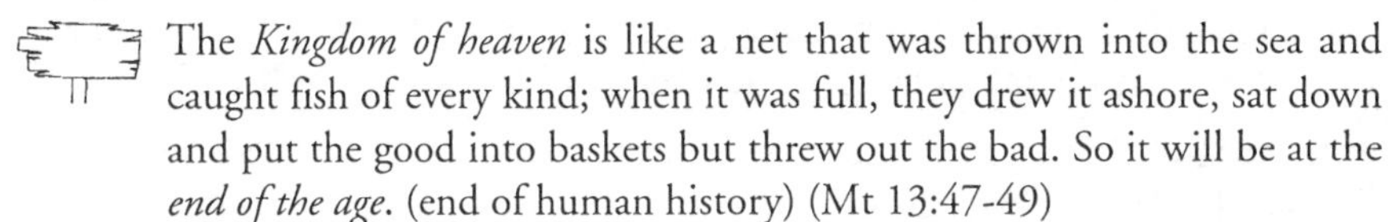

The *Kingdom of heaven* is like a net that was thrown into the sea and caught fish of every kind; when it was full, they drew it ashore, sat down and put the good into baskets but threw out the bad. So it will be at the *end of the age*. (end of human history) (Mt 13:47-49)

There will be a separation of the good and the bad – generally known as 'general judgment' to precede the coming of the Kingdom of God. That scenario is calendared for the end of human history.

Jesus said to her, Your brother will rise again. Martha said to him, I know *that he will rise again in the resurrection on the last day.* (Jn 11:23-24)

The resurrection, one of the foremost Kingdom-blessings, will be a reality 'at the last day.'

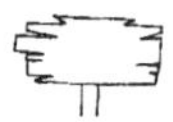

> *Then comes the end* (i.e., of human of history) *when he (Jesus) hands over the Kingdom to God the Father* after he has destroyed every ruler and every authority and power. (1 Cor 15:24)

There will then be a 'mission accomplished' ceremony in which Jesus hands over the final Kingdom – at the 'end,' referring to the end of history.

> When he was sitting on the Mount of Olives, the disciples came to him privately, saying, 'Tell us, when will this be, and what will be the sign of *your coming and of the end of the age*?' Jesus answered them, "Beware that no one leads you astray. For many will come in my name, saying, 'I am the Messiah!' and they will lead many astray. And you will hear of wars and rumors of wars; see that you are not alarmed; for this must take place, but the end is not yet. For nation will rise against nation, and kingdom against kingdom, and there will be famines and earthquakes in various places: all this is but the beginning of the birth pangs ... And this good news of the kingdom will be proclaimed throughout the world, as a testimony to all the nations; and then *the end* will come." (Mt 24:3-14)

In this passage, this end is associated with the coming again or parousia of Jesus.

The Kingdom of God then, in so far as it is still future, will be experienced not when you and I die, but at that moment in world history when humankind will arrive at the 'end.' That is the message of such expressions as 'the close of the age,' 'on the last day,' 'end.'

Where Are We Going?

The All-Important Moment. There was a time when, as a priest, I was psychologically and theologically geared to the moment of death as the all-important moment. As soon as a human being was born, my quite praiseworthy concern was to administer baptism, i.e. to prepare that baby for death (!) and for eventual beatific vision. Now, without minimizing the importance of the moment of death, I have come to realize that my view was too narrow. For, Jesus and the Bible speak of another moment as the all-important and decisive moment: the close of the age or the end-time, the climax of history, the coming of the definitive Kingdom.

Ultimate Goal of Salvation History. It is therefore at the consummation of human history that the Bible locates our ultimate destiny and final salvation. Where are we going? – this is indeed a very consequential question. What is our ultimate destiny? What is the ultimate goal of salvation-history? Where is it all leading? Heaven after death? Or Kingdom of God at the end-time? The answer is clear for the First Look.

Where to Direct Our Steps Today. Knowing what our final goal is, we know where to direct our steps today. That future Kingdom of God at the end-time, and not just the lone moment of the individual's death, is what we should work towards, now. That future fullness of life should, in some provisory way, become a reality through our deeds and life here and now. So it was in the deeds and life of Jesus. So it is in that of our host, the dying human rights worker.

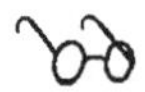

Why Talk about the Future? What is the use of talking about the Kingdom of God as future? Should we not just talk about it as present? Well, a bit of patience will help until our next stop exhibits roadsigns about the Kingdom as present. Meanwhile, we devote attention to its future aspect for two reasons. First, in order to be faithful to the biblical data. Second, our future goal determines the kind of Christian life and practice we engage in today. A Church whose goal is heaven-after-death will be content to send souls to heaven. It will be concerned for life after death. A Church whose goal is the coming Kingdom of God will dedicate itself to total salvation for humans and nature today. It will (also) be concerned for life before death as it journeys towards the Kingdom.

Co-Travelers Along the Road to the Future. We Christians are not alone on this road to the future. We have co-travelers. In fact, others, of different Faiths and faiths, have gone ahead of us—more courageous and more committed even. 'Kingdom of God' is our Christian vocabulary for the new world, new history. Others have their own. What's in a name? The new world, that longed-for 'Utopia,' by any other name, works like a potent magnet for people with vision and love. Our host is one of them.

What Kind of World?

What Kind of World? The Kingdom of God is a future new world at the end of human history.

Our question now is: what kind of a world? Is it heavenly? This very earth transformed? Another earth? There is no uniform view.

We can discern three different views.

The New World Is Heavenly. It is something already existing in heaven, to be manifested at the end-time or the parousia of Christ:

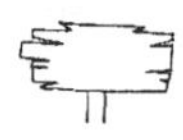

> Blessed be the God and Father of our Lord Jesus Christ! By his great mercy he has given us a new birth into a living hope through the resurrection of Jesus Christ from the dead, and into *an inheritance* that is imperishable, undefiled, and unfading, *kept in heaven* for you, who are being protected by the power of God through faith for *a salvation ready to be revealed in the last time.* (1Pet 1:3-5. You may also see: Col 1:1-5, 3:4; Mt 25:34; Rev 21:2; Gal 4:26; 1Pet 1:4.)[44]

[44] Note that it is not heaven itself, but 'assets,' so to speak, 'kept in heaven.'

This Present Earth Transformed. Another view is that it is this very earth of ours but totally transformed! A re-born creation! Luke's Kingdom is a new world or reborn creation in Matthew:

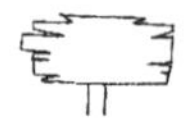

And I confer on you, just as my Father has conferred on me, a *kingdom*, so that you may eat and drink at my table in my kingdom, and you will sit on thrones judging the twelve tribes of Israel. (Lk 22:29-30)

Truly I tell you, *at the renewal of all things*, (in Greek: *paliggenesia*, transformed creation) when the Son of Man is seated on the throne of his glory, you who have followed me will also sit on twelve *thrones, judging the twelve tribes of Israel.* (Mt 19:28)

Blessed are the meek, for they shall *inherit the earth.* (Mt 5:5)

Also: Rom 8:18-23; Rev 5:10.

Another World. A third view is that it is another world to take the place of the present one after its destruction.

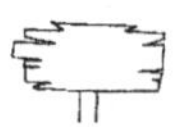

But the day of the Lord will come like a thief, and then *the heavens will pass away with a loud noise, and the elements will be dissolved with fire, and the earth and everything that is done on it will be disclosed.* Since *all these things are to be dissolved in this way*, what sort of persons ought you to be in leading lives of holiness and godliness, waiting for and hastening the coming of the day of God, because of which the heavens will be set ablaze and dissolved, and the elements will melt with fire? But, in accordance with his promise, *we wait for new heavens and a new earth*, where righteousness (justice) is at home. (2 Pet 3:10-13)

Why the Variety of Views. Why is it not easy to provide an accurate floor plan of the new world of the end-time? Because no one has yet experienced it empirically. Thus, even the biblical authors have various expressions for their faith-intuitions. In spite of the diversity, however, there is common intuition here. They all share the view of a full and integral life for people and nature at the consummation of history (and not simply a heaven-and-beatific-vision for the soul).

Life After Death Now

Life after Death before the Coming of the Final Kingdom. Finally, we take up that view, very familiar to us from childhood catechism: going to heaven after death.

If our final destination is the Kingdom at the end-time, what happens to a person before the coming of the Kingdom? When a person dies today, is there life-after-death *now, before* the final Kingdom of the end-time? Our sign-posts speak of people who die now:

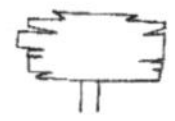

The poor man died and was carried by the angels to *be with Abraham.* (Lk 16:22)

To the good thief Jesus said: today you will be with me in *Paradise.* (Lk 23:43)

> I am hard pressed between the two: my desire is to depart [i.e., to die] *and be with Christ*, for that is far better. But to remain in the flesh [i.e., to stay alive] is more necessary on your account. (Phil 1:23)

Also perhaps: Jn 14:2; 2 Cor 5:8(?)

According to these roadsigns then, is there a life *sometime* after death *now, before* the final Kingdom of the end-time? Yes. there is *life-after-death before the end-time Kingdom.*

Terminology for Life-after-Death. But we must pay attention to the terminology used. What are some of the names/expressions given to this life-after-death? Here:

- 'to be with Abraham,' i.e., to be re-united or recline at table with the ancestor
- 'paradise, i.e., a lovely place full of bliss
- 'to be with Christ,' i.e., to be re-united with Christ in the next life.

Going to Heaven, Anyone? Are you ready for a shock? The terminology 'going to heaven' after death is *not* found in the New Testament! Jesus never used that phrase.

Try verifying this; fine-comb the New Testament for the phrase 'going to heaven.' It could mean an exciting, if sleepless, night of research in Seattle or Manila or anywhere you are. But be on your toes! I am not saying that people do not go to heaven. They do, because what Scripture calls 'to be with Abraham,' 'paradise,' 'my father's mansions,' etc. are the same thing as heaven. So, people do go to heaven after death, but the *terminology* 'going to heaven' is not found in the Scriptures. The term 'heaven' is found. The term 'kingdom of heaven' is found. But the term 'going to heaven' is not.

'Going to heaven' is a phrase that developed after biblical times. And it is what we are accustomed to in our standard catechisms today.

Heaven Is *Not* the Kingdom of God. A sigh of relief. There *is* then a heaven after death. (Our host, the dying human rights worker, is an excellent candidate for heaven.) But – and this is a significant point—*this heaven-after-death is not referred to as Kingdom of God* by the First Look. Heaven is *not* the Kingdom of God. Heaven is not identical with the Kingdom of God. This is so, notwithstanding inaccurate contemporary liturgical formulations, stemming from unawareness of the biblical meaning. For example, 'Grant us the peace and unity of your Kingdom where you live forever and ever.'

Going to Heaven or Entering the Kingdom? Recall that the phrase 'going to heaven' is absent in the New Testament. Accordingly Jesus' language was always 'entering the Kingdom of God.' That means that *strictly speaking* Jesus never invited or challenged us to go to heaven! His invitation was not to heaven but always to the Kingdom of God.

Heaven Not Our Final Goal. Now, back to the question of goal. Where are we going? People indeed do go to heaven, but it is clear by now that that is *not the* *final goal.*[45] I am amused and saddened to see well-meaning Christians expend their best efforts 'in order to go to heaven,' as if that is all there was to living the Christian life. 'Ever since I joined a certain Church organization,' said one, 'my life ceased to be an ambition to make millions and became a single-minded passion to go to heaven.' So much energy chasing clouds when you can shoot for the stars!

Not Much on Life-after-Death. Quite differently from us today, the First Look did not talk much about life-after-death before the end-time. Mark, for example, never once refers to this, always to the Kingdom of the end-time. Why? Because, for the most part, the expectation was that the end-time Kingdom would come soon, within their own lifetime.

But as we have seen, the First Look did indeed believe in a life-after-death. Yet while having that belief, the First Look never lost sight of the Kingdom perspective.

Our situation today is the opposite. We focus on going to heaven after we die, but forget the journey to the Kingdom of the end-time.

Summary Points.

The First Look does by all means speak, though rarely, about life-after-death *now*, before the final Kingdom of the end-time. However, we must expand our understanding. This life-after-death is not given the name Kingdom of God. Heaven is not the Kingdom of God! The characteristic biblical way of speaking is not 'going to heaven' but 'entering the Kingdom.' The final goal of salvation history is the Kingdom of God! Finally, unlike us today, the First Look generation, in their belief in a life-after-death, never lost sight of the Kingdom.

In later post-biblical centuries, Christian consciousness focused on the life-after-death and practically forgot the Kingdom of the end-time. We developed a spirituality and pastoral practice of merely saving souls for heaven. Little or nothing was said about going to the Kingdom and participating in Kingdom-promoting history.

Once More with Feeling: Heaven and Kingdom

Heaven and Kingdom of God Not the Same. The customary mix-up of heaven and Kingdom calls for some recalls and elaborations. Biblically speaking, heaven is not the same as Kingdom of God. Scripture does speak of both heaven and Kingdom of God. But these two entities are not the same.

1. For the Bible, there *is* definitely a reality called heaven.Thus:

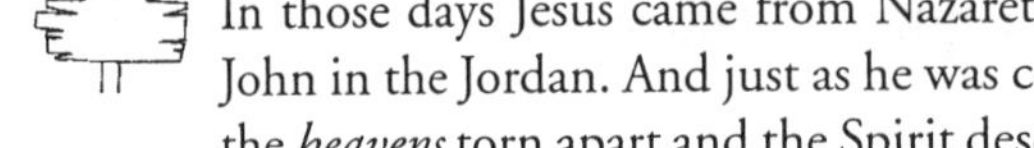

In those days Jesus came from Nazareth of Galilee and was baptized by John in the Jordan. And just as he was coming up out of the water, he saw the *heavens* torn apart and the Spirit descending like a dove on him. And a

[45] Unless read *in context,* Heb 11:16, at first blush, *might seem* to be an exception to this.

> voice came from *heaven*, 'You are my Son, the Beloved; with you I am well pleased.' (Mk 1:9-11)
>
> Take care that you do not despise one of these little ones; for, I tell you, in *heaven* their angels continually see the face of my Father in *heaven*. (Mt 18:10)
>
> He has made known to us the mystery of his will, according to his good pleasure that he set forth in Christ, as a plan for the fullness of time, to gather up all things in him, things in *heaven* and things on earth. (Eph 1:9-10)

2. But heaven is *not* the same thing as Kingdom of God! The principal meaning of heaven in the bible is: the abode of God above. (Remember the pre-scientific understanding as heaven being above and earth below.)

> Let your light shine before others, so that they may see your good works and give glory to *your Father in heaven*. (Mt 5:16)
>
> If you then, who are evil, know how to give good gifts to your children, how much more will *your Father in heaven* give good things to those who ask him! (Mt 7:11)
>
> Take care that you do not despise one of these little ones; for, I tell you, *in heaven* their angels continually see the face of *my Father in heaven*. (Mt 18:10)
>
> Pray then in this way: *Our Father in heaven*, hallowed be your name (Mt 6:9)

3. Heaven is also where God's messengers (angels) are (Mt 19:10; 22:30; 24:36). Heaven is also where the righteous go after the moment of death.

4. But heaven is not spoken of as a new world or transformed creation of the end-time (Mt 19:28) where there is food for the hungry (Lk 6:21), resurrection for the dead (Jn 11:25; Mt 11:5), unity in Christ of all created things in the universe (Eph 1:10), etc., which is what the Kingdom of God is.

5. Another tell-tale detail. The language that is sometimes used for the Kingdom of God is suggestive. It is 'coming' to us, rather than we are 'going' to it. We 'go' to heaven, rather than heaven comes to us, right? On the other hand, the Kingdom of God—a new world—can more readily be conceived of as 'appearing' or 'coming' to us.

> 'I will not drink of the fruit of the vine until the *kingdom of God comes*.' (Lk 22:18)
>
> 'Father, hallowed be your name, your *kingdom come*.' (Lk 11:2)
>
> ... He was near Jerusalem, and ... they supposed that the *kingdom of God was to appear* immediately. (Lk 19:11)
>
> Jesus was asked by the pharisees when the *kingdom of God was coming*, and he answered, 'The kingdom of God is not *coming* with things that can be observed.' (Lk 17:20)

The *Word* 'Heaven'. It will help, therefore, to be clear about the *word* or *term* 'heaven,' as used in the Bible. When you meet the *word* heaven in the Bible—

1. it can refer to the blue dome above where (or above which) God was thought to dwell. This is the *normal* use. Examples: 'Our Father, who *are in heaven*,' ' … give glory to *your Father who is in heaven*.'

2. or it can function as a substitute-word for the word God; in this case it does not refer to the abode of God. This is the *special* use. Example: 'Father, I have sinned against *heaven* (=against *God*) and before you …' (Lk 15:18)

If You Miss Your Step

Where God Does Not Want Us to Go. It is clear by now that we are going to God's abode after death, and to the new earth at the end of time. Well, suppose you miss a step or lose your way? Where are we headed for then? Hell? Purgatory? We will not dwell long on these topics, for I am interested more in where God wants to bring us rather than where he wants us not to go! I remember, however, that these were concerns, actually points of obsession, in my childhood catechism. And perhaps still in catechisms today. And so, they need corresponding attention.

If you (decide to) lose your way, could you find yourself in hell? Did Jesus speak of hell? Jesus did warn about a place or state of punishment. He called it 'hell' or 'gehenna.' Gehenna, or more precisely, *Ge Hinnom*, referred to the Valley of Hinnom, a ravine running along the south side of Jerusalem. It was what our Smokey Mountain once was, the city garbage dump. There, fire burned and worms thrived.

In later times, over-resourceful imagination—popular, artistic and even theological—threw in non-biblical details.[46] But we will not, since, as I take it, none of us is planning a trip there, much less, make our permanent residence there.

But one thing we can pause to note. Although Jesus seldom says what kinds of sin will get people to hell, the one that is most dramatically portrayed is found in Matthew 25:41-45:

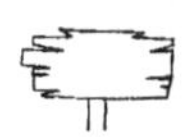

> Then he will say to those at his left hand, '*You that are accursed, depart from me into the eternal fire* prepared for the devil and his angels; *for I was hungry and you gave me no food, I was thirsty and you gave me nothing to drink, I was a stranger and you did not welcome me, naked and you did not give me clothing, sick and in prison and you did not visit me.*' Then they also will answer, 'Lord, when was it that we saw you hungry or thirsty or a stranger or naked or sick or in prison, and did not take care of you?' Then he will answer them, 'Truly I tell you, just as you did not

[46] A similar fate has befallen 'heaven.' According to the biblical records, Jesus spoke of heaven only as the abode of God and his messengers, the angels. We, over-imaginative catechists and theologians know more about heaven than Jesus.

> do it to one of the least of these, you did not do it to me.' And *these will go away into eternal punishment*, but the righteous into eternal life.

Favorite Halfway House. And what about that "favorite halfway" house for Catholics, purgatory? Well, purgatory is not mentioned in the New Testament, although there might be some oblique hint in 2 Macc 12:43-45. Later tradition arrived at this notion through a theological logic. If a person is not ready to enter heaven due to some imperfection, he/she must first undergo purgation. And this is done in a place aptly called 'purgatory,' a place of cleansing. Prayers for the deceased are part of accepted Catholic practice.

Ultimate Object of Hope

So, back on biblical track and safer ground ...

If I had been asked a few years ago what I thought of a religion whose ultimate object of hope was a new world, a new history, a new humanity, I would have thought it to be an interesting religion or philosophy but it would not be the Christian religion. Here is where I was mistaken. This *was* the Christian religion for Jesus and the first Christians, the religion of the New Testament. The question 'Where are we going?' is answered by the biblical tradition: to a new world, a new history, a new humanity at the end of time. Samples and partial realizations of that future new world, however, should be experienced through our actions and deeds here and now.

At this juncture in our journey, we can whisper a short prayer of thanks for people like our host, the human rights worker. They know where to go. They can show us the way.

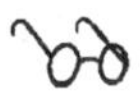

In this stopover we have let our mind and imagination race through time and space up to their utmost limits. It is time perhaps to let the 'no-mind' do the same without effort, without fatigue ...

Be Still and Know ...

Stopover 11

Gathering of People's Organizations (The Kingdom of God As a Present Reality)

OUR HOST: People's Organizations

Is the new earth, which the Kingdom of God is, a mere mirage of the future? An Asian gathering of people's organizations say an emphatic 'no.' Our present hosts—organizations of youth, environmentalists, women, workers, peasants, mothers, overseas workers, drug and alcohol rehab teams, indigenous peoples, small vendors, urban poor and other grassroots organizations—assert in word and action that something of the new earth has got to be visible and tangible today. 'The Kingdom of God is already in the midst of you,' Jesus announced to the people of his time. He pointed to his actions. He pointed to the blessings he wrought in people's lives. Jesus-followers can find challenge and inspiration from Jesus' practice.

The Kingdom of God As Present

Our current signposts point to the Kingdom of God in its *present* aspect.

Learn Something from the Parables of Growth. The parables of growth, although not designed to illustrate the presence of the Kingdom of God, do in fact imply it.

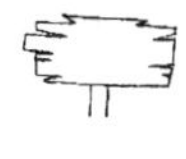

> With what can we compare the *Kingdom of God*, or what parable shall we use for it? It is like a grain of mustard seed, which, when *sown upon the ground*, is the smallest of all the seeds on earth; yet when it is sown it grows up and becomes the greatest of all shrubs, and puts forth large branches, so that the birds of the air can make nests in its shade. (Mk 4:30-32)
>
> The *kingdom of God* is as if *someone would scatter seed on the ground*, and would sleep and rise night and day, and the seed would sprout and grow, he does not know how. (Mk 4:26-27)
>
> The *kingdom of heaven* is like *yeast that a woman took and mixed* in with three measures of flour until all of it was leavened. (Mt 13:33)

It is implied in these parables that the Kingdom has already begun, therefore is already present. It is like seed already planted, or like leaven already placed in the dough. These parables, however, do not say in what concrete way the Kingdom of God is already a present reality. We find that information in the next roadsigns.

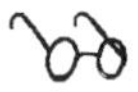

'Among You' or 'In the Midst of You.' At one point in his life, Jesus told the pharisees not to look for signs—like apocalyptic signs in the heavens or some kind of certifying credentials.

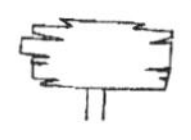

> Once Jesus was asked by the pharisees when the kingdom of God was coming, and he answered, "The kingdom of God is not coming with things that can be observed; nor will they say, 'Look, here it is!' or 'There it is!' For, in fact, *the kingdom of God is among you.*" (Lk 17:20-21)

The Kingdom of God was already in the midst of them. It was already present. It was in the here and now of Jesus' contemporaries.

Among, Not Within. And now, let me make a parenthetical, but important remark, not about the 'when' but about the 'how' of the Kingdom. It is a warning about a mistranslation. In some of your English or vernacular Bibles, you find the faulty translation: The Kingdom of God is *within* you. This incorrect translation reduces the Kingdom to an interior reality in the heart. The better translation of the Greek *entos* is: 'among you' or 'in the midst of you,' that is, you see and hear it *around* you. How? The blind see, the lame walk, etc.

The Reign of God in our hearts—'within you'—is indeed a precious reality, highly esteemed in the Bible. However, in the New Testament, this reign of God in our hearts is not referred to as the Kingdom of God. Of course, after a good grounding in the basic meaning of the Kingdom of God, God's reign in our hearts can be included among the prime blessings of the Kingdom. It remains a fact, however, that for Jesus the Kingdom of God was 'in the midst of you,' or 'among you'—that is, in health for the sick, life-giving energy to the dead, the jubilee year, etc.

In the Defeat of Satanic Forces. The Kingdom of God was already present in Jesus' action of casting out of devils.

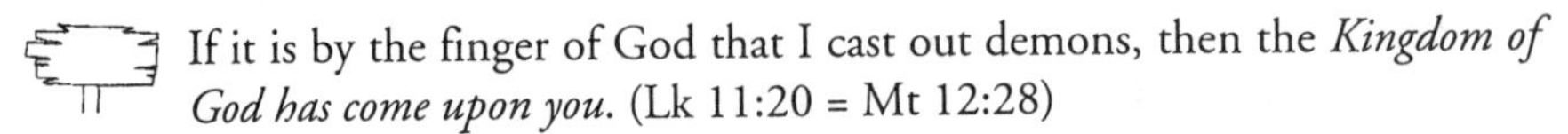

If it is by the finger of God that I cast out demons, then the *Kingdom of God has come upon you.* (Lk 11:20 = Mt 12:28)

Recall that for apocalyptic circles in the first century, definitive salvation was to consist in the destruction of the reign of Satan by the Reign of God. Satan exercised his rule over individuals, over history and the world, causing sin, sickness, suffering and death. People were hoping that Satan's reign would be destroyed by the coming Reign of God. Against this religio-cultural background, Jesus meant that, through his casting out of devils, he was destroying the reign of Satan, and that therefore the Kingdom of God was already present.

What You Hear and See.

When John heard in prison what the Messiah was doing, he sent word by his disciples and said to him, '*Are you the one who is to come, or are we to wait for another?' Jesus answered them, 'Go and tell John what you hear and see*: the blind receive their sight, the lame walk, the lepers are cleansed, the deaf hear, the dead are raised, and the poor have good news brought to them. And blessed is anyone who takes no offense at me.' (Mt 11:2-6 = Lk 7:18-23)

When he came to Nazareth, where he had been brought up, he went to the synagogue on the sabbath day, as was his custom. He stood up to read, and the scroll of the prophet Isaiah was given to him. He unrolled the scroll and found the place where it was written:

The Spirit of the Lord is upon me,
because he has anointed me
to bring good news to the poor.
He has sent me to proclaim release to the captives
and recovery of sight to the blind,
to let the oppressed go free,
to proclaim the year of the Lord's favor.
And he rolled up the scroll … then he began to say to them,
'*Today this scripture has been fulfilled in your hearing.*' (Lk 4:16-21; cf. Isa 61:1-2)

'Tell John what you see and hear ...' 'Today this Scripture is fulfilled in your hearing.' The Kingdom is present. How so? Although the words 'Kingdom of God' are not found, we know that our signposts give a catalogue of Kingdom-blessings according to Jesus based on Isaiah. Mt 11 and Lk 4 are about the Kingdom of God. That Kingdom and its blessings are seen and heard by Jesus' contemporaries in their 'now.'

The Kingdom of God Present in Life-Blessings

Life-Blessings. What do they see and hear? Blessings that give life. Blessings that uphold and further life. In short, life-blessings. The Kingdom of God was present in life-blessings that included healings, exorcisms, propounding the jubilee year. Our hosts share some Kingdom-blessings experienced in our time: ancestral lands reclaimed, a drug-addict rehabilitated, demolition of poor homes stopped, dictators toppled, more women's rights promoted—these are some of the big and small victories shared among our hosts. In his time Jesus points to blessings he brings about in people's lives. The Kingdom is not just for tomorrow. It is now—in actual fact (Mt 11) or at least, as an intended program of action (Lk 4), perhaps aborted by an early death.

At this juncture, our hosts take me aside for a little side-chat. They say: 'It just occurred to us that whereas Jesus' activities want to set people up for life, many of your typical Church activities prepare people for death! A stunning thought. Is our Church more concerned for life after death than for life after birth?

The Three-Dimensional World of Jesus. According to an interpretation I was once taught, our Mt 11 signpost speaks about the 'spiritually blind' to truth, 'spiritual lepers,' deaf to the word of God, dead in mortal sin, oppressed by sin and the devil, the poor in spirit. How deep the inroads of a non-biblical theology! Our hosts, who are playing more and more the role of a devil's advocate, now half-jestingly remark: 'Oh, that a too, too rarefied theology would put on flesh and repossess the three-dimensional world of the biblical Jesus!' No, in these passages, Jesus was not talking about the spiritually blind, poor, etc. He was talking about the really and truly and physically blind, poor, dead, oppressed! What is the basis for saying this? The simplest and the most obvious. Here Jesus is simply giving a summary of his ministry. In the length and breadth of the gospel accounts, it was the really and truly blind, the deaf,and lepers that Jesus healed! Watch:

> When they had crossed over, they came to land at Gennesaret and moored the boat. When they got out of the boat, people at once recognized him, and rushed about that whole region and began to bring the *sick* on mats to wherever they heard he was. And wherever he went, into villages or cities or farms, they laid the *sick* in the marketplaces, and begged him that they might touch even the fringe of his cloak; and all who touched it were healed. (Mk 6:53-56)

Forgiving Sins. At this point in our journey, we take a look at another action of Jesus, the forgiving of sins. It is curiously not included in his key pre-crucifixion mission statements. Nevertheless, we may certainly consider it a Kingdom work of Jesus.

Jesus said to the paralytic, Son, your sins are forgiven. Now some of the scribes were sitting there, questioning in their hearts, Why does this fellow speak in this way? It is blasphemy! Who can forgive sins but God alone? (Mk 2:5ff)

In the Concrete Life Context of Jesus. Jesus' concrete state of life in his time was that of a healer, exorcist, prophet-teacher. It was in his actions within that vocation that he gave concrete manifestations of the Kingdom. The Kingdom of God was present in the life-giving blessings of health, joy, forgiveness, good news to the poor which people experienced through actions proper to his specific calling.

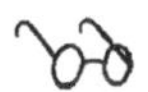

Principal Kingdom-Works of Jesus. What then were the principal Kingdom-works of Jesus—actual or programmatic—during his lifetime, and what can we learn from them? By now we can make this comprehensive summary:

health to the sick
life to the dead
good news (of justice and liberation) to the poor
release to captives
liberty to the oppressed
jubilee year of the Lord (restoration of property, release of slaves, cancellation of debts, rest for the land)
(Mt 11:2-5; Lk 4:16-21)
casting out demons (Lk 11:20)
forgiving sins (Mk 2:5ff)

Life For People. We have just identified the principal Kingdom-works of Jesus and his Kingdom-blessings. It is time to look a bit more closely and ask: what are these Kingdom-works concerned about? It is clear that they are not narrowly concerned about sanctifying grace for the disembodied soul. They are more broadly concerned about *life* (health, resurrection, justice, divine life, forgiving sins) for the *human being* (the blind, the lepers, the poor, the sinner).

One Human Being. Jesus' Kingdom-blessings were directed to the human being, not to the soul. How is it with us today? Our perceptive hosts have made this observation: after Vatican II in the 1960s, we started putting together body and soul. We realized that up to then we had put them asunder. We realized that we had been too preoccupied with the soul and downgraded the body. We began to talk about integral salvation and integral evangelization. We even talked about total human development. We said that we should be concerned not only with the soul but with body and soul together. Thus we arranged a marriage. Body and soul shall tie the knot. The two shall become one flesh. We had a difficult time in the process, and still do.

Jesus and the First Look viewers never had such a problem. The human being was never an assembly of two components.[47] There was always the one human being, breathing, throbbing, alive. And Jesus' Kingdom-blessings for the human being were various forms of life.

Objection. Jesus said to Pilate: 'My Kingdom is not from this world' (Jn 18:36). Is not Jesus saying that his Kingdom has to do with grace/life for souls only? This seems to imply a distinction between body and soul.

No. Jesus' statement does not mean: 'My Kingdom is about souls and spiritual grace.' Rather, it means: 'My kingly power does not derive from the principles of this world, but rather (implied) from God.'

Jesus is not contrasting 'spiritual' vs. 'material.' Jesus, in an exchange with Pilate, is contrasting this world vs. God; worldly things vs. godly things. The 'world' in John's Gospel is sometimes considered evil. The contrast is between what comes from this world and what comes from God.

Pilate and this world	Jesus and Godly things
untruth	truth
naked power	the power of God
power for subjugation, tyranny, conquest	(add: health for the sick, food for the hungry, freedom for the oppressed, divine life)

The Opposite of Spiritual. It is time for us to grapple with the following First Look view: the opposite of 'spiritual' is not 'material.' For the First Look, the opposite of 'spiritual' may be expressed in phrases such as:

- 'merely human'
- 'of the natural human condition'
- 'not of God'
- 'not from the Spirit'
- 'ungodly'

---

[47] After our several wrestling bouts with such notions as 'physical' and 'psychical,' I hope the following observation will be food for curiosity and promote more learning rather than confusion: 'physical' (Greek: *physis*), which we would think means 'bodily,' actually simply means '*natural*' or '*according to one's nature*'; 'psychical' (Greek: *psyche*), which we would think means 'spiritual,' likewise simply means '*natural*' or '*according to one's nature,*' that is, pertaining or according to one's nature.

Thus, if we marshall all our accumulated learnings, we would understand Paul's expression, 'physical body' (1 Cor 15:44). He means the human being ('body') according to his/her nature ('physical'), or, in his/her naked natural condition, without the Spirit of God.

Recall moreover, that 'spiritual' in the Bible simply means 'where the Spirit of God' is. The opposite is simply where God's Spirit is absent.

As you read the following selection, recall our analysis in 'A Thorough Going Over',[48] where *sarx* is equivalent to: human being, human nature; human condition; old self without God, weak, sin-prone, or sinful.

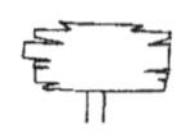

And so, brothers and sisters, I could not speak to you as *spiritual* people, but rather as people of the *sarx*, as infants in Christ. I fed you with milk, not solid food, for you were not ready for solid food. Even now you are still not ready, for you are still of the *sarx*. For as long as there is jealousy and quarreling among you, are you not of the *sarx*, and behaving *according to human inclinations?* For when one says, 'I belong to Paul,' and another, 'I belong to Apollos,' are you not *merely human*? (1 Cor 3:1-4)

Clearly, 'spiritual' is contrasted not to 'material' but to 'according to human inclinations,' 'merely human.'

The same contrast, using other words, is found in Jesus' rebuke of Peter: 'Get behind me, Satan! For you are setting your mind not on *divine things but on human things*' (Mk 8:33).

Samples:

Merely human, 'of the natural human condition,' 'not of God,' 'not from the Spirit,' 'ungodly,' and the like	**Spiritual**
feudal land system	land reform
producing grain for sole profit; dumping overproduced surplus into the sea	producing grain to feed people
power to control and dominate	power to heal
genetic piracy and patenting for profitmaking	gene research to promote health and prevent disease
education for mere self-advancement	education to help the nation
'subduing' and exploiting nature	caring for mother-earth
prayer to show off	unconditional worship and thanksgiving
loveless sex	sex as expression of love between husband and wife

[48] See page 78.

Where to Locate the Kingdom of God

Exact Location of the Kingdom of God. If you were roaming the streets of Palestine in the time of Jesus, where would you pinpoint the exact location of the Kingdom of God? This is not such an idle question, when you consider that often we look for the Kingdom everywhere except where it is. In heaven? In peoples' hearts? Is it a religious institution like the Church? Is it Jesus himself? Attention to the biblical evidence would prompt us to say: none of the above. Rather the Kingdom of God in the time of Jesus was to be found *in blessings of life for the human being* (health to the sick, life to the dead, justice to the poor, forgiveness to the sinner) and *mediated through Jesus' actions*; through his works; through his practice. (Our hosts, people's movements and organizations are happy with this thought.) What none-too-subtle message could we here pick up for our own Kingdom-practice today?

Some Jottings

Two Misconceptions. While we are on the subject of Jesus' works, we take note of a couple of misconceptions.

(1) The wonderful healings of Jesus, it is alleged, were intended to be proofs of his divinity; Jesus performed miracles in order to show that he was God.

(2) Still another view is that his healings served merely as pre-evangelization or pre-gospel; Jesus performed them only to prepare people for the more sublime message about salvation of souls.

Both views are incorrect. These marvelous works of Jesus were manifestations of the presence of the Kingdom of God in action. They *are already* the gospel and the evangelization of Jesus! Remember that Jesus went about all of Galilee and Judea proclaiming the *gospel, the evangel of the Kingdom.* And what was the Kingdom but life-blessings, such as his healings?

To Be Saved. At this juncture, we can also pause to hold up to the light for a still closer look, the simple word 'save.' As a Second Looker I used to associate it with (1) *eternal* salvation (2) *moral* salvation from sin (3) and, of course, with the *soul.*

In the Greek language (*sozo*), as perhaps in all languages, 'to be saved' means to be kept safe and sound, to be restored to health, to be rescued from danger or injury, and, of course, to attain eternal salvation. In the Bible 'to be saved' refers to moral and eternal salvation (Mt 10:22; Mt 18:11; Mt 19:25; Jn 10:9, etc.). But for a hemorrhaging woman, 'salvation' also means, to be made healthy (Mt 9:21); to preserve life and not to kill (Mk 3:5); to be rescued from sinking in water (Mt 14:30); to save one's life or lose it (Mt 16:25); to be spared the death on the cross (Mt 27:40-42; Mk 15:31; Lk 23:37); to heal a blind man (Lk 18:42); to be saved from shipwreck (Acts 27:43).

A Curious Fact About Forgiving Sins. Let us round out our reflection on Jesus and forgiving sins. Did Jesus forgive sins during his lifetime? Yes, the gospel records say so. Now an interested researcher will notice a curious fact. Contrary to all expectation, the gospels record only two instances where Jesus forgives sins.

One is the story of the paralytic, reported by Matthew, Mark and Luke (Mk 2:1-12; Mt 9:1-8; Lk 5:17-26). The other story is found only in Luke (7:36-50). This is all the more striking in the light of the fact that (1) almost every other episode talks rather about healings, exorcisms, feedings, conflicts with authorities, speaking in parables, eating with tax-collectors and sinners – all sorts of things except forgiving sins; (2) the mission statements do not mention forgiving sins; (3) the summaries of Jesus' activities do not mention it. For example:

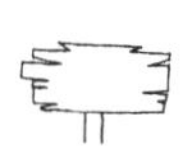

> Jesus departed with his disciples to the sea, and a great multitude from Galilee followed him; hearing all that he was doing, they came to him in great numbers from Judea, Jerusalem, Idumea, beyond the Jordan, and the region around Tyre and Sidon. He told his disciples to have a boat ready for him because of the crowd, so that they would not crush him; for *he had cured many, so that all who had diseases pressed upon him to touch him. Whenever the unclean spirits saw him, they fell down before him and shouted, 'You are the Son of God!'* But he sternly ordered them not to make him known. (Mk 3:7-12; also Mk 1:32-34)

This fact ought to help create a profile of Jesus that is closer to the biblical accounts. It also ought to serve as a motivation for lay people whose Kingdom-activity has nothing to do with sacramental forgiving of sins.

Jesus' religion was not played out only in individual souls, doing good and avoiding evil, hoping one day to scale the heights to heaven. It is more than the psycho-spiritual drama of the individual soul seeking personal fulfillment and helping others to seek the same salvation.

One more word about a theology that revolves around Jesus-sin-forgiveness-me. One would expect that it would burst into a spirituality of endless thanksgiving and joy. More often than warranted, however, it has produced a disproportionate 'sin complex,' and paved a guilt trip to heaven. Could the reason for the resultant long-faced spirituality be this: we preachers and theologians have blown out of proportion the sin-and-me part of it? The Jesus-forgives part would engender a more joyous and healthy spiritual life.

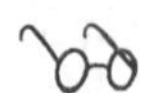

Behind the Kingdom-Blessings. You have perhaps, noticed that in reporting on the Kingdom-blessings of Jesus I have not talked about 'human dignity,' 'the value of relationships,' 'restoring persons back to their rightful place in the community,' 'asserting a counter-culture.' Does this mean that these and similar values were absent in Jesus' Kingdom practice? Far from it. These were behind every act of Jesus. Thus, when with his own hands, he touched the leper and healed him, he was, at the very least, loudly affirming his human dignity and restoring him back to his rightful place in the human community. However, I have advisedly not moved to that level of interpretation. This, for at least two reasons.

The first is that books and articles have spoken about Jesus' concern for human dignity without sufficiently telling us that such a concern of Jesus often takes the form of bread and fish. Incidentally, if Kingdom-blessing translates into global food, then inversely, the global hunger suffered by 70% of humans today must have to be a great Kingdom-crime. A frightening thought—especially for the global profiteers and their accomplices in and out of government. Of course, Jesus used simpler and more straightforward language: 'Away from me, you accursed ones, to everlasting fire. For I was hungry and you did not give me to eat.' (Mt 25:41-42)

The second is that I wanted to hew closely to Jesus' language and let that speak for itself—a practice which we can hardly overdo in our Christian theology. At any rate, it appears to me that Jesus was not one to discourse lengthily on 'dignity,' 'personhood,' 'relationships,' though they were most important for him and underpinned his every move. He did not talk about them. He did them. And the reader of the gospels could do well to tease out what lies just beneath that woodwork.

An empathetic reading of Jesus will lay bare the values that Jesus held, without need of further commentary. These values were, in many instances, diametrically antithetical to the officialdom of his day. These values were certainly *for* the human being and his/her primacy—over and above, say, the sabbath and tradition. Jesus certainly offered counter-values, affirming the value of human dignity. He offered a *counter-culture*. Although enough of this counter-culture should have filtered through our roadsigns so far, we will see more of it in the coming stopovers, especially 12, 14, 15 and 16.

Now, a word about us today. Because we are not Jesus, the following caution may be opportune. Since the value of human dignity and relationships are behind every Kingdom-act of Jesus, it would, of course, be grave irony and gross misunderstanding for Jesus-followers today to work for the Kingdom-blessings of rice, fish and land for reasons less than human dignity and relationships.

The *Anima* of Jesus

***Splagchnizomai*: a Footnote on the Kingdom-Spirituality of Jesus.** The gospels record little about the emotions of Jesus. In addition, Jesus has been chided for not laughing. Well, of course there is scant written record of that. Yet, it is hard to imagine Jesus, having a merry good time with the simple folk, sporting a long face.

Be that as it may, Jesus more than makes up for it with an emotion, very characteristic of him. It is recorded in the Greek word *splagchnizomai*. I give the Greek word first, because it has connotations which our modern technological age finds hard to match.

Splagchnizomai represents an emotion that is in the inner parts of the person – loins, womb, guts, bowels, heart – and is usually rendered as 'compassion.' It is the *anima*, the feminine side in Jesus.

Because They Were Sheep with a Shepherd. One would think that after days of going about all the cities and villages, teaching in synagogues and proclaiming the Kingdom, healing all sorts of infirmity, he would be emotionally drained. But no: 'When he saw the crowds, he had compassion for them, because they were harassed and helpless, like sheep without a shepherd' (Mt 9:36). Sheep here refers to the people; shepherd, to their religio-political leaders. The scene has a very contemporary ring, does it not?

And Packed Lunch Too. No less human is a story from Mark. His disciples had just come back, reporting on their hectic sortie into the towns and villages. Jesus invites them to a secluded place for a rest. But there were so many people 'coming and going, and they had no leisure even to eat' (Mk 6:31). Jesus and the disciples attempted an escape by boat. But people spotted them and ran to the same place on foot and got there ahead of them. As he went ashore he saw a large throng, did he get fed up with them? Well, the story goes on to say that 'he had compassion on them, because they were like sheep without a sheperd.' And he proceeded to teach them and to have them fed, five thousand of them, with twelve baskets left over. And '... if I send them away hungry to their homes, they will faint on the way; and some of them have come a long way' (Mk 6:30-44; Mk 8:3). Jesus' compassion is something you can touch and eat.

After giving life to a girl, He strictly ordered them that no one should know this, and told them to *give her something to eat.* (Mk 5:43)

They Ask for It. People instinctively know what you can and want to give. People seem to know what Jesus can and wants to give. And so they know what to ask for: 'Have mercy (*eleeo*) on us, Son of David!' (Mt 20:30) And they get it: 'Jesus had compassion (*eleeo*) on them, and touched their eyes' (Mt 20:34).

In Mk 1:41 it is a leper that arouses his *splagchna*.

Among the Best Stories Told by Jesus. You have such a stock of something that many of the best stories you tell are about that something. Here, according to Matthew and Luke, are stories told by Jesus about *splagchna*.

A servant owes the king a large amount, is ordered to be sold with his wife and children, falls on his knees, begs for patience. The king forgives him – out of pity. The same servant turns to his fellow servant and puts him in jail for not paying a small sum. The king ruefully addresses the servant: 'should not you have had mercy on your fellow servant, as I had mercy on you?' (Mt 18:33)

The other two stories are all-time favorites and the lines have a familiar ring.

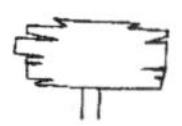

> But a Samaritan while traveling came near him; and when he saw him, he was *moved with pity.* (Lk 10:33)
>
> So he set off and went to his father. But while he was still far off, his father saw him and was *filled with compassion; he ran and put his arms around him and kissed him.* (Lk 15:20)

Compassionate and Strong. While we are on the subject of the *anima* of Jesus, let us listen to words he addressed to the darling city of his people. Better, press your palm gently on his throat. Do you feel the tremor?

> O Jerusalem, Jerusalem ... how often would I have *gathered your children together as a hen gathers her brood under her wings,* and you would not! (Mt 23:37)

Does all this make a wimp of Jesus? If tempted with that bad thought, picture the Jesus at the temple mall, using whip and tongue to good advantage (Jn 2:15). Or feel the air as you come close enough to a Jesus 'enraged' by the hardness of heart of his enemies (Mk 3:5).

And the Disciple's Role?

My Responsibility. Our journey takes us to a point where we begin to ask: 'What is my role in all this?' To put it simply: if the Kingdom is something that should be present, do we have a role in bringing about Kingdom-blessings in our time? Are Kingdom-works in our time only God's, not ours? Have our present hosts, the people's organizations, gone astray in working hard to re-invent our planet and our history? Are the movements and organizing efforts by the poor themselves towards awareness building and empowerment off the mark? Fortunately, even while sophisticated theologians agonize over the question, the First Look answer is unconvoluted and clear: Jesus mandated his followers to proclaim the Kingdom in word and action.

> He called the twelve and began to send them out two by two, and gave *them authority over the unclean spirits....* So they went out and proclaimed that all should repent. They *cast out many demons, and anointed with oil many who were sick and cured them.* (Mk 6:7-13)
>
> Then Jesus summoned his twelve disciples and gave them authority over unclean spirits, to cast them out, and to cure every disease and every sickness.... As you go, *proclaim the good news, 'The kingdom of heaven has come near.' Cure the sick, raise the dead, cleanse the lepers, cast out demons.* (Mt 10:1-8)
>
> And he appointed twelve, whom he also named apostles, to be with him, and to be sent out to *proclaim the message, and to have authority to cast out demons.* (Mk 3:14-15)

See also Lk 9:1-6 and Lk 10:9.

Healing the sick, raising the dead, cleansing lepers, casting out demons were the typical Kingdom-works in the time of Jesus. And the disciples of Jesus were told to perform the same works. From hence come our mandate, inspiration and motivation.

It may be that the future definitive Kingdom of the end-time will be brought about only by God. But no matter. As for the Kingdom today there can be no question: Kingdom-works are a task and a responsibility of today's disciples of Jesus.

Our signposts are to be considered mission texts—missioning of disciples. Note that this is a missioning given by Jesus *during his lifetime, before his death and resurrection.* This missioning to proclaim the Kingdom is *different* from another missioning of disciples, given after his death and resurrection, which has to do with baptizing and teaching.[49]

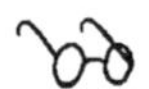

Task and Goal. Is the Kingdom a task or a goal? It is both. Jesus speaks of it sometimes as goal. At other times, as a task.

Jesus speaks of the Kingdom as a goal or reward or inheritance to be attained:

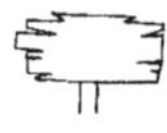

> And if your eye causes you to stumble, tear it out; it is better for you *to enter the kingdom of God* with one eye than to have two eyes and to be thrown into hell. (Mk 9:47)

He also speaks about it as a job to be busy about:

> As you go, proclaim the good news, 'The kingdom of heaven has come near.' *Cure the sick, raise the dead, cleanse the lepers, cast out demons.* (Mt 10:7-8. See Lk 9:2-6; 10:9-10; Mk 6:7-12)

In this respect, therefore, there are two aspects of the Kingdom of God. Frequently it is spoken of as a new world to enter into in the future. It is a goal, a reward, an inheritance, in much the same way as heaven is the goal and reward for the Second Look viewers/disciples/readers.

The Kingdom of God is, as we have just seen, also spoken of in terms of Kingdom-works to be performed today: It is something to be busy about.[50]

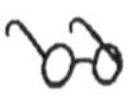

Our Kingdom-Works Today. What form or shape should our Kingdom-works take today? Obviously our Kingdom-works today cannot be a photocopy of Jesus' in his

---

[49] 'All authority in heaven and on earth has been given to me. Go therefore and make disciples of all nations, baptizing them in the name of the Father and of the Son and of the Holy Spirit, teaching them to observe all that I have commanded you; and lo, I am with you always, to the close of the age' (Mt 28:18-20).

[50] Admittedly, our present signposts contain a commissioning, limited to the Jews of Jesus' time. Still it is not amiss to derive inspiration from them for our wider commissioning today.

time. Of course, if we too can make the blind see, the lame walk, let this be one form of our Kingdom-practice. But our Kingdom-practice need not and cannot be limited to this. Nor can it be exactly the same as Jesus' Kingdom-practice. Why not? Because he was God and we are not? No. Because he could perform miracles and we cannot? No. Rather, it is because we live in a different historical context from that of Jesus and we have different historical challenges. But one thing we do have in common with Jesus and the First Look: the concern for total life and well-being (not just divine life for the soul) for the human (not just soul), and for creation.

Serious Analysis of the Social System. Thus, like our present hosts, we need to seriously scrutinize the signs of our own times (Cf. Mt 16:3). For this we need the help of contemporary tools, foremost among which is social analysis. The patient is seriously sick. Flowers and smiles are not enough. A battery of hi-tech medical diagnostic tools is indispensable. Large doses of good will, shiploads of flowers and smiles may turn to bitter regret, when in the end, all they did was to make the patient's certain death somewhat comfortable!

We need to discover the structures and systems—including culture—that undergird society. All this, together with a good measure of the biblical *checed* (compassion), are indispensable components for pastoral work, catechesis, theology and spirituality today.

The HIV of the World. What is the illness? At the time of writing, and perhaps for some time to come, the diagnosis points to a world-wide disease that goes by the name 'globalization.' Pope John Paul II, in a visit to Mexico, "attacked free-market policies for their neglect of the poor and their 'purely economic conception of man (sic).' He blamed globalization for the growing gap between rich and poor," —so runs an editorial of even a widely-circulated First World newspaper.[51]

The HIV-like virus of globalization is deceptive and treacherous because it seems to carry a blessing. It globalizes information which has become instantaneous, massive and worldwide. But it is deadly because it also globalizes the exploitation and destruction of human beings and nature. It is a tenacious parasite-like virus because a few millionaires in the world live by it, make profit by it and swear by it.

The heart of this virus, as I understand it, is this: capitalist enterprises—transnational corporations with the inter-active partnership of the IMF,[52] World Bank and the WTO[53]—extract mega-profits from the peoples of the globe and from the resources of nature.

What Globalization Does to Humankind and Nature. Here are some of the visible effects of globalization:

---

[51] *The New York Times*, January 27, 1999.

[52] International Monetary Fund.

[53] World Trade Organization.

- The already all too familiar growing gap between the rich and poor people, rich and poor nations is widening.
- The workers are experiencing unemployment, job insecurity, loss of benefits, contractualization, the destruction of unions.
- The farmers lose their lands in favor of industrial sites, golf courses, recreational facilities for the rich. They have to compete with the products of rich countries, not to mention problems that chemical fertilizers and pesticides bring to them.
- The ordinary fisherfolk may no longer get food from the seas which have now been taken over by sophisticated trawling ships.
- Women, especially working women, experience intensification of their manifold exploitation.
- Indigenous peoples' right to ancestral lands is undermined by the incursion of multinational plantations, mining and logging enterprises.
- Environment, where profit has prime priority, is among the prime victims of globalization. The deadly effects include climate change, ozone depletion, air and water pollution, ocean resource depletion and pollution, deforestation, extinction of species and cold-blooded genetic manipulation.
- Human rights are sidelined. The priority given to the business interests abets violations of people's rights—economic, social, cultural, political and civil.
- States and governments are subjected to the dictates of transnational business. Legislation, even constitutions, are changed to promote the gains of these businesses.

Globalization is the antithesis of the Kingdom of God. Motivated by Jesus' summons, let us join our present hosts—organizations of youth, environmentalists, women, workers, peasants, mothers, overseas workers, drug and alcohol rehab groups, indigenous peoples, small vendors, urban poor and other grassroots organizations—who assert, in word and action, that something of the new earth has got to be visible and tangible today. Kingdom-work means to join in the global project to find alternative paradigms for living and being in the globe, our home. Like our hosts and like Jesus, may we be able to say: 'The Kingdom of God—or something of it—is already among us.'

In Touch with the Source

Twenty Four Hours with Jesus. Let us keep Jesus company for twenty four hours. Was it all work? All action? Did he not burn himself out? Whence the energy? Did he immerse in the Fountainhead and soak up the waters of compassion? Whence the clarity of vision? The sense of purpose? The gospel accounts suggest where to look: Jesus' intimate communion with his Father, his '*abba*.'

After First Day of Work, Dawn Solitude. Mark recounts Jesus' first day of work – a typical day really (Mk 1:14-34). After this hectic day—the call of the first disciples, the teaching and exorcising in the synagogue, the healing of Peter's mother-in-law, healing and exorcising at sundown (Mk 1:16-34)—Mark reports that:

In the morning, while it was still very dark, he got up and went out to a deserted place, and there he *prayed.* (Mk 1:35)

He was buried in that dawn solitude until he was interrupted by friends, eager to show him (off?) to the rest of the world:

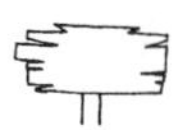

And Simon and his companions hunted for him. When they found him, they said to him, 'Everyone is searching for you.' He answered, 'Let us go on to the neighboring towns, so that I may proclaim the message there also; for that is what I came out to do.' And *he went throughout Galilee, proclaiming the message in their synagogues and casting out demons.* (Mk 1:36-39)

Rhythm. Such seems to have been the rhythm of his life: Action ... prayer ... action ... prayer ...

After a Frenzied Day. Remember the time when Jesus and his disciples were going to a secluded place for rest, how there were so many people 'coming and going, and they had no leisure even to eat,' how Jesus and the disciples attempted an escape by boat, how people spotted them and ran on foot ahead of them to the place where they were sailing, how he steps off the boat, and out of compassion, teaches and feeds them? What follows this frenzied day? Mark says:

Immediately he made his disciples get into the boat and go on ahead to the other side, to Bethsaida, while *he dismissed the crowd. After saying farewell to them, he went up on the mountain to pray.* (Mk 6:45-46)

In Between Critical Moments. Sandwiched between intense bouts with his opponents (Lk 5:17-6:11) and the all-important choosing of his twelve life-companions is this item:

Now during those days he went out to the mountain to pray; and he *spent the night* in *prayer* to God. (Lk 6:12)

Just Connected. What did he do all night? The gospels are reverently silent. Shall we try some spy work and lift the veil of night? Can we even see through the night—and without irreverence—into his being? Let us not dare.

Let us just guess. Why, he is doing nothing! No words. No thinking. Just centered. Just aware. Just connected.

Our guess is as good as any. There are at least two persuasive pieces of evidence. One, when Jesus taught prayer, his counsel was not to use many words (Mt 6:7). Two, it is difficult to conceive a night-long prayer other than a prayer of silent communion. A third possible reason, a shot in the dark, is that Jesus was not too far from the Asia of silent meditation. In that Asia, you learn to be in touch with the Source in a non-verbal and non-cerebral way.

Was It? Did He? Was it during these nights, in the innermost chamber of his being, that he 'knew' that 'I and the Father are one'? Was he in touch with the Source from which the wise man draws out treasures old *and new*? Did he plumb the underground Springs that connect with the vast ocean of existence? Did he make contact there with the volcanic fire that burns up the ego and ignites the lips, frozen in terror, to say: 'let this cup pass from me ... yet not what my ego desires ...'?

The Jesus Follower. Can the Jesus-follower do less than make his own Kingdom-spirituality a chemistry of deed and contemplation, action and silence?[54]

The Flame. At this juncture, one of our activist-hosts shares her experience and understanding of Asian meditation:

The 'essence' of Asian meditation, as I understand it, she says, is awareness. One is aware. One who is in meditation has gone beyond thinking. Awareness is not thinking. One has a surface 'me' that thinks. One's deepest self is simply aware. Like a candle that is lit, it is simply aflame. The flame does not pass judgment. It does not engage in reflection. It does not analyze. It does not talk. It just shines. It shines on anything it falls on. Awareness does not think. It is simply aware—of anything, of itself, of the breath, of the sounds, of the feel of things, of one's thoughts even, of one's feelings. That flame is really the Christ in me. Its native language is silence. The only 'utterance' it knows is 'Abba.' And it utters 'Abba' without words. In silence, therefore. For it utters it in *language too deep for human words.* Paul describes this:

> God has *sent the Spirit of his Son into our hearts, crying, 'Abba! Father!'* (Gal 4:6)
>
> ... that very Spirit intercedes *with sighs too deep for words.* (Rom 8:26)

Or, awareness is like the eye. It just looks. It does not think. It does not judge. It just looks. It just sees. And the marvelous thing is that just by pure seeing, so many marvelous things happen ...

In meditation one has gone beyond the noise of the mind. One has moved into the stillness of awareness. Pure consciousness, which is our deepest and most real self, brings gifts that transcend all expectations.

[54] Hopefully, with such a formula, we may steer clear of these words: "Not everyone who says to me, 'Lord, Lord,' will enter the kingdom of heaven, but only the one who does the will of my Father in heaven. On that day many will say to me, 'Lord, Lord, did we not prophesy in your name, and cast out demons in your name, and do many deeds of power in your name?' Then I will declare to them, 'I never knew you; go away from me, you evildoers.'" (Mt 7:21-23)

Jesus and Us.

It is evident from the gospels that this unique person, Jesus, felt within himself certain real powers to destroy evil in the lives of people: the sick, suffering and possessed. He felt the power of God's Spirit (*ruah*)—God's breath, life, energy—within him, a power which no doubt sprang from a deep silent communion with his Father. He healed. He cast out demons. He announced a program of far-reaching liberation. He saw in these actions and blessings tangible presences (not just 'signs') of the Reign of God. The question for us, Jesus-followers today, is whether the new world, its justice and life, is felt and experienced through our contemplation and deeds. That new world would include the self-determination of the poor and the creating of alternatives to globalization. The Kingdom of God is not just something to wait for. It is something to be busy about today.

Stopover 12

PCP II
(A Kingdom Blessing: Good News to the Poor)

OUR HOST: PCP II

Central but Neglected. 'Good news to the poor' is an innocent little phrase in the gospel tradition. Its most remarkable characteristics are (1) the centrality it occupies in the consciousness and practice of Jesus, and (2) the disregard, neglect, and misconception it has suffered in the Church for centuries.

Biblical Basis for Philippine Church. Do you remember meeting 'good news to the poor' in our journey? Well, it is one of the Kingdom-blessings.[55] Happily 'good news to the poor' – notwithstanding our somewhat thoughtless handling of it in our tradition— is in fact the secure basis for two key-axioms of our contemporary Philippine Church. These two axioms that we profess are (1) We are the Church of the Poor; and (2) Our Church has a preferential option for the poor.

[55] See page 35 and 'Principal Kingdom-Works of Jesus,' page 118.

Our roadmap takes us now along the banks of the Pasig river where in the early months of 1991, the Second Plenary Council of the Philippines (PCP II) solemnly declared that we are the Church of the Poor. PCP II is our present host.

Two Questions

Who and What. The phrase 'good news to the poor' is artlessly simple and clear. Yet it has been made either invisible or prettified with such an overlay of misconceptions or rationalizations that patience is needed to restore it to its natural condition. We will work away with the help of two questions: *Who are the poor? What is the good news?*

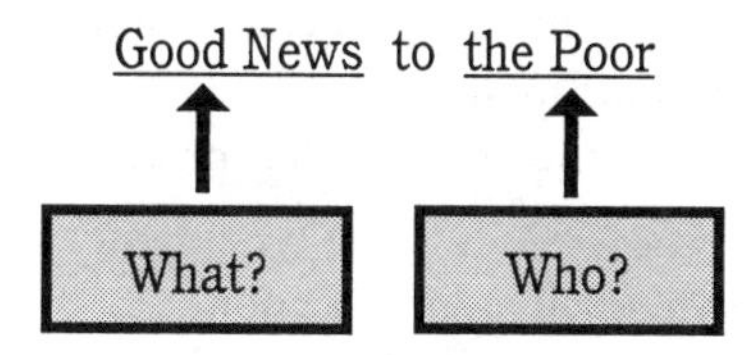

Unreflected Responses. Who are the poor? In the past, we, religious and clergy, living in relative comfort, were too quick to reply 'poor in spirit.' Thank God, this situation is changing.

And what is the good news? 'But, of course, the good news is the Word of God,' – might go an unreflected response, followed by a spirited distribution of Holy Bibles to the colonies of the urban poor.

Jesus would beg to disagree with both responses.

More than ever, we need our Third Look eyeglasses.

The Poor: Who Are They?

When Jesus said he was proclaiming good news to the poor, what poor was he referring to? Which poor? The spiritually poor? Or the really, materially poor?

Our unequivocal answer is: the really poor. Jesus' proclamation of good news was to the really poor. We have three sets of data which point to this: (a) Isaiah, the background and inspiration of Jesus' message, meant the really poor; (b) 'Poor' in the gospels always refers to the really poor, the one exception being Matthew's editorializing addition; (c) When the gospels speak of blessedness and good news to the poor, the standard formulation simply says 'poor.'

Poor in the Book of Isaiah.

The background and inspiration for 'poor' as found on Jesus' lips is the *'anawim* or *'aniyim* in the Book of Isaiah. Recall our past signposts on Jesus and Isaiah. In particular, it is obvious that Jesus' 'good news to the poor' is lifted right out of

Isa 61:1. We must then examine the meaning of 'poor' in the Book of Isaiah. Here are all the texts in which Isaiah mentions the *'anawim* or *'aniyim* .

The Lord enters into judgment with the elders and princes of his people:
It is you who have devoured the vineyard,
the spoil of the *'aniyim* is in your houses. (Isa 3:14)

What do you mean by crushing my people, and grinding the face of the *'aniyim?* says the Lord God of hosts. (Isa 3:15)

Ah, you who make iniquitous decrees,
who write oppressive statutes,
to turn aside the needy from justice
and to rob the *'aniyim* of my people of their right,
that widows may be your spoil,
and that you may make the orphans your prey!
(Isa 10:1-2)

With righteousness he shall judge the poor,
and decide with equity for the *'anawim* of the earth;
he shall strike the earth with the rod of his mouth,
and with the breath of his lips he shall kill the wicked. (Isa 11:4)

What will one answer the messengers of the nation?
'The LORD has founded Zion,
and the *'aniyim* among his people
will find refuge in her.' (Isa 14:32)

For he has brought low the inhabitants of the height, the lofty city.
He lays it low to the ground, casts it to the dust.
The foot tramples it, the feet of the *'aniyim* , the steps of the needy.
(Isa 26:5-6)

The *'anawim* shall obtain fresh joy in the Lord,
and the neediest people shall exult in the Holy One of Israel. (Isa 29:19)

The villainies of villains are evil;
they devise wicked devices to ruin the *'aniyim* with lying words,
even when the plea of the needy is right. (Isa 32:7)

When the *'aniyim* and needy seek water, and there is none,
And their tongue is parched with thirst,
I the Lord will answer them,
I the God of Israel will not forsake them. (Isa 41:17)

Sing for joy, O heavens, and exult, O earth;
break forth, O mountains, into singing!
For the Lord has comforted his people,
and will have compassion on his *'aniyim.* (Isa 49:13)

Therefore hear this, you who are *'aniyim,*
who are drunk, but not with wine:

Thus says your Sovereign, the LORD,
your God who pleads the cause of his people:
See, I have taken from your hand the cup of staggering;
you shall drink no more
from the bowl of my wrath. (Isa 51:21-22)

O afflicted ['*aniyah*] one, storm-tossed, and not comforted,
I am about to set your stones in antimony,
and lay your foundations with sapphires. (Isa 54:11)

... Is it not to share your bread with the hungry,
and bring the homeless *'aniyim* into your house;
when you see the naked, to cover them,
and not to hide yourself from your own kin? (Isa 58:7)

The spirit of the Lord GOD is upon me,
because the LORD has anointed me;
he has sent me to bring good news to the *'anawim*;
to bind up the brokenhearted,
to proclaim liberty to the captives,
and release to the prisoners. (Isa 61:1)

Heaven is my throne and the earth is my footstool;
what is the house that you would build for me,
and what is my resting place?
All these things my hand has made,
and so all these things are mine, says the Lord.
But this is the one to whom I will look,
to the *'aniyim* and contrite in spirit,
who trembles at my word. (Isa 66:1-2)

Isaiah's *'Anawim*: Really Poor. Even without the help of a dictionary, and just by looking at the context, we have the answer. Poor, *'anawim* or *'aniyim* in the Book of Isaiah means, with one possible exception, the really poor, not the spiritually poor. This is so particularly in passages where he speaks of justice, liberation, and joy for the poor.

Furthermore, the more accurate meaning is 'poor *and oppressed*.' Recall that the root word is *'anah,* a word which connotes some form of oppression or suppression.[56] Very frequently this oppression is due, as in the above contexts, to economic poverty. Since Jesus was inspired by Isaiah, Jesus was, more likely than not, talking of good news to the really poor.

[56] See 'Poor and Oppressed,' page 47.

Poor in the Gospels

There are two separate but complementary considerations here: (1) the use of the word *ptōchós*; and (2) the context in which the poor is spoken about.

When the gospels refer to the poor, they use the Greek word *ptōchós* (plural: *ptōchói*). In the world in which Jesus lived, *ptōchói* were people reduced to begging, crouched in helplessness and destitution[57]. Here are all the gospel texts in which *ptōchós* is mentioned; from the contexts themselves, it is clear that the gospels speak of the really poor.

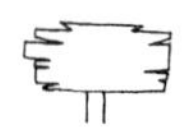

> 'Why was the ointment wasted in this way? For this ointment could have been sold for more than three hundred denarii, and the money given to the *poor*.' And they scolded her. But Jesus said, 'Let her alone; why do you trouble her? She has performed a good service for me. For you always have the *poor* with you, and you can show kindness to them whenever you wish; but you will not always have me.' (Mk 14:5-7 = Mt 26:9-11; also Jn 12:5-8)
>
> You lack one thing; go, sell what you own, and give the money to the *poor*, and you will have treasure in heaven; then come, follow me. (Mk 10:21 = Mt 19:21 = Lk 18:22)
>
> But when you give a banquet, invite the *poor*, the crippled, the lame, and the blind (Lk 14:13); Go out at once into the streets and lanes of the town, and bring in the *poor*, the crippled, the blind, and the lame. (Lk 14:21)
>
> There was a rich man who was dressed in purple and fine linen and who feasted sumptuously every day. And at his gate lay a *poor* man named Lazarus, covered with sores, who longed to satisfy his hunger with what fell from the rich man's table; even the dogs would come and lick his sores. The *poor* man died and was carried away by the angels to be with Abraham. The rich man also died and was buried. (Lk 16:19-22)
>
> Look, half of my possessions, Lord, I will give to the *poor*; and if I have defrauded anyone of anything, I will pay back four times as much. (Lk 19:8)
>
> He looked up and saw rich people putting their gifts into the treasury; he also saw a *poor* widow put in two small copper coins. He said, 'Truly I tell you, this *poor* widow has put in more than all of them; for all of them have contributed out of their abundance, but she out of her poverty has put in all she had to live on.' (Lk 21:1-4 = Mk 12:42)
>
> Some thought that, because Judas had the common purse, Jesus was telling him, 'buy what we need for the festival'; or, that he should give something to the *poor*. (Jn 13:29)

---

[57] *Pénēs* is another word for 'poor.' This refers to the poor who have to work for a living. *Ptōchós*, on the other hand, refers to people in poverty so total that people are forced to beg.

Plus the texts we are presently inquiring about:

... the *poor* have the good news brought to them. (Mt 11:5 = Lk 7:22)
... to proclaim the good news to the *poor*. (Lk 4:18)
Blessed are you who are *poor*, for yours is the Kingdom of God. (Lk 6:20)

Poor '*Ptōchoi*' in the Gospels: Really Poor. Poor in the gospels always means the really poor except in the *one* case when Matthew 5:3 introduces an editorial 'in spirit.' Poor are the *really poor* in the gospels, unless it is qualified; and it is qualified only once, and not by Jesus but by Matthew!

The Blessedness of the Poor.

The blessedness of the poor is a gospel theme which is variously expressed as 'good news to the poor' or 'blessed are the poor.' Every time the gospels speak on this theme, the standard formulation always simply says 'poor' except in the one single instance of Matthew's 'poor in spirit':

The *poor* have the good news brought to them. (Mt 11:5)
The *poor* have the good news brought to them. (Lk 7:22)
To bring good news to the *poor*. (Lk 4:18)
Blessed are you who are *poor.* (Lk 6:20)
Blessed are the *poor in spirit.* (Mt 5:3)

The Old and Standard Formulation. In other words, the formulation or language for this fragment of early Christian tradition is normally 'good news to the *poor*,' not some other idiom, such as 'good news to the poor in spirit.' What does this evidence indicate? It is a strong indicator that Jesus and the tradition spoke simply of the really poor and that Mt 5:3, 'poor in spirit,' in keeping with a Matthean tendency to moralize, is an editorial modification by Matthew. It is worth noting, by the way, that even Matthew himself says simply 'poor' in reporting out this tradition in Mt 11:5.

Other Instances

Evidently the Really Poor. We may add the following reflection. There are other occasions when the gospels talk about good news, blessing or happiness for the poor, and, evidently, to the really poor:

The poor man, after death, is to be with Abraham. (Lk 16:22a)

Zacchaeus gives half of his possessions to the poor. (Lk 19:8)

God fills the hungry with good things. (Lk 1:53)

Jesus counsels the rich young man to give to the poor. (Mt 19:21; Mk 10:21)

The Poor in Jesus' Time. As you walk through the gospel pages, you will meet:

- beggars (Mk 10:46)
- casual workers (Mt 20:1-9)
- tenants (cf. Mt 21:33)
- slaves (Mt 8:6)
- people in debt (Lk 16:5)
- the poor of the land (Jn 7:49)

These are examples of the *'anawim* in Jesus' time. And no wonder such people existed, if we keep in mind some features of the life of the common people:

- Payment of taxes and tribute. It was double taxation: (a) tithes and other dues paid to the temple and priests, and (b) tribute and other taxes paid to Rome.
- Indebtedness. This was quite common and widespread in Jesus time (see Lk 16:5).
- Loss of land. This too had been a perennial problem for some centuries.
- Dislocations due to the raiding activities of Roman armies in towns and villages.
- Breakdown of traditional village-based social structure; for example, the destruction of family and clan economic unity.
- Peasants being reduced to becoming debt slaves, tenants, day laborers, or unemployed (see Mt 20:1-9), while the native aristocracy increased land-holdings and power.
- Absence of common people's political participation.

The Clear Lines on Their Faces. I hope that our efforts at restoration have helped to flick away some of the incrustations of a long tradition and brought out some of the clear lines on the faces of Jesus' 'poor.' It was to the really poor that Jesus wanted to bring good news. And now we turn to the other question: What? What was his good news to them?

The Good News: What Is It?

Difficulty. What good news did Jesus want to announce to the poor? An easy task has been rendered difficult by the phrase 'good news' itself.

We have been so used to equate good news or gospel with the 'word of God' or 'the Christian Faith' or 'the saving death and resurrection of Christ' that 'good news to the poor' has come to mean bringing the Bible to the poor or to catechize them about the truths of the Christian Faith. Under certain circumstances, that may or may not be the best news for the poor, but in any case that is not what Jesus would mean or do.

'Good news,' in the time of Jesus, could refer to the birth of a future emperor or his arrival in a city. It was a secular word.

In its religious usage, it could refer to the saving death and resurrection of Christ; this is St. Paul's use of the word (1 Cor 15:1-3).

Jesus never used it to refer to his death and resurrection. Like Isaiah, he used it, first, to refer to the coming of a new earth, the Kingdom of God.

Secondly, in this stopover, we encounter *still another use* of 'good news' in the phrase *'good news to the poor.'*

Misleading Platitudes. The difficult task turns out to be rather easy. Food, land, homes, security, human rights, justice, liberation from poverty—that is what good news to the poor is. It is the most obvious meaning ... and the most correct! Third Look eyeglasses should have been superfluous. However, experience has shown that we should be careful with some well-meaning but misleading notions. These usually take the form of platitudes, spoken and unspoken:

'Jesus is with you in your poverty. (Subconsciously: You can remain in your poverty.) With Jesus you can bear it all.'

'You are God's special favorites. God loves and blesses the poor. You can bear your poverty with the strength he lavishes on you.'

'Jesus loves you in a special way and died for your sins on the cross.'

Wait for the Second Statement. In passing, let us make ourselves conscious of a certain ambivalence of many of our conventional platitudes. We say: 'God is good.' 'God loves you,' etc. Any such statement can have two possible meanings and *depends on a second statement for its real meaning*. For example, the first statement 'God loves you,' is clarified by a second statement which can either be 'Therefore, be patient in your suffering,' or 'Therefore, God is in solidarity with you in your organizing and struggle.' When we preachers or theologians say something which has the ring of a religious adage, the listener should wait or ask for the next sentence.

Many Kinds. There are many kinds of good news. There is good news for students, for teachers, for peasants, for mothers, for business people. For the poor there is still another. Is Jesus' Sermon on the Mount the good news to the poor? No. That is not specifically good news to the poor. That is good news for everyone (including, of course, the poor). What about the dogmatic truths, packaged during seminary days and repackaged for diocesan catechisms and homilies? Not so, either. Assuming it is good theology—an assumption that needs to be tested—it would be good news for *all* Christians.

Gospel to the Poor: Justice and Liberation. The gospel to the poor is the good news to the poor of any era: food, land, homes, health. In summary, justice and liberation from poverty and oppression! The gospel to the poor and oppressed must at least include this. Many other blessings, among them moral and religious, go into the making of gospel to the poor, but it cannot be gospel without justice and liberation.

★

A Word to Pastors and Preachers. Therefore, a reminder to us pastors and preachers: proclaiming the 'gospel to the poor' is proclaiming liberation and justice (at least).

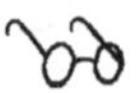

Passion, Not Words. The words 'justice and liberation' are household words in the Church today. The actual *words* 'justice and liberation' are not found on the lips of Jesus. The passion for them is. Words matter less.

A Spiritual Work. Justice for the poor is not just a corporal work of mercy (as opposed to spiritual work of mercy). This should be a familiar notion by now. But because of its importance, I beg indulgence for the repetition. In biblical categories, 'spiritual' is any reality—land, rice, prayer, religious reading, political action, human rights—in which we find traces of the Spirit or God's life-giving energy, and which is therefore animated and transformed by that Spirit.

Greek Split. Greek thought, in which our catechesis and theology have been expressed for so long, splits reality into spirit and matter; spiritual here means a reality which is non-material or things pertaining to the soul. Here, prayer is spiritual; feeding the hungry is corporal. Not so for Jesus and the Bible.

Spiritual and Gospel. Land for the landless, rice for the hungry, justice for the exploited can be the most spiritual concern of a Christian who understands what Jesus was all about. Justice and liberation of the poor, for the Bible, is not a corporal work of mercy, as my former theology used to say; it is a spiritual work! In fact, it was a constituent component of the Kingdom of God and thus of the mission of Jesus. It was part of the gospel of Jesus! All of which makes us ask: and what gospel do we preach in the Church today? PCP II, our present host, is a break-through. But of this, later.

The Poor: Not Mere Beneficiaries of Good Will. 'Good news to the poor' is not to be misconstrued as if the poor were mere recipients and beneficiaries, while the rich and the middle-class are their great benefactors. Not at all. In fact, it is quite the opposite. The poor today are awakening. They are setting up movements and organizations for liberation. They are enabling themselves to move away from centuries of passivity and resignation towards the creation of a more humane history for all of us. The task of the rest of us is to support, to facilitate, to accompany.

In the formation of basic Christian communities among the poor, one may discern the following types: (1) the purely liturgical; the Christian community gathers around the word of God and the sacraments, (2) the developmental; the members engage in activities which improve their life—religio-cultural, economic, political, social—*within* the present social system, (3) the liberational; the members are aware that poverty is the effect of an unjust social system and are committed to change that system. It is especially this third type that offers excellent opportunities for accompaniment to the non-poor who want to be in solidarity with the poor.

Part of Our Christian Heritage? We have just taken a look at the biblical meaning of 'good news to the poor.' How much of this biblical, not any other, meaning, is part of our Christian heritage today? In seminary courses? In religion classes? In catechetical programs? In homilies? In normal consciousness? After PCP II, a case can be made for a qualified positive response. But caution is called for. In order to avoid complacency? Yes, but there are better reasons. One, do we *really* understand PCP II? Do we understand its biblical underpinnings—provocative underpinnings? Two, do we *do* it?

In any case, I think one can safely say that 'good news to the poor' – understood as justice and liberation – is not normally seen as part of the 'core teachings' of our Faith. We normally do not take it to be central to our Faith. Jesus does. Pry open Jesus' consciousness and you will find it there.

Look carefully likewise at his *practice* and you will find it there. We will now proceed to do this with the help of roadsigns that contain (1) Jesus mission-statements; and (2) his actions and teaching.

Good News to the Poor: How Central for Jesus?

In Mission Statements

Central in Jesus' Mission Statements. Let us once more look at his mission statements and review the listing of the various Kingdom-blessings. With or without your eyeglasses, you will notice that there is one, and only one, item which is always mentioned and never omitted: 'good news or blessing to the poor.' Conversely, the other items—for example, sight to the blind—is mentioned in one recital but not in another. And we are dealing, not with secondary or off-the-cuff statements. They are key-statements, the mission statements.

The blind receive their sight,
the lame walk,
the lepers are cleansed,
the deaf hear,
the dead are raised,
and the *poor have good news brought to them.* (Mt 11:2-6 = Lk 7:18-23)

To *bring good news to the poor,*
He has sent me to proclaim release to the captives
and recovery of sight to the blind,
to let the oppressed go free,
to proclaim the year of the Lord's favor.'
And he rolled up the scroll, gave it back to the attendant, and sat down.

> The eyes of all in the synagogue were fixed on him. Then he began to say to them, 'Today this scripture has been fulfilled in your hearing.' (Lk 4:16-21; cf. Isa 61:1-2)
>
> *Blessed are you who are poor,* for yours is the Kingdom of God.
> Blessed are the hungry ...
> ... the sorrowful
> ... the pure in heart,
> ... etc. (Lk 6:20 = Mt 5:3)

Always Mentioned. Every time Jesus opens his mouth to talk about his mission, good news to the poor is always on his lips! *Bukang bibig,* as we would say in Pilipino. An obvious but overlooked fact.

Privileged Position. Take note, too, of a small but significant detail. 'Good news to the poor' is always in a noteworthy position in the enumeration. It is either the climactic last or the prominent first.

Still another little detail to note: in the gospel of Luke, it is Jesus' very first words in the very first public statement of his adult life.

Etched in Jesus' Consciousness. There it is, tattooed in Jesus' consciousness and chafing to find outward expression in his mission statements. And yet it is hardly a passing thought in our present theology, preaching, and catechism.

In His Actions

Action among the Sick, Possessed, Multitudes, Sinners. Mission-statements, even those of Jesus, are words and nothing more, unless they are backed up by deeds. So what about Jesus' actions and teachings? Were these good news to the poor? Let us put his practice to the test. For this, we sample a typical day:

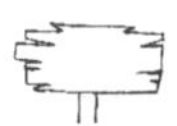

> Jesus departed with his disciples to the sea, and *a great multitude* from Galilee followed him; hearing all that he was doing, they came to him *in great numbers* from Judea, Jerusalem, Idumea, beyond the Jordan, and the region around Tyre and Sidon. He told his disciples to have a boat ready for him because of the crowd, so that they would not crush him; for he had *cured* many, so that all who had diseases pressed upon him to touch him. Whenever the *unclean spirits* saw him, they fell down before him and shouted, 'You are the Son of God!' But he sternly ordered them not to make him known. (Mk 3:7-12)

Here we see Jesus stretching his healing hand over the sick, the possessed, and the multitudes. 'Sinners' may be added to this list.

Not All but Many of Them: The Poor of Palestine. Who are these people in fact? Are not most of them the poor of the Palestine of Jesus' time? In a sociologically poor area like Palestine, the majority of such people, though admittedly not all, would have been the poor. The sick would have been the malnourished poor, vulnerable to various illnesses. The 'possessed' would have been the mentally ill, victims of malnutrition and poverty. The multitudes: these were mostly the unschooled poor of the land attracted by a popular preacher and wonder worker.

And 'Sinners' Too. Many of the so-called sinners would have also been, not necessarily people of evil morals, but rather the poor. We can discern about three categories of people to whom the label 'sinners' was given:

1. real sinners, i.e., those that can be presumed to have moral guilt, e.g., Mk 2:5;
2. people forced into dubious professions due to *poverty*, e.g., prostitutes, thieves;
3. the uninstructed *poor* who did not know their 'catechism' who were considered sinners by the religious establishment.

Categories 2 and 3 tell us that frequently, in the gospels, 'sinners' are really the poor. It is the flesh-and-blood poor who frequently lie concealed behind the word 'sinners.'

Jesus' Actions and Good News to the Poor. Since the gospel pages depict the healing touch of Jesus on the sick, possessed, multitudes, and sinners, we can say that Jesus' actions and ministry were good news to the poor of his time.

Poverty, Not Morals. Did Jesus proclaim good news to the poor because they were subjectively good, simple or holy, or for any other moral qualification? No, he proclaimed good news to them primarily because they were poor. The focus of Jesus' remarks (cf. e.g., Lk 16:19-31; Lk 6:20; Mk 10:21, etc.) was not the goodness of the poor but the poverty of the poor.

Non-Poor Outcasts. Did Jesus' concern and care also go out to outcasts who were not poor? Yes, of course. Tax-collectors, lepers, children, women, possessed, sinners, the sick—these suffered from various forms of marginalization: cultural, psychological, religious. Jesus cared for anyone who, in any way, was suffering, oppressed or outcast.

Not to Apply the Word 'Poor'. However, it is not wise to apply the word 'poor' to these non-poor outcasts. The reason is that strictly speaking, biblical terminology, reserves 'poor' (*ptōchós*) to the really poor and oppressed. We thus avoid unnecessary confusion. It is advisable to reserve 'poor' to the really poor and oppressed. We would also avoid awkward statements such as a pastor's: 'I play golf every other day with Mr. Millionaire because after all he is poor in so many ways.'

Jesus, Children and Feminism. One of the truly praiseworthy developments of our time is the concern for women and children. That Jesus had a special regard for children is a common knowledge (Mk 10:13-16).

The multi-layered oppression of women in history, not excluding Church history, is breaking more and more into our consciousness. We are seeing through to the inhumanity of patriarchy, the institutional domination of females by males with the conscious or unconscious claim that the male is normative for humanity. In response, both women and men have espoused feminism, a movement which seeks to restore to women their equal rights as humans.

Was Jesus a feminist? Did his Kingdom-practice include what we would consider feminist concerns today? Perhaps not in the way and to the extent that is expected today. The gospels have left us a handful of indicators. The evangelists credit Jesus with the following actuations. In his dealings with women he went beyond or against the accepted ways of his time. Women could become his disciples and close followers (Mk 15:40-41). He didn't seem to subscribe to the levirate custom of successive brothers having to take the same woman as wife (Mk 12:18-24). The hemorrhaging woman was not only cured but also endearingly addressed 'daughter' (Mk 5:34), while male disciples often came in for a scolding (Mk 8:17-21). The prominence and intelligence of women in the passion and resurrection scenes (Mk 15:40-41; Lk 23:27, 49, 55; 24:10; 22, 24) seem to be not only a faithful recording of fact but also a (delayed?) tribute both to the women and to Jesus who allowed them to be among his disciples. Jesus used feminine metaphors and parables. There would seem enough to permit the claim that Jesus and his women disciples, as archived in the gospel records, sowed the first small grain of feminism in the Christian tradition.

Jesus and Rich Outcasts. What would Jesus' attitude be towards a rich outcast, e.g., a tax-collector? Jesus would care for him in so far as he is an ostracized tax-collector. At the same time, Jesus would put his wealth to the test: 'Sell what you have and give to the poor.' (cf. Mk 2:14; Mk 10:17-21; Lk 19:1-10)

In His Teaching

Jesus' Prophetic Teachings on Property and Possessions. Both his mission statements and his practice were good news to the poor. They have weathered our scrutiny.

But did Jesus' healing touch alleviate the poverty of the poor? It would seem not, at least not directly. And so we turn to his teachings. After all Jesus was not just a healer. He was also a prophet-teacher. We inspect his teachings, particularly on riches and poverty, on property and possessions.

> And Jesus said *to a rich man,* 'You lack one thing; go, *sell what you own, and give the money to the poor,* and you will have treasure in heaven; then come, follow me.' (Mk 10:21)
>
> *Sell your possessions, and give alms.* Make purses for yourselves that do not wear out, an unfailing treasure in heaven, where no thief comes near and no moth destroys. (Lk 12:33-34)

> *Blessed are you who are poor*, for yours is the Kingdom of God. But *woe to you who are rich*, for you have received your consolation. (Lk 6:21 and 24)
>
> There was *a rich man* who was dressed in purple and fine linen and who feasted sumptuously every day. And at his gate lay *a poor man* named Lazarus, covered with sores, who longed to satisfy his hunger with what fell from the rich man's table; even the dogs would come and lick his sores. The *poor man died and was carried away by the angels to be with Abraham.* The *rich man also died and was buried. In Hades, where he was being tormented*, he looked up and saw Abraham far away with Lazarus by his side. (Lk 16:19-23)
>
> *No one can serve two masters;* for a slave will either hate the one and love the other, or be devoted to the one and despise the other. *You cannot serve God and wealth.* (Mt. 6:24)
>
> Take care! Be on your guard against all kinds of greed; for one's *life does not consist in the abundance of possessions.* (Lk 12:15)
>
> The *land of a rich man* produced abundantly. And he thought to himself, 'What should I do, for I have no place to store my crops?' Then he said, 'I will do this: I will pull down my barns and build larger ones, and there I will store all my grain and my goods. And I will say to my soul, 'Soul, you have *ample goods laid up for many years; relax, eat, drink, be merry.' But God said to him, 'You fool!* This very night your life is being demanded of you. And the things you have prepared, whose will they be?' So it is with those who store up treasures for themselves but are not rich toward God. (Lk 12:16-21)
>
> *How hard it is to enter the kingdom of God!* It is easier for a camel to go through the eye of a needle than for *someone who is rich* to enter the kingdom of God. (Mk 10:23-25)

Director of the Department for the Alleviation of Poverty. Such prophetic utterances would make Jesus an ideal director of the Department of the *'Anawim*. In our time there is a suspicion that some government institutions, professedly set up to safeguard the interests of labor, spend more energy defending the interests of capital. There is no mistaking Jesus. He has blessings for the poor and warnings for the rich. He comes in strong against acquisitiveness and the consumerist spirit. He advocates sharing goods with the poor. 'Alms' in his time was an exercise of justice (What is given to the beggar really belongs to him!), not of charity.

His is a prophetic voice in the first century, not the methodical analysis of a twenty-first century economist. But there is no doubt for whom his good news is. If you were among the *'anawim* in Jesus' time, would not his words have a happy ring in your ears? Would they not be addressing your situation of poverty?

Substantial or Structural Liberation? Since Jesus is doing quite well, let us press a little further. Did Jesus' actions and teaching offer structural liberation and justice to the poor and oppressed? Did his actions and teaching liberate the poor by changing social and economic structures?

Here we ask the question about what Jesus did in the economic, not cultural, sphere. Of course, any change in cultural attitude in favor of the poor, such as that fostered by Jesus, would be a contribution to economic change. But in order to make our inquiry satisfactory, I choose to limit inquiry to the economic domain. We examine Jesus' teachings more closely and scrutinize his stand or platform on such questions as possessions and property, social justice.

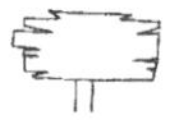

> Jesus, looking at him [the rich man] loved him and said, 'You lack one thing; *go, sell what you own, and give the money to the poor*, and you will have treasure in heaven; then come, follow me.' (Mk 10:21)
>
> *Sell your possessions, and give alms.* Make purses for yourselves that do not wear out, an unfailing treasure in heaven, where no thief comes near and no moth destroys. For where your treasure is, there your heart will be also. (Lk 12:33-34)

What is Jesus' stand on possessions, assets, goods, wealth? Distribute. Share. It is disarmingly simple. Naive? Let us approach the matter this way. These words of Jesus constitute a *prophetic* view of things, for Jesus was a prophetic figure, *not* an economist. *But* if this prophetic vision of Jesus were to provide inspiration for a modern-day economic program, what kind of human community would emerge?

To Each According to Need. Whatever our answer to that might be, his words did provide stimulus to a group of first century Christians. They attempted to translate his prophetic vision into actual life (Acts 2:42-47; 4:32-35; 5:1-10). What happened?

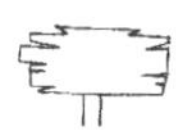

> They had all things in common.
>
> They sold their possessions and goods, like land and houses (from each according to his capacity), and distributed them to all, as any had need (to each according to his need).
>
> No one said that any of the things which he possessed was his own.
>
> There was not a needy person among them.

Vision, Not Speculation. Some western interpreters say that this was an ideal which was never practiced. Or, this practice was motivated by the expectation of the imminent return of Christ. That might be. But the issue before us does not concern deductions and speculations. It concerns a question. Can the spirit of Jesus' vision capture the imagination of Christian societies today?

Did Jesus Talk About Social Justice?

Social Justice. The phrase 'social justice' is part of our standard vocabulary today. It means justice for workers, peasants, the jobless, women, children, indigenous peoples and other targets of injustice in society. Our roadsigns thus far clearly indicate that Jesus was emphatic about social justice. But did Jesus say or teach anything more explicit on it? Well, he did. But it has been locked up in the bodega and waits for an honorable release.

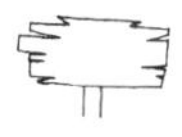

Woe to you, scribes and pharisees, hypocrites! For you tithe mint, dill, and cummin, and have neglected the *weightier matters of the law: justice and mercy and faith*. It is these you ought to have practiced without neglecting the others. You blind guides, straining out a gnat and swallowing a camel! (Mt 23:23-24)

Word Combination. The core message of Mt 23:23 is simply this: the more important matters of religion are social justice. How so? Because *justice and mercy and faithfulness* in that statement of Jesus is equivalent to what we know today as 'social justice.' This meaning will emerge when we do some dusting of antecedents in the Hebrew Scriptures. Taken singly, here are Hebrew words with their corresponding meanings:

ts^e^daqah [*tsdq*]	=	justice or righteousness
mishpat [*mshpt*]	=	justice or right
checed [*chcd*]	=	compassion, mercy or steadfast love
'emet or 'emunah [*'emn*]	=	truth, faithfulness

A combination of two or more of these words means justice in society for the poor, marginalized and oppressed, social justice.

On the other hand, there is no *tsedaqah*, *mishpat*, *checed*, *'emet* where there is shedding of innocent blood, unjust laws and court, oppression of the poor, widows, the fatherless. The following texts are instructive:

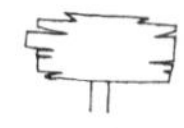

For your hands are defiled with blood,
and your fingers with iniquity;
your lips have spoken lies,
your tongue mutters wickedness.
No one brings suit justly [*tsdq*],
no one goes to law honestly [*'emn*];
they rely on empty pleas, they speak lies,
conceiving mischief and begetting iniquity....
Their works are works of iniquity,
and deeds of violence are in their hands.
Their feet run to evil,
and they rush to shed innocent blood;
their thoughts are thoughts of iniquity;
desolation and destruction are in their highways.

The way of peace they do not know,
and there is no justice [*mshpt*] in their paths.
Their roads they have made crooked;
no one who walks in them knows peace.
Therefore justice [*mshpt*] is far from us,
and righteousness [*tsdq*] does not reach us;
we wait for light, and lo! there is darkness;
and for brightness, but we walk in gloom....
We all growl like bears;
like doves we moan mournfully.
We wait for justice [*mshpt*], but there is none;
for salvation, but it is far from us...
transgressing, and denying the LORD,
and turning away from following our God,
talking oppression and revolt,
conceiving lying words and uttering them from the heart.
Justice [*mshpt*] is turned back,
and righteousness [*tsdq*] stands at a distance;
for truth [*'emt*] stumbles in the public square,
and uprightness cannot enter.
Truth [*'emt*] is lacking,
and whoever turns from evil is despoiled.
The LORD saw it, and it displeased him
that there was no justice [*mshpt*]. (Isa 59:3-15)

How the faithful city has become a whore,
she that was full of justice [*mshpt*]!
Righteousness [*tsdq*] lodged in her, but now murderers....
Your princes are rebels and companions of thieves.
Every one loves a bribe and runs after gifts.
They do not defend the orphan,
and the widows' cause does not come before them. (Isa 1:21-23)

For the vineyard of the Lord of hosts is the house of Israel,
and the people of Judah are his pleasant planting;
and he expected justice [*mshpt*],
but saw bloodshed;
righteousness [*tsdq*] ,
but heard a cry! (Isa 5:7)

Salvation in the future means the presence of *tsedaqah*, *mishpat*, *checed* and *'emet*:

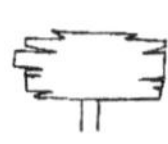

And I will restore your judges as at the first,
and your counselors as at the beginning.
Afterward you shall be called the city of righteousness [*tsdq*], the faithful city.

Zion shall be redeemed by justice [*mshpt*],
and those in her who repent, by righteousness [*tsdq*]. (Isa 1:26-27)

For a child has been born for us, a son given to us;
authority rests upon his shoulders;
and he is named
Wonderful Counselor, Mighty God,
Everlasting Father, Prince of Peace.
His authority shall grow continually,
and there shall be endless peace
for the throne of David and his kingdom.
He will establish and uphold it
with justice [*mshpt*] and with righteousness [*tsdq*]
from this time onward and forevermore.
The zeal of the LORD of hosts will do this. (Isa 9:6-7)

Until a Spirit is poured out on us from on high,
and the wilderness becomes a fruitful field,
and the fruitful field is deemed a forest.
Then justice [*mshpt*] will dwell in the wilderness,
and righteousness [*tsdq*] abide in the fruitful field. (Isa 32:15-16)

The Lord is exalted, he dwells on high;
he filled Zion with justice [*mshpt*] and righteousness [*tsdq*]. (Isa 33:5)

And I will take you for my wife forever;
I will take you for my wife in righteousness [*tsdq*]
and in justice [*mshpt*], in steadfast love, and in mercy [*chcd*].
I will take you for my wife in faithfulness;
and you shall know the LORD. (Hos 2:19-20)

To do *mishpat* and *chcd*: this is what life is all about:

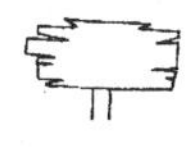

He has told you, O mortal, what is good;
and what does the Lord require of you
but to do justice [*mshpt*], and to love kindness [*chcd*]
and to walk humbly with your God. (Mic 6:8)

Yahweh himself gives a self-definition in terms of *tsedaqah*, *mishpat*.

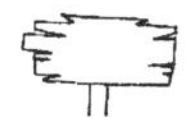

Let those who boast, boast in this,
that they understand and know me, that I am the LORD;
I act with steadfast love [*chcd*], justice [*mshpt*]
and righteousness [*tsdq*] in the earth,
for in these things I delight, says the LORD. (Jer 9:24)

From the above sample texts, it is clear that:

- *tsedaqah*, *mishpat*, *checed* and *´emet* in one or other combination is equivalent to justice in society or social justice

- *tsedaqah*, *mishpat*, *checed* and *'emet* are central to the message of the prophets.

Jesus and Social Justice. And how does it stand with Jesus? He lays the following charge on his adversaries: 'you tithe mint and dill and cummin, and have neglected *the weightier matters of the Law, justice and mercy and faith*' (Mt 23:23).

The 'Law,' or better the 'Instruction,' refers to the Torah, the first five books of the Hebrew Scriptures, attributed to Moses. Clearly it contains more than laws; it contains history. The Torah functioned as the religio-civil constitution of the Israelite people. According to Jesus, the weightier matters of such a Torah is social justice.

Dill, mint and cummin are tiny herbs and spices. Jesus suggests that his adversaries put more importance on small things and forget the bigger issue of social justice. The pharisees are blind guides, filtering out a small insect and swallowing a camel!

Tithing—the giving of one tenth of one's produce or income to the temple and priests, and at least, indirectly to God—was a sacral duty in Jesus' culture. Of greater moment than that sacred duty – according to Jesus – is one's practice of social justice.

Weightier than Worship. In fact, social justice is so weighty that, in certain situations (Mt 9:13;12:7), it is weightier than worship of God! Jesus makes his own the words of Hosea: 'Go and learn what this means, I desire mercy [*checed*], and not sacrifice' (Mt 9:13;12:7; Hos 6:6).[58] Sacrifice here refers to the offering of animals in the temple, signifying worship of God.

Jesus Was Serious. Was Jesus serious? Evidently. Your fate as a goat destined for eternal fire or as a sheep destined for the Kingdom is decided by 'compassion,' and perhaps, we may add, 'rather than worship.' Compassion takes the form of food, drink, clothing, comfort you held out or withheld to the least of his brethren. (Mt 25:31ff).[59] Compassion takes the form of agrarian reform, cancellation of debts, release of slaves, rest for the land (Lk 4:16-20).-

Are We Serious? And so, in a way, it is a wonder that the justice apostolate has had to be thrust on the Church, as it were, by the circumstances of history, and considered by some as a passing fad. One may be allowed to wonder, too, how much interiorization and owning there have been of the many Church statements in behalf of justice and the poor of the past decades.

---

58 A contemporary equivalent would go thus: God would rather see you treat your househelp humanely than see you in Church on Sunday!
The clear statement of the entire biblical tradition is: God prefers justice to worship-without-justice. It will well pay your effort to reflect on the following: Isa 1:10-17; 58:3-10; Jer 7:4-7, 6:18-21; Hos 6:4-6; Mic 6:6-8; Amos 5:21-25; Mt 5:23-4; 9:13; 12:7; 23:23; 1 Cor 11:20-22; 1 Jn 4:20; Mt 25:31-46 (compare Mt 7:21).

59 Although Mt 25:31ff is found only in the gospel of Matthew, by now we have enough affinity with Jesus to say that it is a trustworthy mirroring of Jesus' spirit.

The Weightier Matters for a Typical Christian. It would be educational to ask even a well-educated Christian today what he would consider the weightier matters of religion. As for me, these consisted at one time in certain abstract truths such as three persons in one divine nature, the divinity and humanity of Christ and similar truths. I have since discovered that God and Jesus can very well take care of themselves and that there are co-humans who could use a little more *tsedaqah* in their lives.

What About the Rich?

We may well wonder at this point: why is it all so heavily in favor of the poor? And we wonder with reason. We search for an answer to this phenomenon. My own search ends with two realizations: (1) We cannot invent the gospel story. We cannot create another gospel story. (2) This phenomenon allows us a peek into the heart of Jesus.

Jesus' Relationships with the Rich. Now we ask solicitously: what was Jesus' view of the rich or the non-poor? How did he relate to them? The rich in Jesus' life seem to be one of the following:

1. critiqued by Jesus, e.g., 'Woe to you rich' (Lk 6:24; 16:19-31; Mt 6:25-33);
2. challenged by Jesus, e.g., the man/ruler who was asked by Jesus to sell his possessions and share with the poor (Mk 10:21). Such a challenge does not mean antagonism on the part of Jesus. On the contrary, according to Mark, 'Jesus looking upon him, *loved* him' (Mk 10:21);
3. converted and shared his/her riches, e.g., Zacchaeus (Lk 19:1-10), like a significant few wealthy ones in our time;
4. had faith in Jesus (and presumably, in everything Jesus stood for, including justice and liberation for the poor), and not an oppressor, e.g., the women who followed Jesus (Lk 8:2); the Roman centurion (Lk 7:1-10).

In virtually every instance, even the friendliest encounter with the non-poor, for example, at dinner with the pharisees, there is a moment of critique or challenge or conversion or faith.

Jesus Died for Rich and Poor. But did Jesus not die for rich and poor alike? Yes, he eventually died for rich and poor. But while he was living, he stood for justice and liberation for the poor, and this stand for the *'anawim,* in all likelihood, had something to do with his death at the hands of the powerful and wealthy of his time.

Kingdom Proclaimed to Rich Also. And did not Jesus proclaim the good news of the Kingdom to all, rich and poor alike? Was salvation not offered to all alike? Yes, he proclaimed the good news of the Kingdom to all alike. Few of Jesus' emotions are recorded, but Mark, as we have just noted, goes out of his way to depict Jesus' love for a rich person. There is no lack of genuine love and concern for the rich in the New Testament. The invitation to the kingdom is *for all.* But because of the nature of the Kingdom and its demands, it was often uncomfortable news for the wealthy and powerful (e.g., Mk 10:21-22; Lk 14:15-24.).

Ministry to the Rich. Since Jesus also had a solicitude for the rich, should not the Church today also minister to the rich? Yes. The only question is 'how?' It is not enough that the rich appropriate the merits of Jesus' death in baptism and nurture it in the sacraments. The rich must also be asked to live according to the Kingdom summons of Jesus. Playing golf or tennis with the rich while saving their souls would not exactly be Jesus' ministry to the rich of his time.

Good News to the Poor and the Philippine Church

PCP II and the Church of the Poor. PCP II outdoes itself. Its declaration that we are a Church of the Poor must be a fruit of its sensitivity to the signs of the times and to the Spirit. Never mind that it does not base itself on the exegesis of Jesus' 'good news to the poor.' This is more to its credit than debit. For PCP II drew life intuitively and directly from the love of the poor and from God. Here are some of the more substantive statements of this remarkable group of people, who notably belonged not only to the middle class and the rich, but also to the poor.

- In the Philippines today, God calls us most urgently to serve the poor and the needy. The poverty of at least half of the population is a clear sign that sin has penetrated our social structures (par. 122).
- Poverty in the sense of destitution is not God's will for anyone. Vatican II teaches that 'every man has the right to possess a sufficient amount of the earth's goods for himself and his family.' To the shanty dwellers of Favela dos Alagados, Pope John Paul II forcefully asserted: "Do not say that it is God's will that you remain in a condition of poverty, disease, unhealthy housing; that is contrary in many ways to your dignity as human persons. Do not say, 'It is God who wills it' " (par. 122).
- In the Scriptures, the poor are blessed. 'Blessed are you who are poor, for the Kingdom of God is yours.' It is not their poverty that is 'blessed.' Nor are they blessed because they are necessarily better Christians than their prosperous brothers and sisters (par. 123).
- While PCP II counsels, as it should, 'the evangelical spirit of poverty, detachment from possessions, a profound trust in the Lord as the sole source of salvation, poverty of spirit' (par. 125), its emphasis is on 'special love for the poor ... the suffering, and those undergoing persecution for sake of justice' (par. 126).
- 'The 'Church of the Poor' is one that will be in solidarity with the poor. It will collaborate with the poor themselves and with others to lift up the poor from their poverty....' (par. 130)

- The 'Church of the Poor' means, in the words of Pope John Paul II, that: 'Before today's forms of exploitation of the poor, the Church cannot remain silent. She also reminds the rich of their precise duties. Strong with the Word of God, she condemns the many injustices which unfortunately, even today, are committed to the detriment of the poor.' Pastors and members of the Church will courageously defend and vindicate the rights of the poor and the oppressed, *even when doing so* will mean alienation *or persecution from the rich and powerful* (par. 131).

Grounding and Meaning. Need anything more be said? Those, however, who are looking for a firm biblical grounding for the Church of the Poor, will, I hope, find it in Jesus' proclamation of 'good news to the poor.' In other words, what is the biblical basis for the Church of the Poor? It is Jesus' proclamation of justice and liberation for the poor.

In fact, it provides not only grounding; it also supplies the only possible serious meaning to the 'Church of the Poor.' In other words, what is the serious meaning of Church of the Poor? It is a Church that proclaims good news of justice and liberation for the poor. A Church can claim to be a 'Church of the Poor' only when, like Jesus, it stakes its life and its fortunes on behalf of the poor and their well-being. Otherwise, it is all a play with words.

Preferential Option. Something similar can be said for that oft-repeated axiom 'preferential option for the poor.' Why preferential option? Is this not an unwarranted bias? Again, we cannot re-write the gospel story according to our image and likeness. The Church must have this option, because Jesus did.

'Good news to the poor' had an axial position in the mission statements, in the practice and in the teaching of Jesus. Need we find a sounder proof of Jesus' preferential option for the poor – except to add that, in the case of Jesus, such option evidently amounted to something like obsession?

As Jesus-followers, we cannot let all that centrality and preoccupation of Jesus go to waste. Thus our much celebrated but little practiced 'preferential option for the poor' is not optional but the duty of a Church that wants to follow Jesus.

Questions To Ponder

A Question for The Christian Conscience. In the spirit of our host, PCP II, I would like to end with a couple of questions. In the practically 500 years of conventional Catholic and Reformation theologies, we have listed all the deeds of Jesus before, during, and after his earthly life except, or hardly ever, his proclamation of liberation and justice to the poor.

I look for serious treatments of 'good news to the poor' in theology manuals and catechetical modules—and most of the time, in vain.

And yet, it is mentioned in the principal mission statements. It is the only act of Jesus that is constantly mentioned in different mission statements. Therefore, it is the bone and marrow of his message and mission! His teachings on property and possessions and on social justice are plain and clear.

Why then has the gospel of liberation and justice for the poor not been part of the Christian conscience for several hundred years? Can we make up for lost time – especially we theologians and clergy who have been largely responsible for our Church's limited recall of Jesus' message?

The Poor Judge the Church. Let us conclude with a simple though weighty question. The most serious question that still faces the Church in our day is this: Will the *'anawim* of the Third World today judge the Church to be good news to the poor? Is our witness and practice as Jesus' Church today good news to the poor? Yes, happily, in the case of certain good and tried friends of the poor. But these same people beckon to their Church brothers and sisters to shed off the pomp, the titles, and the obeisances of medieval times . . . and get on with the Jesus-business of our day.

Will You Also Go Away? At this point in our journey, the signposts could very well read: after this many of his disciples drew back and no longer went about with him. Jesus said to the twelve: Will you also go away? (Jn 6:66-67)

But Why Suffering?

Why Is There So Much Suffering in the World? Jesus and his God want life-blessings, not suffering. That is a growing persuasion for us by now. But if so, why is there so much suffering in the world? This is the age-old question, is it not? As far as I know, no one has given a completely satisfactory answer. I will not attempt one. As I fumble in the dark, the following thoughts serve as tiny candle-lights standing vigil around this question of human suffering: (1) Jesus and his God want life-blessings, not suffering. (2) It is we humans who invent much of our sufferings. They are either sufferings we impose on ourselves, or, sufferings we impose on other humans and on nature. (3) Uninvited, unplanned, unavoidable suffering—these are tear-drenched offerings we are sometimes called to bring to our altars. These altars belong to *this our* dimension of existence. They are not angelic or extraterrestrial altars. They are *human* altars, bearing the cup of *truly human* pain. I will say more on this, especially when we encounter the death and cross of Jesus.

Be Still and Know ...

Stopover 13

Under a Tree, Beneath Clear Skies (A Catechetical Pause)

Looking Back

A Pause. Our roadsigns thus far have been pointing to some answers to only two principal questions: 'What was the mission of Jesus?' and 'What is the Reign-Kingdom of God?' But since we have gathered a good bit of lore, we pause for some possibly useful summary and inventory. Let us then, just by ourselves, have a catechetical pause.

What was the mission of Jesus? What was the life-purpose of this person?

In the earlier phase of his life, initially, originally, Jesus' mission was the proclamation of the Reign-Kingdom of God.

What is the Reign-Kingdom of God?

It is a new world, new history, new humankind.

- Isaiah and Jesus have the following indicators for it:

  good news of God's Reign-Kingdom
  blind see
  lame walk
  deaf hear
  lepers are cleansed
  dead are raised
  good tidings of liberation and justice to the poor and oppressed
  poor rejoice
  liberty to captives
  freedom to the oppressed
  the year of the Lord's favor or the final jubilee year
  someone anointed by God's Spirit who will:
    announce good news to the poor
    establish justice on the earth

- The beatitudes picture it in terms of:
  justice and liberation for the poor and oppressed
  food, rice for the hungry poor
  laughter and joy for the sorrowing poor
  earth, land for the meek
  experiencing mercy
  seeing God
  being sons and daughters of God
- It is sitting at table, eating, drinking, meal, feast, banquet, bread, rice.
- It is resurrection of the dead.
- It is the destruction of Satan and satanic forces.
- It is a new heaven and a new earth: new universe, new world, new creation in which justice dwells.
- It is a new history for humankind, an 'age-to-come.'
- As a future reality, it will be realized at the end-time.
- As a present reality in Jesus' time, it took the form of life-giving blessings through Jesus' actions.
- A preeminent blessing in it is justice and liberation (good news to the poor).

What are some inadequate or mistaken understandings of Reign-Kingdom of God?

- It is heaven above where souls see God face to face after death.
- It is the Reign of God in human hearts as a purely interior reality.
- It begins on the cross, that is, the Reign-Kingdom of God is realized when Christ atones on the cross for the sins of humankind.
- It is Jesus himself.

If the Reign-Kingdom of God and the cross are not identical, are they related? How?

- Yes. Briefly, for now, Jesus' death is a consequence of the Reign-Kingdom proclamation.

In a Nutshell. Final-and-definitive salvation for the first century Jews and for Jesus was not the heaven of average Christian theology today with its connotations of beatific vision for souls. Rather, salvation for them was a new world, where, under God's Reign, a new humankind, individually and collectively, will experience a new history.

The features of this final-and-definitive salvation include: total well-being for people, a transformed earth, a new capital city, victory over death through resurrection, banquet, justice, comfort and joy for the *ʿanawim* (=poor and oppressed), the vision of God, divine filiation, the destruction of all evils, God dwelling among the people.

As a future reality, it will be realized on the last day of history. It was already present in Jesus' time in his actions which promoted life-blessings for people and justice to the poor.

It is present in our time through the actions of people who produce life-blessings for our troubled world.

Historical, Social, Individual. Jesus had a historical and societal purview, for the Reign-Kingdom of God really was a new world and a new history. Jesus was in the line of the Hebrew-Jewish tradition for whom salvation had a historical, social and individual character. Historical, because this tradition saw salvation as a new history. Social, because the blessings—peace, justice, joy, health—are not just for individuals but for society, humankind and the world. And individual, because salvation was for the individual too.

Be Still and Know ...

Stopover 14

A Visit with Human Rights Lawyers (The Precept-Aspect of Biblical Religion)

On the Ethics of the Kingdom

Human rights lawyers will be our hosts this time. Why so? It is because we are going to talk about 'laws,' precepts, requirements, ethical demands, rules of conduct. Up to this juncture in our journey, we have considered the *proclamation*-aspect of Jesus' message; in this stop-over we are making the acquaintance of the *precept*-aspect. These two aspects are present in biblical religion generally.

The Old Testament has a classical expression of this proclamation-precept combination. 'I am the Lord, thy God, who brought you out of the slavery of Egypt' would be the proclamation-aspect. 'Therefore, *obey my statutes and ordinances'* would be the *precept-aspect.*[60] The proclamation-part announces salvation. The precept-part puts down the ethical demand on the Israelite.

---

60 See Ex 20:22ff.

This same pattern is found in the New Testament. Read Mk 1:14-15 thus:

Proclamation-Part Announcing Salvation	Precept-Part or Ethical Requirement
After John was arrested, Jesus came into Galilee, proclaiming the *gospel* of God, and saying, 'The time is fulfilled, and *the Kingdom of God is at hand ...*	*... repent, and believe in the gospel.'*

Let us gain this insight into the proclamation and precept aspects by taking a preliminary step, that is, by first recalling an aspect of the Kingdom of God, namely, that it is a *goal.*

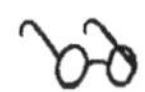

Kingdom As Task and Goal. We have seen that the Kingdom is both task and goal. As task, it is something to be busy about. It means that disciples are to generate life-blessings for the whole household of humans and nature.

As goal, it is a destination to be reached, a reward to be attained by the individual, a prize to be won, a treasure to be enjoyed. It is a finish line to be arrived at, a final home to go to, a new earth to inherit, a definitive salvation to be possessed.[61]

Kingdom As Goal: Prominent in the New Testament. Although today many of us perhaps find the task-aspect more appealing because we like to put in our bit to the Kingdom work, it is the goal-aspect that is more prominent in the New Testament.

Jesus announces the Kingdom as a definitive salvation to be possessed and invites people to attain it. Earlier the Jews were in expectation of the coming of the Kingdom of God as a salvation to be attained. Jesus then responded to this expectation and invited people to enter into it. The following New Testament signposts speak of the Kingdom of God as a goal to be reached, as a definitive salvation to be attained, as a possession to be inherited, as something to enter into:

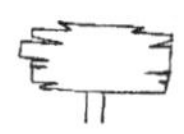

'The tax collectors and the prostitutes *are going into the kingdom of God* ahead of you.' (Mt 21:31)

"Not everyone who says to me, 'Lord, Lord,' will *enter the kingdom of heaven,* but only the one who does the will of my Father in heaven." (Mt 7:21)

'Whoever does not receive the kingdom of God as a little child will never *enter it.'* (Mk 10:15)

'No one who puts his hand to the plow and looks back is *fit for the kingdom of God.'* (Lk 9:62)

[61] In much the same way as the Second Look would see heaven as a goal.

Flesh and blood cannot *inherit the kingdom of God*, nor does the perishable inherit the imperishable. (1 Cor 15:50)

Corresponding Ethics. *Corresponding* to the Kingdom-as-goal are *precepts, moral requirements, conditions for entry, a moral code.* These constitute a code of behavior for individuals to participate in that final salvation. Jesus would say: 'If you want to enter into the Kingdom of God, this is what you do. Be this. Do this.' Much of the Sermon on the Mount would belong to the precept-part, but not, as we have insisted, the beatitudes.[62]

This then is the *precept-aspect* of the Jesus message. With the help of our new hosts, human rights lawyers, this will be the focus of our current stopover.

Samples of the Precept-Aspect

I will now simply enumerate representative ethical teachings of Jesus. After you go through the list, you will perhaps sympathize with certain scholars who say that this is the ethical teaching of one who was expecting the imminent end of the world. It is an impossible ethic!

Others would say it is a radical and demanding ethic which, with gritted teeth, will power and the grace of God, one must grin and bear. I tried this kind of spirituality in my years of formation. I found it to be a 'rubber band spirituality.' Pull, stretch, strain, force and the rubber band either breaks or I snap back to where I started and 'tell the same sins to the priest!'

Could there be another way of comprehending these 'ways of acting and being'? Are they perhaps natural rain-drops when the cloud is full? Are they not the most spontaneous drizzles, nay, outpours, of a cloud that is seeded with the Spirit of God? Is this not what one would 'instinctively' do and say if in touch with the Source? Read and see these samples from Matthew:[63]

Leave your gift there before the altar and go; first be *reconciled* to your brother or sister. (5:24)

If your right eye *causes you to sin*, tear it out and throw it away. (5:29)[64]

If any one strikes you on the *right cheek, turn* to him *the other also.* (5:39)

Love your enemies and pray for those who persecute you. (5:44)

When you give alms, do not let your *left hand* know what your *right hand* is doing. (6:3)

---

62 See pages 39, 51. The beatitudes are proclamations.

63 I take these samples from Matthew, especially the Sermon on the Mount, since it is he who records many of Jesus' ethical teachings.

64 Allow for poetic language here.

Whenever you *pray, go into your* room and shut the door and pray to your Father who is in secret. (6:6)

When you are *praying, do not heap up empty phrases* ... for your Father knows what you need before you ask him. (6:7)

Do not store up for yourselves *treasures on earth*, where moth and rust consume and where thieves break in and steal; but store up for yourselves *treasures in heaven* .... For where your treasure is, there your heart will be also. (6:19-21)

No one can serve *two masters* ... You cannot serve *God and wealth.* (6:24)

Do not worry about your life, what you will eat or *what you will drink*, or about your body, *what you will wear.* Is not life more than food, and the body more than clothing? (6:25)

First take the *log out of your own eye*, and then you will see clearly to take the speck out of your neighbor's eye. (7:5)

Ask, and it will be given you; search, and you will find; knock, and the door will be opened for you. (7:7)

In everything *do to others* as you would have them do to you; for this is the law and the prophets. (7: 12)

Not everyone who says to me, 'Lord, Lord,' will enter the kingdom of heaven, but only the one who *does the will of my Father* in heaven. (7:21)

Follow me, and let the *dead bury their own dead.* (8:22)

Neither is *new wine put into old wineskins* ... but new wine is put into fresh wineskins, and so both are preserved. (9:17)

You received without payment; *give without payment.* (10:8)

Be *wise as serpents and innocent as doves.* When they hand you over, do not worry about ... what you are to say; for what you are to say will be given to you at that time; for it is *not you who speak, but the Spirit of your Father* speaking through you. (10:16-21)

Everyone who *acknowledges me* before others, I also will acknowledge before my Father in heaven; but whoever denies me before others, I also will deny before my Father in heaven. (10:32)

Whoever loves father or mother more than me is not worthy of me; and whoever loves son or daughter more than me is not worthy of me; and whoever does not *take up the cross* and follow me is not worthy of me. Those who *find their* life will lose it, and those who *lose their life for my sake* will find it. (10:37-39)

Woe to you, Chorazin! Woe to you, Bethsaida! For if the deeds of power done in you had been done in Tyre and Sidon, they would have *repented* long ago in sackcloth and ashes. (11:21)

I desire mercy, and not sacrifice. (12:7)

Either make the tree good, and its fruit good; or make the tree bad, and its fruit bad; for the *tree is known by its fruit.* (12:33)

So, for the sake of your *tradition,* you have made void the word of God. You hypocrites! (15:6-7)

What comes out of the mouth proceeds from the heart, and this is *what defiles.* For out of the heart come evil intentions, murder, adultery, fornication, theft, false witness, slander. These are what defile a person, but to eat with unwashed hands does not defile. (15:18)

Blessed are you, Simon son of Jonah! For flesh and blood has not *revealed* this to you, but my Father in heaven. (16:17)

Get behind me, Satan! You are a stumbling block to me; for you are setting your mind *not on divine things but on human things.* (16:23)

If any want to become my followers, let them *deny themselves and take up their cross* and follow me. For *those who want to save their life* will lose it, and those who *lose their life* for my sake will find it. For what will it profit them if they *gain the whole* world but forfeit their life? Or what will they give in return for their life? (16:24-27)

If you have *faith* the size of a mustard seed, you will say to this mountain, 'Move from here to there,' and it will move; and nothing will be impossible for you. (17:20)

'Lord, if another member of the church sins against me, how often should I *forgive*? As many as seven times?' Jesus said to him, 'Not seven times, but, I tell you, *seventy-seven times.*' (18:21-22)

Let the *little children* come to me, and do not stop them; for it is to such as these that the kingdom of heaven belongs. (19:14)

If you wish to be perfect, go, *sell your possessions,* and *give the money to the poor,* and you will have treasure in heaven; then come, follow me. (19:21)

It is easier for a camel to go through the eye of a needle than for someone who is *rich to enter the kingdom of God.* (19:24)

And everyone who has *left houses or brothers or sisters or father or mother or children or fields, for my name's sake,* will receive a hundredfold, and will inherit eternal life. But many who are *first* will be last, and the *last* will be first. (19:29-30)

Are you able to *drink the cup* that I am about to drink? (20:22)

You know that the rulers of the Gentiles lord it over them, and their great ones are tyrants over them. It will not be so among you; but whoever wishes to be *great among you* must be your *servant,* and whoever wishes to be *first* among you must be your *slave*; just as the Son of Man came not to be served but to serve, and to give his life a ransom for many. (20:25-28)

'You shall *love the Lord your God* with all your heart, and with all your soul,

> and with all your mind.' This is the *greatest and first* commandment. And a *second* is like it: 'You shall *love your neighbor* as yourself.' On these two commandments hang all the law and the prophets. (22:37-40)
>
> For you tithe mint, dill, and cummin, and have neglected the weightier matters of the law: *justice and mercy and faith*. It is these you ought to have practiced without neglecting the others. You blind guides! You strain out a gnat but swallow a camel! (23:23-24)
>
> You on the outside look righteous to others, but inside you are full of *hypocrisy* and lawlessness. (23:27-28)
>
> Keep awake therefore, for you do not know on what day your Lord is coming. (Mt 24:42)
>
> Keep *awake* therefore, for you know neither the day nor the hour. (25:13)
>
> Come, you that are blessed by my Father, inherit the kingdom prepared for you from the foundation of the world; for *I was hungry and you gave me food*, I was thirsty and you gave me something to drink, I was a stranger and you welcomed me, I was naked and you gave me clothing, I was sick and you took care of me, I was in prison and you visited me.' (25:34-36)
>
> Unless your *righteousness* exceeds that of the scribes and pharisees, you will never enter the kingdom of heaven. (5:20)
>
> Be *perfect*, therefore, as your heavenly Father is perfect. (5:48)
>
> Everyone then who *hears these words of mine and acts* on them will be like a wise man who built his house on rock. The rain fell, the floods came, and the winds blew and beat on that house, but it did not fall, because it had been founded on rock. And everyone who hears these words of mine and does not act on them will be like a foolish man who built his house on sand. The rain fell, and the floods came, and the winds blew and beat against that house, and it fell—and great was its fall! (7:24-27)

By Being, Not by Doing. Irrational! Impossible! Indeed. But we must reckon with the author of this ethic. He was in touch with the Source. He was always a pregnant cloud. And perhaps he expected his followers to be the same. And our excuse for failing? Because he was divine and we are not? Such 'bad thoughts' are not to be entertained. Let us try this: He was in touch. We are not … or less in touch. Our cloud is less seeded …

And remember, a cloud is silent. The rains may come down hard and strong and loud, but the cloud is always still.

This is the kind of ethic that you don't try hard to follow by *doing*. It is more the kind of ethic that happens to you by just *being* … being in touch. For, the best kind of spirituality is one that happens to you rather than one that you make happen. This is so in the best of Asian religious traditions. Be in touch and there are no longer precepts— only the spontaneous dance-movements of the heart.

Some Non-Moralistic Ways of Being Moral

The Most Basic Precept: *Metanoia*, a Change of Life. We have nearly forgotten our hosts....

Our hosts, outstanding human-rights lawyers, who know their theology more from life and practice than from speculation on human nature, begin our session by asking this question: 'What is the most basic precept of Jesus?' We go into a huddle and, after a rather long interval and many discussions, finally come to a consensus: Jesus' most basic precept is 'conversion.' Our hosts are both amused and pleased. Amused, because it took us a long time to arrive at an answer. Pleased, because we gave the correct answer.

We go on to share that the original Greek word, *metanoia*, is an excellent word, meaning precisely, 'self-transformation,' 'total change of life,' 'basic reorientation of one's life-values,' 'radical sharing of one's wealth.' Our hosts are too modest to say that they practice this *metanoia*, for many of them do not make a living out of their practice in behalf of human-rights victims. We also noted that *metanoia* is poorly translated as 'repent,' or 'be sorry for one's sins' and that it means infinitely more than 'going to confession to a priest.'

We agreed that *metanoia* is seen in lawyers like Jose Diokno and Evelio Javier. In the time of Jesus, it was practiced by his first followers who gave up their boats, nets, parents, servants (Mk 1:18,20), their tax-collection business (Mk 2:14), their wealth (Lk 8:2).[65]

Dissolving the Darkness. One of our hosts makes this remark: Conversion or self-transformation is really going from darkness to light. We then discuss various ways of doing this. One of us shares an excellent way which she learned from an Eastern sage. It is the meditation of silence. In that meditation one is directly in touch with the Source. That Source is not only living water. It is also light. The sage said: Now, in a dark room, you do not get rid of the darkness by throwing it out of the window. You dissolve the darkness—and that ever-shadowy ego—by simply lighting a candle. And the lighted Candle is in you, is you. You just have to stir and quicken the flame—in silence.

The Greatest. The next question was both expected and easy. What is the first and greatest commandment? We are almost too ashamed to say the self-evident: love God. And close on its heels: love your neighbor.

In addition, however, we were all puzzled by another self-evident observation: after 2000 years of Christian love, among the most loveless and exploitative societies are Christian societies.

---

[65] An example of a negative practice is found in Mk 10:21-22.

Another Weighty Commandment. Our hosts go on to the next question: Is the 'law of love' the only premier commandment of Jesus? Having forgotten one of our hard-earned learnings, we say 'yes.' We expect warm affirmation. Instead we get half-approval. They open the New Testament. They point out that we have given only one half of the correct answer. For Jesus, in addition to the love of God and love of neighbor (Mk 12:28-34), *tsedaqah, mishpat, checed and 'emet* or social justice (Mt 23:23) constitute 'weightier matters of religion.' It is *weightier* than giving one-tenth of your livelihood for religious purposes. Thus for Jesus social justice is also a chief commandment.[66]

Some in our group justify our half-erroneous answer by saying: but (the concept of) love includes (the concept of) justice; when you love, you do justice. Our hosts are not impressed. They say they are not philosophers and are not wont to reduce biblical texts to syllogisms. They say they can discuss history better, either contemporary history, in which they are involved, or past history. We trace the past history of 'Christian love' and are led to see once more this somewhat embarassing picture: after centuries of love, it is in Christian societies that you see the shanties of the destitute rubbing walls with the rich man's mansion or the bishops palace or a religious house.

Our hosts give a broad hint to pastors and priests: give a moratorium to 'love' and give 'justice' a chance. We have a good lead from the 1971 Synod of Bishops: 'Action on behalf of justice and participation in the transformation of the world fully appear to us as a constitutive dimension of the preaching of the Gospel.'[67]

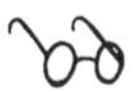

Our hosts, who do a lot of forensic work in law courts in behalf of the poor, are curious about the parable of the 'last judgment' of Mt. 25. Here is the heart of the parable.

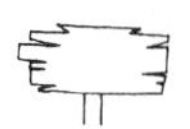

> Come, you that are blessed by my Father, inherit the kingdom prepared for you from the foundation of the world; for *I was hungry and you gave me food, I was thirsty and you gave me something to drink, I was a stranger and you welcomed me, I was naked and you gave me clothing, I was sick and you took care of me, I was in prison and you visited me.'* (Mt 25:34-36)

We have encountered this signpost in passing. Now we take a look at it as part of the ethic of the follower of Jesus.

It is straightforward and clear: Open your heart and hand to another human in need. If you do, you are the sheep that will possess the Kingdom. If you don't, you are the goats that will wind up somewhere else.

It is noteworthy for being the only saying of Jesus that explicitly spells out criteria for belonging or not belonging.

---

66 See page 150.

67 Synod of Bishops, 30 November 1971, *Justice in the World.*

There are two dubious readings of this signpost, however. First, some scholars say that the 'least of my brethren'[68] did not refer to the poor, but to the disciples of Jesus, whom Jesus had called his brothers elsewhere in Matthew's gospel. This *may* be so and we need not make this a point of contention. However, using our Third World glasses, what do we see? We see a Jesus who was obsessed with 'good news to the poor.' Would such a Jesus be loathe to call the poor his brothers and sisters and make compassionate deeds to them a criterion for salvation?

Second, we are witness to the following kind of spirituality. 'Seeing Christ in others.' 'Doing good for the sake of Christ.' 'I help the sick, the needy and the poor, because I see Christ in them': Well, what if Christ were not to be found in them? You would then not lift a finger? In any case, what we have here is a mis-reading of Matthew 25. Jesus did say that as long as you did it to the poor, you did it to him, but he did not say, 'because you saw me in the poor.' On the contrary, the startled sheep and goats are thoroughly baffled: 'When did we see you hungry ...?' This, I take it, indicates that when they fed/did not feed the hungry, they did/did not see Jesus in the hungry, much less feed them 'because we saw Christ in them.' So these are people who fed the hungry without seeing Jesus in them. And the parable might even suggest—though this might be stretching it too far—that Jesus would be happiest when you thought he was not there and you did it anyway! After all, he can very well take care of himself. Our hosts, particularly the women-lawyers, relish this particular insight.

Perhaps we would do well to see in the poor what Jesus and God saw in the poor: the human being. Our hosts agree.

Interpellating Moralistic Spirituality. Somewhat mortified and chastened, but not entirely crushed, we are ready for more conversation with our hosts. We decide to take the initiative and make small talk about the law profession. How is Philippine law practice and do they enjoy being lawyers? To our surprise, they do not have much time or liking for law, or precisely, law for law's sake. It is their turn to take the offensive once more. Why, they want to know, is it that for the typically good Christian, religion consists in the precept aspect? Religion is identified with commandments. Religion and life tend to be moralistic. Fortunately, our journey has equipped us with enough resources for a sensible response. We agree with their observation. And we say that a Jesus-inspired religion would dwell equally, if not more, on the proclamation aspect. We explain that the proclamation aspect has to do with food, land, health, justice, peace, human rights. They smile. Wanting to impress, we throw in a few big words: integral salvation and evangelization, mission of Jesus, fullness of life, life-blessings, new heaven and new earth, Kingdom of God. Talk of getting off the hook! And with lawyers! Delicious, if you can take it from the first mouthful.

[68] Mt 25:40 and 46 (RSV).

Our hosts, with an impish look, now ask our permission to play a guessing game. We oblige. Guess, they ask, what quote or inscription do you frequently find in Filipino church patios and sanctuaries? We think for a few moments and almost altogether burst out into embarassed laughter. In Church premises we often find, in big, big letters and written in big, big tablets, the ten commandments of Moses! A religion of commandments indeed! Lurks a police-God behind?

We wonder whether instead of the decalogue of Moses, the beatitudes of Jesus, as some churches have them, would be an improvement. We are not sure, for a moralistic interpretation on the part of the beholder would in fact be more disastrous. It would lead one to abet not only moralism but also oppression![69] Our hosts are too kind and too polite to remind us that their motto and acronym, FLAG, carry a different tone and spirit: Free Legal Assistance Group. No police-God here. Rather, a counsel for the oppressed.

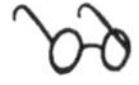

Moral Conversion Is Not Kingdom of God. By this time we, the lawyers and us, are more at ease with each other. We return to an old point which we earlier met.[70] Hopefully it will make more sense at this juncture.

Some pastors and catechists tend to talk of the Kingdom of God as moral conversion. The Kingdom of God consists in repentance or conversion of hearts. That is incorrect. This is perhaps due to a misunderstanding of one of our key-passages: The Kingdom of God is at hand ... repent and believe in the gospel (Mk 1:14-15). Repentance or conversion is a response/requirement for entering the goal, the Kingdom of God. It is not the Kingdom of God itself. The Kingdom is a new world, new history, new humanity. Conversion is precept. Kingdom of God is proclamation.

Proclamation	Precept
the kingdom [new world, new history]	repent, convert, change, believe [response/requirement]

The Kingdom of God Is Blessings, Not Moral Acts. This is the place to further sharpen our understanding of the Kingdom of God. This point has been implicit. It is time to make it explicit. Below are two columns. One of them is the Kingdom of God. The other, *strictly speaking*, is not.

69 See page 51.
70 See page 24.

A (Life-Blessings)	B (Good Moral Acts and Virtues)
Food, land, good health, education, jobs, wages, decent housing, security, contentment, resurrection, total liberation, just socio-economic system, just world order, gender equality, healthy environment, blue skies, clean rivers, divine filiation, vision of God, etc.	Kindness, humility, simplicity, trust, faith, hope, charity, good will, loyalty, compassion, conversion, courage, prayerfulness, selflessness, zeal, openness, generosity, love, dedication, temperance, patience, perseverance, cheerfulness, honesty, uprightness, honor, chastity, etc.

What is the difference between the two columns? Column B is about good moral acts and virtues. In Column A are life-blessings.

Well, the Kingdom of God, strictly speaking, is not moral acts and virtues. It is about life-blessings. Of course, they are closely related, and in actual life, the life-blessings of the Kingdom of God are usually realized through the practice of good moral acts and virtues. Yet, the two are not the same. Thus, for example, our bodily resurrection is a blessing we will enjoy and experience rather than a moral act we will exercise.

Good moral acts and virtues are, of course, desirable and salutary. But in a retreat, for example, preaching about good moral acts is not necessarily preaching about the Kingdom. 'Let us practice Christian love, selflessness, generosity, kindness, fair-play, honesty and respect, for that is what the Kingdom of God is....' Well, that may be a good homily on the practice of virtues, but it is not, strictly speaking, about the Kingdom of God as such. For, as we have seen again and again, Kingdom of God means rice, health, land, jobs, fresh water and fresh air, sunshine and rain, the indwelling Spirit, a just world order.

So then, do you see the difference between preacher A who says: "Let us love one another for that is the Kingdom of God," and preacher B who says: "Authentic land distribution, viable alternatives to globalization, self-determination for the powerless, rights for women and children, well-being of Mother Earth—these are God's summons to us today. God dares us to invent a just and humane global order, for the Kingdom of God for our time is just that: a planet in which we anticipate the experience of 'the new heaven and the new earth in which justice dwells'" (2 Pet 3:13).

If Jesus were walking this earth today, he would probably not say: 'The Kingdom of God is faith, hope and charity.' Rather he would most likely say: 'The Kingdom of God is food, jobs and security.'

Some Name-Dropping. We end this session in a light note. We do a mock recitation by doing some name-dropping. We say we should not mix up *kerygma* with *paraenesis,*[71] proclamation with precept, the declarative with the imperative, virtue to be practiced with blessing to be enjoyed. Our hosts are 'properly' impressed by this bit of erudition.

[71] *kerygma* = proclamation; *paraenesis* = exhortation

Stopover 15

A Summit With Old Friends (Conflict in Jesus' Practice)

Conflict

Trouble on First Workday and Beyond. What do you say of a man, who on his first day of work is headed for trouble? He walks into the prayer-and-study house, the synagogue. He gives a talk. How unlike our gurus, theologians, canonists—people say. Such wisdom! Such authority! Waves of astonishment and delight surge through his hearers. Unorthdox, fresh, original. Different from their scholars. He invites trouble, this potentially dangerous person, and overnight his fame begins to spread throughout the area! (Mk 1:21-28)

Early next morning, while it is still very dark, he gets up and goes out to a deserted place, and there he prays. But, soon after that, after people find him, he is at it again giving his talks all over that territory (Mk 1:36-38).

A little later, he is healing a leper. Watch how he goes about it. Only priests may bless a leper. Jesus is a layman. Lepers – according to the ritual regulations laid down by the theologians – are ritually impure and no one may touch them. Jesus touches the leper. The narrator suggests that in contrast to the religious personnel, Jesus in this situation is 'moved with compassion.' Finally, Jesus sends the leper to bring an offering to the priests. But for what purpose? In compliance with the Mosaic regulations? No! Rather, as a 'testimony *against* them.' As a protest against the pastoral style of the priests! (Mk 1:40-45).[72] The leper, despite Jesus' injunction not to tell anyone, announces his cure to everyone so that people pour in from all quarters to this Jesus, a growing threat to the establishment. He can no longer go into towns openly, but has to stay in the outskirts.

[72] The same Greek expression is used in Mk 6:11 and Lk 10:11. 'Even the dust of your town that clings to our feet, we wipe off *in protest against* you.'

Eventually he gets home. He finds a paralytic. He forgives his sins. He heals him. But the watchful scribes are present. They level an accusation at Jesus: Blasphemy! Yet Jesus continues to excite amazement and admiration: 'We have never seen anything like this!'

Shortly thereafter, we find him having lunch with tax collectors and sinners. The pharisees object. Jesus clarifies: 'Those who are well have no need of a physician, but those who are sick; I have come to call not the righteous but sinners.'[73]

The next thing we know, he is being interrogated about, of course, fasting. 'Why do the disciples of John the Baptist and of the pharisees fast, but your disciples do not fast?' Jesus takes this occasion to register a critical comment on their tradition: Your bankrupt tradition is beyond redemption. No one, he says, uses an unused piece of cloth to patch an old cloak. No one puts new wine into old wineskins; otherwise, the wine will burst the skins, and the wine is lost, and so are the skins; but one puts new wine into fresh wineskins. Their tradition is not good enough to be recycled!

No sooner is this confrontation about eating over than we find him in a debate about his disciples plucking corn. This time the issue is the sabbath. Jesus' disciples are doing what the law forbids. But Jesus poses a question: what do you do when people are hungry and want to eat? Remember David (1 Sam 21:1-6)? He broke into the temple and ate the sacred bread reserved for priests, and gave it to his hungry companions. From the lips of Jesus then falls an axiom which expresses his view on life, law, tradition: 'The sabbath was made for humankind, and not humankind for the sabbath.'

To Save Life. The cycle of conflictive events ends with a final confrontation. I will let the evangelist himself tell the story.

> Again he entered the synagogue, and a man was there who had a withered hand. They watched him to see whether he would cure him on the sabbath, so that they might accuse him. And he said to the man who had the withered hand, 'Come forward.' Then he said to them, *'Is it lawful to do good or to do harm on the sabbath, to save life or to kill?'* But they were silent. He *looked around at them with anger; he was grieved at their hardness of heart* and said to the man, 'Stretch out your hand.' He stretched it out, and his hand was restored. The *pharisees went out and immediately conspired with the Herodians against him, how to destroy him.* (Mk 3:1-6)

To save life or to kill – are our choices really limited to that? So Jesus seems to say. If we do not promote life, we destroy it.[74] Jesus held this axiom with passion. He was angered and grieved at its opposite, hardness of heart. A rare display of emotions. To save life (*psyche*), not souls – that's what it is all about, Jesus would say.

---

[73] See page 20 for our interpretation of this text in 'Back to Mk 2:17; Mt 9:13: An Alternative Reading.'

[74] Here's a less elegant version: If you are not part of the solution, you are part of the problem.

To save life – could very well be the inscription on Jesus' tombstone.

An ominous statement ends this cycle: the religious leaders conspire with the political leaders. They plot his destruction!

Conflictive Practice. We have followed Jesus through a couple of days of his life, as chronicled by Mark. If anything, that experience will have taught us that we cannot stereotype Jesus. He is indeed the 'meek and humble' Jesus. But that is not all there is to him. His passion for the Kingdom and its life-blessings drew him into conflict with the authorities and power structures of his time.

At this stage in our journey, we focus on Jesus' conflictive practice. Of this we generally know little, except for his practice of calling the pharisees 'hypocrites.' Yet, without this conflictive practice, his death would be unintelligible. In fact, without it, even his life would lack intelligibility.

Our hosts for this stopover will be all the people who have taken us in thus far. We have met them successively from the fisherfolk of Stopover 2 to the human rights lawyers of Stopover 14. We are having a summit with them. We are discussing with them a matter which was real for Jesus and is a real possibility for a serious follower of Jesus, *conflict*. They will take turns leading and moderating the various discussions.

Jesus and the Pharisees and Scribes

(Moderators: Human Rights Lawyers, People's Organizations)

Here we get acquainted with the actors of the drama.

Pharisees and Scribes. *Pharisees,* in the time of Jesus, were an association of 'middle class' Jews, of strict religious observance regarding, for example, the sabbath, ritual purity, tithing. Their zeal was aimed at influencing the Jewish people towards the observance of the Law of Moses or the Mosaic Torah.

There is a certain historical core in the conflicts reported in the gospels. But in the interest of historical accuracy and in fairness to the pharisees and scribes, we note (1) that in their origins, 200 years earlier, the pharisees were a courageous and 'prophetic' group, protesting the corruption of priests and kings; (2) that our gospel records, as they stand, are colored by an antagonistic spirit of a time later than Jesus; (3) that not all of the pharisees and scribes were 'bad'; and that a good number had a view of things similar to that of Jesus and vice versa. Compared to sadducees, whom we shall meet shortly, pharisees were liberal, progressive and populist. They had contact with the common populace.

Scribes were the scholars or intellectuals, experts in the Torah. They produced oral interpretations, commentaries, rules and regulations for contemporary life, based on their understanding of the Torah. They thus provided the system of values and meanings, ideology if you will, which governed Jewish life. They were also known as the rabbis.

Pharisees and scribes together exercised authority, power and leadership in religious and civil matters.

Herodians were people associated with the governor of Galilee, Herod Antipas: relatives, political cronies, members of Herod's court, friends and hangers-on.

Issues. Our signposts above have described typical collision-events between these people and Jesus. They also contain the typical matters of contention between Jesus and his opponents, such as putting primacy on the human being and human life over against the accepted tradition and law.

In addition, the following critical remarks of Jesus are recorded in Matthew's gospel. They might contain more of Matthew's bias against the pharisees and scribes than the original Jesus confrontation, but they serve to convey the intensity of the conflict. Imagine that you are a missionary to whom Jesus addresses these charges: 'You shut the doors of the Kingdom of heaven to yourselves and to people who want to enter. You go to foreign missions to make converts, and when they convert, you make them doubly a child of hell as you. You are the children of those who murdered the prophets.' We are familiar with Jesus' censure—reported not only by Matthew but also by Luke—for the pharisees' neglect of social justice.

> Woe to you, scribes and pharisees, hypocrites! For you lock people out of the kingdom of heaven. For you do not go in yourselves, and when others are going in, you stop them. (Mt 23:13)
>
> Woe to you, scribes and pharisees, hypocrites! For you cross sea and land to make a single convert, and you make the new convert twice as much a child of hell as yourselves. (Mt 23:15)
>
> Woe to you, scribes and pharisees, hypocrites! For you build the tombs of the prophets and decorate the graves of the righteous, and you say, 'If we had lived in the days of our ancestors, we would not have taken part with them in shedding the blood of the prophets.' Thus you testify against yourselves that you are descendants of those who murdered the prophets. Fill up, then, the measure of your ancestors. You snakes, you brood of vipers! How can you escape being sentenced to hell? (Mt 23:29-33)
>
> Woe to you, scribes and pharisees, hypocrites! For you tithe mint, dill, and cummin, and have neglected the weightier matters of the law: justice and mercy and faith. It is these you ought to have practiced without neglecting the others. (Mt 23:23; Lk 11:42)

JESUS AND THE CHIEF PRIESTS, ELDERS, SCRIBES
(MODERATORS: Women and Nature-Carers, Protesters Against War Weapon Production, Sorsogon Folk)

We now make the acquaintance of other prominent personages in the conflictive life of Jesus:

Chief Priests, Elders, Scribes. The *elders* were the heads of families, particularly prominent and influential families. They probably numbered among the economic, political, and social aristocracy of Palestine. Their economic base would have been land and/or large-scale commerce.

Chief priests were the elite priests. They resided in Jerusalem, the capital city. The first among them was the high priest. Differentiate them from the simple poor priests who lived and worked in the countryside.[75]

Ever since the Persian colonial period, 500 years earlier, when instead of kings, high priests, under various imperial powers, became the heads-of-state, the high priestly class enjoyed supreme social, political and economic power. The main sources of their wealth were land, commerce, and the profitable temple income from tithes, donations, temple banking and business enterprises. In the time of Jesus, the high priest shared supreme political power with the Herodian kings and the Roman procurator. The high priest was the head of the Sanhedrin, the Jewish supreme council, the highest political body in Palestine for domestic national affairs.

Scribes were the intellectual elite, experts in their religious tradition. We have already met them. When associated with the chief priest and elders, the designation refers principally to the sophisticated *urban* scholars, specialists in the Torah.

Aristocracy. These three groups—the chief priests, scribes and elders—constituted the aristocracy of Palestine: economic, political, cultural, intellectual, and religious. Moreover, from these groups were drawn the members of the Sanhedrin, their supreme council which wielded the highest political authority, though subject to Rome of course. Religio-political leadership was in the hands of these people.

Jesus and the Religio-Political Leadership. What did Jesus have to say to the religio-political leadership? Was Jesus in sharp conflict with the religio-political authorities of his time? Listen to a message addressed by Jesus to them: Yahweh entrusted you with the care of the Israelite people whom he loved very much. From time to time, Yahweh sent prophets to check. You had nothing to show. Instead, you tortured and murdered the prophets. And now he sends his son, thinking you would respect him. But no, you will conspire to kill and will actually kill him.

---

[75] Zachary, the father of John the Baptist, is an example of these minor priests from the countryside. (See Lk 1:5-23.)

What will Yahweh then do? (What do you think, dear reader, Jesus' verdict will be?) God will come and destroy them! No light indictment! That is the gist of Jesus' message. He tells it more graphically and forcefully through his favorite medium, the parable:

> Then he began to speak to them (the chief priests and scribes and the elders of Mk 11:27) in parables. "A man planted a vineyard, put a fence around it, dug a pit for the wine press, and built a watchtower; then he leased it to tenants and went to another country. When the season came, he sent a slave to the tenants to collect from them his share of the produce of the vineyard. But they seized him, and beat him, and sent him away empty-handed. And again he sent another slave to them; this one they beat over the head and insulted. Then he sent another, and that one they killed. And so it was with many others; some they beat, and others they killed. He had still one other, a beloved son. Finally he sent him to them, saying, 'They will respect my son.' But those tenants said to one another, 'This is the heir; come, let us kill him, and the inheritance will be ours.' So they seized him, killed him, and threw him out of the vineyard. *What then will the owner of the vineyard do? He will come and destroy the tenants* and give the vineyard to others." (Mk 12:1-10)

God Will Destroy You. The chief priests, elders and scribes, whom Jesus was addressing in the vineyard-parable, held the religio-political leadership and social power in Jesus' time. They were murderers of the prophets. They were worthless leaders of God's people. God would destroy them! Strong words—little expected from a stereotype wimpy Jesus.

Jesus and the Temple

(Moderators: PCP II Participants, Barrio Fiesta Folk, Mother and Child)

Jesus did not spare the temple. His assault was double barreled – in word and in action.

The Temple in Jesus' Time. What was the temple? Of course, it was a religious institution. It was the principal one, because there was only one temple for the whole nation. It was only in the temple that sacrifices were offered. It was situated in the capital city of Jerusalem. The synagogues in the countryside were places for study and prayer only.

In a society where there was no sharp distinction between the religious and political spheres, the temple served, like the modern flag, as a principal national symbol. It also had political associations. The Sanhedrin met within the temple complex. Those in charge of the temple were the chief priests, leading political figures.

It was also a principal economic institution. Revenues flowed freely here, what with the sale of sacrificial animals, fees and taxes, donations, money-exchange.

It was also, of course, the special domain of the priestly aristocracy.

The temple, therefore, was the major religio-cultural, political and economic institution.

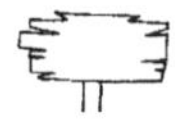

Then they came to Jerusalem. And *he entered the temple and began to drive out those who were selling and those who were buying in the temple, and he overturned the tables of the money changers and the seats of those who sold doves; and he would not allow anyone to carry anything through the temple.* He was teaching and saying, "Is it not written, *'My house shall be called a house of prayer for all the nations'? But you have made it a den of robbers."* And when the chief priests and the scribes heard it, they kept looking for a way to kill him ... (Mk 11:15-19)

Focus of Jesus' Action against the Temple. Clearly Jesus' complaint was about all the goings-on that restyled a place of prayer into a place of commerce. Looking closely, however, notice that he singles out segments which are related to the poor: money changing and the sale of doves. Money-changing was especially hard on the poor. Doves were the offerings of the poor. Jesus gave special attention to these. The temple, which was supposed to serve the poor, has become a den of thieves!

Jesus' Verbal Attack on the Temple. Jesus also pronounced some threatening words against the temple.

As he came out of the temple, one of his disciples said to him, 'Look, Teacher, what large stones and what large buildings!' Then Jesus asked him, 'Do you see these great buildings? *Not one stone will be left here upon another; all will be thrown down.'* (Mk 13:1-2)

Imagine threatening the cathedral today with utter destruction. Jesus' threat was consequential enough to constitute one of the charges against him during his trial.

"We heard him say, '*I will destroy this temple* that is made with hands, and in three days I will build another, not made with hands.' " (Mk 14:58)

This was the taunt leveled at him on the cross.

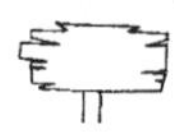

Those who passed by derided him, shaking their heads, and saying, 'Aha! *You who would destroy the temple and build it in three days save yourself,* and come down from the cross!' (Mk 15:29-30)

This oft-repeated mention of Jesus' verbal attack makes it one of the few historical facts about Jesus. It did much to pave the way to the cross.

Jesus and Rome

Was Jesus anti-Roman? There is not enough evidence about Jesus' stance towards Rome. His oft-quoted 'Give to Caesar the things that are Caesar's' is not necessarily an endorsement of Rome. The statement could mean: Give to Caesar what belongs to him. But nothing belongs to him. Everything belongs to Yahweh in this nation.... What is clear is his repudiation of imperial values (Mk 10:42-45). There is enough data, not about Jesus' attitude towards Rome, but about Rome's attitude towards Jesus. From the point of view of the Romans, he probably was regarded as a rebel. At a time when certain Jews led rebellious movements against Rome and were regarded as Jewish kings, Jesus was given the title 'King of the Jews' (Mk 15:2-3; Lk 23:38). Jesus was executed by crucifixion, a capital punishment meted out to rebels against Rome. He was crucified between, and therefore associated with, two 'thieves,' or better, 'bandits.' The excessively oppressive imperial regime produced social bandits among the peasantry. Social bandits—many of whom were considered 'Robin Hoods' by the peasantry—were a regular feature of the Roman times. Barabbas may have been a social bandit.

Underlying Dynamics

(Moderators: Fisherfolk, Fruit and Vegetable Growers, Indigenous People)

We now attempt to understand an underlying pattern or dynamic in Jesus' conflictive activity.

It's been sometime since we have adjusted our eye-glasses. Perhaps this is a good time.

The Elite and the Common People

The Palestine of Jesus' time was a Palestine of the economic, political, cultural elite, on the one hand, and of the impoverished and voiceless common people, on the other.

The Elite and Their Economic, Political, Cultural Power

The main sources of wealth were land and commerce.

Access to political power was through political office, family lineage, wars of conquests, social connections and manipulation, economic standing.

Moreover, social privilege was determined by blood: Jew or non-Jew, noble or common, pure or impure.

The dominant culture was largely shaped by people who were recognized to have the authority to interpret traditions, customs, values and meanings based on the Torah; these were principally the scribes, but also the pharisees and priests.

In the pages of the gospels we meet the *economic elite*. They go by the names *elders and chief priests*.

We meet the *socio-political* elite. These are the *chief priests, elders and scribes*. Many of these were members of the highest Jewish authoritative body in Palestine, the Sanhedrin, though subject to the Roman empire.

We meet people who wielded *religio-cultural authority and power*. We recognize them as the *scribes and pharisees, and also the priests*. They produced the system of values and meanings (religio-cultural ideology). They prescribed the rules and regulations about the Sabbath, purification, tithing and many other matters.[76]

These—elders, priests, scribes, pharisees—constituted the privileged economic, socio-political, cultural, religious elite of Palestine.

Religio-Cultural Ideology: Anti-Poor

The following is important for our study of Jesus. It would appear that in New Testament times, this religio-cultural ideology was anti-poor and anti-outcast. Its net message to the poor and outcast would be: '*You do not know the Torah. You do not obey the Torah. You do not observe the purification laws. You do not follow the tradition. You are adulterers, murderers, thieves. You are sinners. You are the accursed masses*' (cf. Jn 7:49). It taught the poor and the outcasts to despise themselves and to accept the prevailing system of the institution as good and willed by Yahweh, when in fact it had lost the life-giving spirit of the ancient law. It, at least tacitly, blessed the domination of the elite and its power, privilege and authority. It was an oppressive ideology.

The Common People and Their Two-Fold Domination

On the other hand, we have the poor and outcast sector. The common folk suffered under a two-fold domination:

(1) *Roman* imperial domination through:

a. *Political occupation* either by direct rule of the Roman procurators or by indirect rule through Herod the Great and his sons.

b. *Military occupation*. The Roman garrison in Jerusalem was adjacent to the temple. The Roman procurator's residence and fort in coastal Caesarea were just some hundred kilometers from Jerusalem.

Roman armies raided villages and massacred people suspected of rebellion against Rome.

---

[76] The elite, mostly of the priestly class, had an association, the *sadducees*. This was an aristocratic and wealthy group, conservative and fundamentalist. They accepted only written tradition. They were not open to new beliefs. Unlike the pharisees, they failed to gain the sympathy of the common people. They generally collaborated and compromised with foreign power.

c. *Tribute*. Tribute to the imperial powers (Assyria, Persia, Greece, Rome) had been for a long time a part of the life of the Palestinian peasantry. In Roman times, non-payment of tribute and taxes was considered rebellion.

d. *Cultural colonialism*. This type of domination did not seep as much into the common folk as into the elite who took on Graeco-Roman political and cultural forms, language and education.

(2) Domination by the *local Jewish elite* through:

a. Elite control of *land and big commerce*.

b. Elite control of *political power.*

The prime holders of power were kings like Herod as well as the high priestly class, heads of aristocratic families, and scribes, many of whom belonged to the Sanhedrin.

c. *Religio-cultural domination* by the scribes, pharisees, and priests.

In the gospel pages, we meet the poor under several guises. We meet:

- the *multitudes*, many of whom were the poor of the land.
- the *sick*, many of whom must have been the malnourished poor.
- the 'poor of the land,' the *'am ha aretz.*
- *'sinners,'* most of whom were the poor who were too uneducated to know the Torah and the rabbinic prescriptions, and did not practice them. Frequently in the gospels, then, when you meet the word 'sinners,' you may understand 'the poor' or 'the unschooled poor.'

We meet the *tax collectors*: they were despised by the elite as marginals and outcasts because of their shady profession and their connection with Rome.

[Therefore the phrase 'tax collectors and sinners' practically means 'the outcasts and the poor.']

Pattern in Jesus' Behavior with the Privileged and the Under-Privileged. From the social profile we have just sketched, it is clear that we can speak of two groups in Jesus' time:

Privileged Group	Under-Privileged
(the privileged elite)	(the poor and outcast sector)
chief priests	the poor of the land (the multitudes, sick, sinners, *`am ha aretz*)
elders	tax-collectors and sinners
pharisees and scribes, etc.	

Let us now discern a pattern in Jesus' relationship with *the privileged group* and *the under-privileged group*. What was his typical attitude, behavior, valuation of each of them? Does Jesus offer *counter-practice*, that is, an alternative way of acting and being? Does Jesus have a counter value-system or a counter-ideology, that is another set of values?

Sample 1:

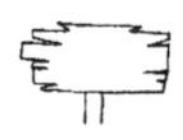

'We ***[Jesus and his disciples]*** played the flute for you, and you did not dance; we ***[John the Baptist and his disciples]*** wailed, and you did not mourn.'

For John came neither eating nor drinking ***[John the Baptist observed the Pharisaic rules on fasting]***, and they say, 'He has a demon'; the Son of Man [Jesus] came eating and drinking ***[Jesus did not observe the Pharisaic rules on fasting; counter-practice]***, and they ***[the privileged elite]*** say, 'Look, a glutton and a drunkard, a friend of tax collectors and sinners *[the outcasts and the poor]*!' (Mt 11:16-19)

COMMENT: This episode tells us a few things about Jesus' relationship with *the privileged group* and *the under-privileged group*.

Towards the under-privileged: Jesus was reputed to be their friend, a member of their gang (*barkada).*

Towards the privileged: 1. Jesus did not follow their practice of fasting; he offered a counter-practice. 2. Jesus and the *privileged* were not on very friendly terms (Jesus played music to which they did not dance). 3. The *privileged* were critical of Jesus' association with the poor and outcasts.

Sample 2:

Then he told this parable: "A man ***[Yahweh]*** had a fig tree ***[the Jewish nation, the temple and specially the leadership]*** planted in his vineyard; and he came looking for fruit on it and found none. So he said to the gardener, 'See here! For three years I have come looking for fruit on this fig tree, and still I find none. Cut it down! Why should it be wasting the soil?' He replied, 'Sir, let it alone for one more year, until I dig around it and put manure on it. If it bears fruit next year, well and good; but if not, you can cut it down.'" (Lk 13:6-9)

COMMENT: Here we find Jesus' opinion or judgment of the nation and its leadership. The nation, particularly, *the privileged group*, was like a barren fruit tree that bore no fruit and deserved to be cut down. The vinedresser petitions a reprieve.

Sample 3:

"What do you think? A man had two sons; he went to the first ***[the `am ha `aretz, tax collectors, sinners who do not know nor practice the rabbinic prescriptions of the Torah]*** and said, 'Son, go and work in the vineyard today.' He answered, 'I will not'; but later he changed his mind and went.

> The father went to the second *[the privileged elite who know the Torah]* and said the same; and he answered, 'I go, sir'; but he did not go. Which of the two did the will of his father?" They said, "The first." Jesus said to them, "Truly I tell you, the tax collectors and the prostitutes *[the outcasts and the poor]* are going into the kingdom of God ahead of you. For John came to you in the way of righteousness and you did not believe him, but the tax collectors and the prostitutes believed him; and even after you saw it, you did not change your minds and believe him." (Mt 21:28-32)

COMMENT: The first son is *the under-privileged group*. He initially said 'no' to God's order but later actually performed it. The second son is *the privileged group.* He said he would, but did not. *The privileged group* gets a negative valuation; *the under-privileged group*, a positive one.

Sample 4:

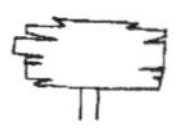

> He also told this parable to some who trusted in themselves that they were righteous and regarded others with contempt: "Two men went up to the temple to pray, one a pharisee *[one of the privileged elite]* and the other a tax collector *[the outcast]*. The pharisee, standing by himself, was praying thus, 'God, I thank you that I am not like other people: thieves, rogues, adulterers, or even like this tax collector. I fast twice a week; I give a tenth of all my income.' But the tax collector, standing far off, would not even look up to heaven, but was beating his breast and saying, 'God, be merciful to me, a sinner! *[conditioned by the system so to pray]*.' I tell you, this man went down to his home justified rather than the other; for all who exalt themselves will be humbled, but all who humble themselves will be exalted." (Lk 18:9-14)

COMMENT: What mark did Jesus give to *the privileged group*? To *the under-privileged group*? Positive for *the under-privileged group*. Negative for *the privileged group*. This parable is more than just a moral lesson on humility. It is also Jesus' social commentary and appraisal of groups in his society.

Sample 5:

> One sabbath he was going through the grainfields; and as they made their way his disciples began to pluck heads of grain *[counter-practice]*. The pharisees *[producers of value-system]* said to him, 'Look, why are they doing what is not lawful on the sabbath?' *[counter-practice]* And he said to them, 'Have you never read what David did when he and his companions were hungry and in need of food? He entered the house of God, when Abiathar was high priest, and ate the bread of the Presence, which it is not lawful for any but the priests to eat, and he gave some to his companions.' Then he said to them, 'The sabbath was made for humankind, and not humankind for the sabbath *[counter value-system]*; so the Son of Man is lord even of the sabbath.' (Mk 2:23-28)

COMMENT: Note Jesus' principles and actions in relation to *the privileged group*. Jesus provides a counter-practice and a counter value-system against *the privileged group*. Human need has a claim worthier than religious prohibitions. The day of rest was made for people and not the reverse.

Sample 6:

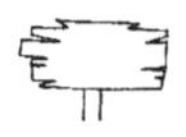

'Watch out, and beware of the yeast of the pharisees and sadducees.' Then they understood that he had not told them to beware of the yeast of bread, but of the teaching of the pharisees and sadducees ***[the value-system of elite]***. (Mt 16:6-12)

COMMENT: Jesus was critical of the religio-cultural ideology of *the privileged group*.

Sample 7:

Now when the pharisees and some of the scribes ***[the makers of the value system]*** who had come from Jerusalem gathered around him, they noticed that some of his disciples were eating with defiled hands, that is, without washing them. (For the pharisees, and all the Jews, do not eat unless they thoroughly wash their hands, thus observing the tradition of the elders; and they do not eat anything from the market unless they wash it; and there are also many other traditions that they observe, the washing of cups, pots, and bronze kettles.) ***[This is the value-system or ideology that is particularly discriminating against the unlettered poor.]***

So the pharisees and the scribes asked him, "Why do your disciples not live according to the tradition of the elders, but eat with defiled hands?" ***[counter-practice]*** He said to them, "Isaiah prophesied rightly about you hypocrites, as it is written, 'This people honors me with their lips, but their hearts are far from me; in vain do they worship me, teaching human precepts as doctrines.' You abandon the commandment of God and hold to human tradition." ***[critique of the religio-cultural ideology]*** ...

Then he called the crowd again and said to them, "Listen to me, all of you, and understand: there is nothing outside a person that by going in can defile, but the things that come out are what defile ***[counter ideology]***....

"Do you not see that whatever goes into a person from outside cannot defile, since it enters, not the heart but the stomach, and goes out into the sewer?" (Thus he declared all foods clean.) And he said, "It is what comes out of a person that defiles. For it is from within, from the human heart, that evil intentions come: fornication, theft, murder, adultery, avarice, wickedness, deceit, licentiousness, envy, slander, pride, folly. All these evil things come from within, and they defile a person." ***[counter value-system]*** (Mk 7:1-23)

COMMENT: Jesus' critique is not only directed against *the privileged group*, but also indirectly favors *the under-privileged group*. The elite's value-system which he is critiquing in word and deed is discriminatory against the poor.

Sample 8:

'Woe to you, scribes and pharisees, hypocrites! For you tithe the mint, dill, and cummin ***[the practice and value-system of the privileged elite]***, and have neglected the weightier matters of the law: justice and mercy and faith ***[counter value-system benefiting the poor and oppressed]***. It is these you ought to have practiced without neglecting the others. You blind guides! You strain out a gnat but swallow a camel!' (Mt 23:23-24)

COMMENT: It is obvious that *the privileged group* is being criticized. It also shows that the remark is favorable to *the under-privileged group*, because for Jesus the weightier things in religion are those that favor *the under-privileged group*, namely, *mishpat-checed-'emet.* (Also Lk 10:29-37)

Sample 9:

And as he sat at dinner in the house, many tax collectors and sinners came and were sitting with him and his disciples ***[counter-practice]***. When the pharisees saw this, they said to his disciples, 'Why does your teacher eat with tax collectors and sinners?' But when he heard this, he said, 'Those who are well have no need of a physician, but those who are sick. Go and learn what this means, 'I desire mercy *[checed]*, not sacrifice.' For I have come to call not the righteous but sinners.' ***[vs. the value-system of the privileged elite]*** (Mt 9:10-13; also 12:1-8)

COMMENT: Much of this is obvious. But note that here Jesus enunciates an important principle which is favorable to the poor and oppressed. Jesus would rather have *checed* than worship. Here Jesus is quoting the God of Hosea 6:6. Recall that *checed* is one of the quadruplets, *tsedaqah-mishpat-checed-'emet,* meaning social justice for the poor. (Also Lk 15:1-32)

Sample 10:

'There was a rich man ***[the privileged elite]*** who was dressed in purple and fine linen and who feasted sumptuously every day. And at his gate lay a poor man named Lazarus, covered with sores, ***[belonging to the under-privileged]*** who longed to satisfy his hunger with what fell from the rich man's table; even the dogs would come and lick his sores. The poor man died and was carried away by the angels to be with Abraham. The rich man also died and was buried. In Hades, where he was being tormented, he looked up and saw Abraham far away with Lazarus by his side.' (Lk 16:19ff)

COMMENT: Positive for *the under-privileged group*. Negative for *the privileged group*. (Also Lk 12:16-21; 14:16-24; Mt 6:24; 25-34. Both Matthew passages refer to the value-system of the privileged elite).

Sample 11:

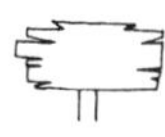

Now the chief priests and the whole council *[the sanhedrin]* were looking for testimony against Jesus to put him to death; but they found none. (Mk 14:55)

The chief priests and the scribes ***[the privileged elite]*** were looking for a way to arrest Jesus by stealth and kill him; for they said, 'Not during the festival, or there may be a riot among the people ***[the `am ha `aretz]*** (**Mk 14:1-2**).' See Mk 3:9; 20; 4:1; Mt 7:28; 9:8; 13:2, etc.

COMMENT: At the time just before Jesus was killed, which these passages describe, we see who Jesus' friends were and who his enemies were. *The privileged group*, his enemies, wanted to arrest Jesus but feared Jesus' friends, the multitude (*the under-privileged group*).

CONCLUSION: Did you discover a consistent pattern, an underlying dynamic, in Jesus' practice? In other words, what was Jesus' general attitude/behavior towards the privileged elite, be it regarding their wealth, political power or their value-system? And what was it towards the poor and the outcast?

NO ANTISEPTIC JESUS

The Immune Jesus. Our average understanding – outcome of our average religious and theological instruction – sees Jesus taking the pharisees to task for their hypocrisy. But this is as far as it goes. For the rest, Jesus is portrayed one-sidedly as the meek and humble Jesus (which, of course he was), a good and personal friend and brother ... and, because he is God, immune to human struggle.

Without Conflict, There Is No Jesus-Story To Tell. And yet, we cannot understand his life *and death* properly without understanding it as a conflictive one. Without conflict, there is no Jesus-story to tell. His Kingdom-practice included the strong (counter)positions he took with regard to the sabbath (Mk 3:1-6), purification laws (Mk 7:1-23), justice (Mt 23:23), poverty-riches (Lk 6:24; Mt 6:24), and especially the temple (Mk 13:1-2; 12:1-12).

Jesus Did Not Die in Bed! Our summit with old friends ends with this reflection: Jesus did not die in bed! Most of us will. Why was his death different from that of most of us? Is it because his life was different from that of most of us? People would normally not be killed for wanting to save souls. But people could want to kill you for proclaiming an alternative world. Such were Purificacion Pedro, Bill Begg, Rey Robles, Joe Tangente, Edgar Jopson, Lorena Barros, Evelio Javier, Tullio Favali, Godofredo Alingal, Emman Lacaba, Rudy Romano, Asuncion Martinez, Satur Neri, Rodrigo Mordeno, Bobby de la Paz, Cecilia Natolin and many others, forgotten by me and unknown to many, known only to their family and close friends and to God. Among these were people who called the alternative world by names other than 'Kingdom of God.' No matter. Those among them who, in their tryst with martyrdom were inspired by Jesus, would pointedly recall Jesus' words: 'A disciple is not above the teacher, nor a slave above the master; it is enough for the disciple to be like the teacher, and the slave like the master. If they have called the master of the house Beelzebul, how much more will they malign those of his household!' (Mt 10:24-25)

Stamina. Stamina—that is what the Jesus of this stopover needed. He must have had it. Was it because he was in touch?

Be Still and Know ...

Stopover 16

With Mother Teresa, Padre Pio, Archbishop Romero and Evelio Javier (The Death of Jesus)

OUR HOSTS: M. Teresa, Archbishop Romero, Evelio Javier and Padre Pio

At last, it is time to let Jesus die.

A Solicitous Query. Let us pause here to note that it took us some time before letting Jesus die. I hope we now see how important his pre-crucifixion mission was. In carrying out our pastoral and spiritual lives, we have to fill in a gap in our official creed. Our official creed,[77] formulated in the 4th century *after* Christ, which we profess every Sunday, omits the Kingdom-proclamation of Jesus and its consequences.

[77] Either the so-called Apostolic Creed, composed in the 4th century of the Christian Era, or the longer Nicene-Constantinople Creed, composed in 325 and 381 C.E.

We believe:
in Jesus Christ,
His only Son, Our Lord,
who was conceived by the Holy spirit,
born of the Virgin Mary,
________?________
suffered under Pontius Pilate,
was crucified,
died
and was buried ...

Jesus has hardly settled in on the crib than he is sent off to the cross. Jesus is hardly born than he is sent off to his passion and death. These are not meant to be facetious remarks. They are solicitous queries about the kind of consciousness which our official prayers must generate among the average Christian.

Look at the words of the creed again. If you were not familiar with the theological controversies that led to the formulation of the creed, you would wonder about the somewhat morgue-ish concern to see Jesus really dead: he was crucified *and* died *and* was buried. Again, no apologies. For far from being a droll remark, my comment is an attempt to probe a bit into our Christian psyche.

Shoes to Wear: Blind Faith or Apologetics? A word in passing about the creed. I was raised to *believe in* these truths about God. Thus the creed was there to help me grow up to believe in these truths, or even, believe in God, but hardly to *experience* God. I make this not-too-incidental remark at this juncture because we are entering a terrain—the death, resurrection, Cosmic Christ—where there are better shoes to wear than blind faith or apologetics....

... But now, at last, it is time to let Jesus die.

A Redundant Statement? This Jesus lived dangerously. He would die dangerously. We know from history and our Faith that he died. Aye, and there's the rub. We know that he died. We do not *really* know that he was killed. Have I just made a redundant statement? Our hosts—two sets of them—will clarify. Archbishop Romero and Evelio Javier[78], who were killed for justice, will tell us why he was *killed*. Mother Teresa and Padre Pio, who had a special devotion to the suffering and crucified Jesus, will tell us why Jesus *died*.

[78] Evelio Javier, at 29, elected by a landslide majority was the youngest provincial governor in the Philippines. He was the untypical politician, using political power not for self-enrichment but for the people. Loved and hero-worshipped by the poor and the youth for his dedication, charisma, courage, and disliked by traditional politicians, he was gunned down not far from the provincial Capitol.

DEATH OF JESUS: HISTORICAL ASPECT.

Jesus' Record in the Book of Life. Archbishop Romero and Evelio Javier will show us Jesus' record in the book of life:

He put primacy on the human being and human life over and against the accepted tradition and law. He violated the sabbath by healing people. 'Is it lawful to do good or to do harm on the sabbath, to save life or to kill?' – was his defense, delivered with anger and grief (e.g. Mk 3:1-6).

He violated the sabbath by letting the hungry pluck corn (Mk 2:23-28). His defense: the sabbath was made for humankind; not humankind for the sabbath.

To him, tax-collectors, sinners, the poor were human beings (Mk 2:15-17; Lk 16:20-22).

He was a rebel against tradition. In the eyes of the institution he was not only a non-conformist. He was a heretic, an apostate. 'Tradition of the elders' (Mk 7:3) is an old wineskin that cannot hold new wine (Mk 2:22). Tradition is an old fabric that cannot be patched with a piece of new cloth (Mk 2:21).

He makes little of the tradition of fasting and the ritual purity laws: 'This people honors me with their lips, but their heart is far from me; teaching as doctrines the precepts of men. 'You leave the commandment of God, and hold fast to the tradition of men.... You have a fine way of rejecting the commandment of God, in order to keep your tradition!' (Mk 7)

He offered a fresh re-reading of the tradition. That is a dangerous thing to do when those in authority are either too entrenched or insecure or both.

He was an uncompromising critic of the value-system or ideology of the establishment. He excoriated the theologians and strict observers for prescribing tithing but neglecting social justice, which for him was the weightier matter of religion (Mt 23:23).

Whereas the institution honored the righteous and despised the sinners, he came not 'to call the righteous, but sinners.' (Mk 2:7; Mt 9:13)

'Beware of the yeast of the pharisees and the yeast of Herod.' (Mk 8:15) – was his warning.

'Justice-and-compassion' would have been the inscription on his phylactery[79] if he had worn one. It was a badge of honor he wore in his heart. 'I would rather have compassion than sacrifice.'

Compassion for the hungry, the tax-collectors and the sinners rather than animal offerings in the temple! – was a cardinal principle for Jesus, as it was for Hosea (Mt 9:13;12:7; Hos 6:6).

---

[79] A small box containing written portions of the Torah, worn on the head and left arm.

For Jesus, the weightier matters of the law were justice and mercy and faith. (Mt 23:23)

He was unabashedly for the poor and stern towards the rich. Good news to the poor was the constant refrain in his mission statements (Mt 11:2-5 = Lk 7:18-23; Lk 4:16-21; Lk 6:20 = Mt 5:3). It was matched by performance.

The rich he critiqued (Lk 6:24; 12:16-21), challenged Mk 10:21), warned (Lk 12:16-21; 16:19-31).

His physical assault on the temple was a loud message in behalf of the poor, addressed to its wealthy custodians (Mk 11:15-19).

He aims and fires at the establishment. He said that their scholars love to walk around in long robes, to be greeted in the marketplace, to have the best seats in the synagogues and places of honor at banquets! They devour widows' houses. For the sake of appearance, they say long prayers (Mk 12:38-40).

More substantial charges were forthcoming. He indicted the religio-political leadership with infidelity to their trust, with unproductiveness and with murder. They killed the prophets and now they were going to do the same to the vineyard's heir (Mk 12:1-10).

He censured the aristocracy. He did not mince words with the temple aristocracy: 'You have made the house of prayer a den of thieves.' (Mk 11:17)

Nor were his accusations against the intellectual-pastoral elite any milder: you shut the Kingdom of heaven against people and make your converts twice as much a child of hell (Mt 23:15).

His words to the king, Herod Antipas, were hardly conciliatory: "Go and say to that fox, 'Behold, I cast out demons and perform cures today and tomorrow, and the third *day* I am perfected'" (Lk 13:31-32).

He staged a double-assault – in speech and feat – against the most massive institution, the temple. Some scholars think that this was what sealed Jesus' death (Mk 11:15-19; 13:1-2).

He wrested from the experts and the erudite their power and authority. These influential men probably sensed the common folk's reaction to Jesus: the people were astounded at his teaching, for he taught them as one having authority, and not like them, the recognized teachers of the community (Mk 1:21-28).

He usurped the status of the priest. Being a lay person, he healed a leper (Mk 1:40-45).

He exposed their hypocrisy and love for externals (Mt 23).

Canonization or Condemnation? With such a record, people like myself would be ready to canonize him. Another Thomas More! Another martyr on the Roman arena, standing head high against the imperial claims. A subversive saint! Just as we are about to canonize him, the aristocratic elite of his time condemn him to death. Understandably, in a way. Would we have done any better ourselves? What with the steady stream of 'irritants' to authority, power, establishment, tradition, wealth, law ... and, lurking behind all of these, the EGO. How do you solve a problem like Jesus?

Why Was He Killed? Jesus was killed. He did not just die. He was executed. Why? Because during his lifetime he wanted to save souls? A friend of mine once remarked, perplexed: 'Such a fine chap. All he wanted to do was save souls. And they did him in!'

Again, why? Because his Father wanted him dead—for our sins? Banish the evil thought!

Why? Because he disappointed people's hopes of a political, military messiah? Hardly, it would seem.

The available data do not permit certainty about the *exact* cause of Jesus' execution. But from all appearances, it was his conflictive Kingdom-activity which set his feet moving toward the cross. A rebel's life courts a rebel's death.

Activism and Contemplation. In the course of our journey, we paused to note that Jesus' life was one of action and contemplation. So should be that of the disciple. We can now introduce a refinement: Jesus' life was one of *activism* and contemplation. That would be more accurate and true to life, would it not?

Jesus, the First Activist. Jesus is the first activist in our Christian history. He stood squarely for life, for the human being, for the poor, for justice, confronting a tradition, a law, an authority that had become meaningless and destructive for people's lives. We ought also to rescue the word 'activism' from attempts to paint it black and despicable. And what is activism? I prefer not to give a dictionary meaning. Read the second sentence of this paragraph. Or better: Read Jesus. Read Jesus well. You are reading an activist. One of the best, if not the best, of the variety.

Other Reasons for Jesus' Execution. The gospel accounts also mention other possible causes or motives. However, it is difficult to tell the real motives and the false charges. These include: (1) Jesus claimed to be the Messiah and the Son of God (Mt 26:63-4); (2) Jesus uttered blasphemy (Mt 26:65); (3) Jesus was delivered by the Jewish authorities out of envy (Mt 27:18); (4) Jesus performed many signs. 'If we let him go on thus, every one will believe in him, and the Romans will come and destroy both our holy place and our nation.' (Jn 11:47-48); (5) Jesus was perverting the nation and forbidding people to give taxes to the emperor, and claiming to be king (Lk 23:2); (6) Jesus was stirring up the people throughout the land (Lk 23:5). These last two charges would make Jesus anti-Roman, a not unlikely fact at all.

We have just reviewed some of the historical situations, people and reasons connected with Jesus' death. Our guides have been Archbishop Romero and Evelio Javier. The signposts were provided mostly by Mark, Matthew and Luke.

Jesus in the Face of Death. How was Jesus in the face of oncoming death? We sometimes harbor a certain ill-considered view. He was God, we say. He foresaw everything. We have an unstated suspicion that he did not go through a real human struggle. He took his death as matter of course, pre-programmed for him from all eternity.

Human Struggle. The fact, however, is he *did* go through a real human struggle. No matter how painful to him or to us, we cannot permit our pious intentions to steal away from him this fragment of life. He avoided places of danger at night. He went around only with his close and trusted friends. He took refuge in safe (hiding?) places like Bethany and Ephraim. Gethsemane, too, might have been a place of hiding, for only Judas, not the arresting soldiers, knew where it was.

He fought; he resisted as long as he could hold out.

Let us follow him during the last days, as Mark tells the story in Chapter 11:8 and following:

He No Longer Went About Openly. Amid *hosannas* and leafy branches Jesus enters Jerusalem. Danger ahead! He is entering the heart of enemy zone. The sanhedrin is there. The Jewish military is there. The unique Jesus Rally of Palm Sunday probably puts his enemies somewhat on the alert.

Jesus enters the temple. It is here that on the morrow, he is going to stage a raid. So what does he do? 'He looks around at everything.' Is this a preliminary survey of the lay of the temple in preparation for the assault?

As it was getting to be late in the day, he leaves. Is he avoiding the city? It is enemy territory; it is not safe even during the day, less so at night. In addition to the Jewish police, there is the Roman garrison overlooking the temple. He slips away from the city.

To where? Watch where he goes. To Bethany. Perhaps because it is a safer place, being a couple of miles away from Jerusalem.

John's gospel even says that Jesus goes underground! 'Jesus therefore no longer went about openly among the Jews.' He then hides in a town called Ephraim far out in the country near the desert.

And with whom? His trusted friends, the twelve.

Thus should we read the following roadsigns:

> And he entered *Jerusalem*, and went into the *temple*; and when he had *looked round at everything*, as it was *already late*, he went out to *Bethany* with the *twelve*. (Mk 11:11)
>
> So from that day on they *planned to put him to death*. Jesus therefore *no longer walked about openly* among the Jews, but *went from there* to a town called *Ephraim* in the region near the *wilderness*; and he remained there with the *disciples*. (Jn 11:54)

The Anguished Semicolon. Event follows event in quick succession: on the following day, he attacks the temple. Then, he engages in verbal tussles with his enemies. Then, he eats the Passover meal with his disciples. All the while his enemies are busy plotting his death.

Did Jesus go to his death like a lamb being led to the slaughter? *No, not until after the anguished semicolon in his life*. In Gethsemane, his whole being was shaken. In distress, agitation, grief, he resisted and warded off his mortal fate. 'Remove this cup from me;' [This is the pivotal semicolon. This is the great divide. Before this he was fighting, resisting, refusing.] 'yet, not what I want, but what you want.'

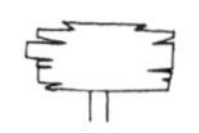

They went to a place called Gethsemane; and he said to his disciples, 'Sit here while I pray.' He took with him Peter and James and John, and began to be *distressed and agitated*. And he said to them, '*I am deeply grieved, even to death*; remain here, and keep awake.' And going a little farther, he threw himself on the ground and prayed that, *if it were possible, the hour might pass from him*. He said, 'Abba, Father, for you all things are possible; *remove this cup from me;* [**the anguished semicolon**] *yet, not what I want, but what you want.'* (Mk 14:32-36)

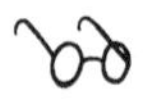

An Aside on the So-called God's Will. Almost drowned in agony, Jesus cries: 'Abba, Father … your will be done.' This is the place for an important aside on 'the will of God.' You will perhaps notice that Jesus hardly spoke about 'God's will.' He normally spoke about a father's will: my father, your father (Mt 7:21;10:29; 12:50). Theological hairsplitting? No. Doing 'God's will' can and does evoke images of a God who is iron-fisted, arbitrary, inflexible, insensitive, distant. But the wish, desire, solicitude, will of a parent—that is something else.

At any rate, I would rather talk in terms of a life-flow. It is like a river. There are parts that are still and pleasant like placid lagoons. There are the turbulent parts where the river crashes against crags and boulders, flaring up into smithereens of pain. Here, crises. There, questionings. Here, abandonment. There, despair. These turbulent parts may not, will not, cannot have the answers. But the whole river does. The river as a whole knows that the entire adventure makes sense, that there is only one place to go, the great ocean, and the river knows with absolute certainty that it will get there.

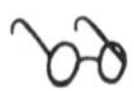

Let us go back now to Jesus and his dying …

Pause Here. And so they killed him on the hill of the skull (Mt 27:33). It is one of the most cruel and most painful deaths invented by men. We can pause here. Say nothing. Do nothing. Just be in touch with the flow that exudes from the core of the Crucified. That energy , shared with us by this unusual Jesus, could eventually become life-giving rivulets for ourselves and others.

Towards a Meaning. We have a high regard for meaningful deaths. That of Jesus'

is without doubt one of the most, if not the most, meaningful deaths in human history. The stakes he played for the sake of human life, the poor, justice would have conferred enough meaning to his death. However, another, more mystical meaning, was given to his death …

Jesus' Death: Theological Aspect

Archbishop Romero and Evelio have just told us why Jesus was *killed.* Mother Teresa and Padre Pio will now take over and tell us why he *died.*

A mystical meaning was given to his death. His death was a sacrificial offering in atonement for sin. He died for the sin(s) of the world.

> For I handed on to you as of first importance what I in turn had received: that *Christ died for our sins* in accordance with the scriptures, and that he was buried, and that he was raised on the third day in accordance with the scriptures…. (1 Cor 15:3-4)
>
> But now, apart from law, the righteousness of God has been disclosed, and is attested by the law…. through faith in Jesus Christ for all who believe…. by his grace as a gift, *through the redemption that is in Christ Jesus, whom God put forward as a sacrifice of atonement by his blood.* (Rom 3:21-25)
>
> and live in love, as Christ loved us and gave himself up for us, *a fragrant offering and sacrifice to God.* (Eph 5:2)
>
> The next day he saw Jesus coming toward him, and said, 'Here is the *Lamb of God, who takes away the sin of the world!'* (Jn 1:29)

Personal and Cosmic. The faith-understanding expressed here can have both a personal and cosmic import. A personal testimony is found in the letter to the Galatians. The cosmic is found in a contemplative insight in the letter to the Colossians:

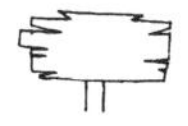

> … the life I now live in the flesh I live by faith in the Son of God, who *loved me and gave himself for me.* (Gal 2:20)
>
> … and through him God was pleased to *reconcile to himself all things,* whether on earth or in heaven, by *making peace through the blood of his cross.* (Col 1:20)

Why Did Jesus Die? Faith Interpretation or Mystical Insight. He died for sin. His death was a fragrant sacrifice for sin. We are dealing here with what can variously be termed faith-interpretation, theological meaning, sacrificial aspect.

But can we be more accurate and also more fair to Paul and other New Testament testimonies about Jesus' atoning death? Yes. Here we are in touch, not with a theological doctrine, but with a faith experience, the fruit of mystical seeing and experiencing. Our pathway to it is likewise mystical insight and experience, not cerebral analysis. Here 'mystical' need not be spelled with capital letters. It is everyone's birthright. For how can touching or drinking *directly* from the Source be a privilege or monopoly of the few? Padre Pio, whose flesh was an engraving of the Crucified, could give us a hand.

A while ago, we paused in silence to drink in the spirit of a rebel. This time, and any other time, we can pause once again, to drink in the Spirit that flows from the altar of the cross. It is a Spirit that cleanses, transforms and animates.

Cultural Background. The view that someone's death could have an atoning value was not strange in a Jewish cultural environment. It was believed that an innocent man or martyr could offer his death for the sins of others. Secondly, in the Jewish religious system, sacrificial blood, usually of animals, was the vehicle for sin-atonement. Thirdly, Isaiah 53 spoke of a servant-figure, originally referring to the people Israel, that suffered for the transgressions of others.

Jesus Himself. The insight into the sacrificial meaning of Jesus' death was discerned by the early Christians who eventually understood his death in the light of the Suffering Servant of Isaiah (52:13-53:12). It is not unlikely, however, that it originated with Jesus himself at a time when the forces of mortal opposition were closing in on him during the latter part of his life. (See Mk 10:45 and Mk 14:24)

Two Aspects of Jesus' Death.

Historical and Theological. Our hosts, Archbishop Romero and Evelio Javier, Mother Teresa and Padre Pio will have clarified for us that there should be at *least two ways of talking about the death of Jesus*:

Why did Jesus *die*? To which the answer is: in atonement for sin. Death-for-sin is the *faith-meaning and theological significance* of Jesus' death.

Why was Jesus *killed*, executed or murdered? The various historical reasons that led to his execution: this is the *historical aspect of Jesus death.*

We would do well to take both aspects seriously and not let the faith-meaning cancel out the historical aspect—under pain of trivializing Jesus' death.

Recover the Historical Aspect. In a very general way of speaking, Second Look consciousness is focused only on the theological significance. 'Why did he die?' to which the correct answer is:'to redeem us from sin.' The historical aspect—'Why was he killed?'—is nearly overlooked. But it is important to recover it – and for several reasons. Because it belongs to the total story, and without it Jesus' death cannot be explained. Because it is particularly meaningful in the Third World today. In our day there are already modern martyrs—whether Jesus-followers or not—whose blood has witnessed to values and 'issues' similar to those of our first martyr, Jesus.[80] Jesus offers the Jesus-followers among them a profile for inspiration and imitation: in his commitment to human life, the human being, and human rights above law and tradition (Mk 3:1-6); in his choice of *tsedaqah, mishpat, checed*

[80] Our first martyr is Jesus, not Stephen! To make Stephen our first martyr is to exempt Jesus from humankind.

as the heart of life and religion (Mt 23:23); in his critique of the establishment, theology, canon law, life-style and practice of his own 'Church' and temple-state; in his clear stance regarding the *'anawim* and outcasts; in his equally clear stance regarding the wealthy and powerful elite. Three of our hosts, Romero, Evelio and Mother Teresa, each in their own way, are imitators of this Jesus in our time—Romero and Evelio in socio-political life, Mother Teresa in her uncommon compassion for the sick and the dying.

Yes To the Open Side. The atoning death of Jesus is a sure constituent of our faith. And today we rightly make the faith-assertion: 'Jesus died for me and my sins.' Paul says, 'I live by faith in the Son of God, who loved me and gave himself for me' (Gal 2:20). It is a precious possession, especially to those for whom it is not just a doctrine to be believed but an open side from whose juices we slake our thirst. That open side of Jesus is also the living spring which flows into the Church's sacraments. But, we must say more, particularly for the information of Christians whose political outlook is progressive but who, theologically, have remained static in a Second Look catechism. And what is this more ...

The More: He Did Not Set Out to Die. In the human history of Jesus, he did not set out on a mission to die (!) He was definitely not a dead man walking, as sometimes he is made out to be—unconsciously and unwittingly. Rather he set out first on a mission 'to proclaim the Kingdom and its justice.'[81] It was this proclamation in word and action which then drew Jesus into mortal conflict with the social, economic, political and religious elite of his time and brought him to his cross. His death was then given a particular meaning—an atoning death for sin.

Playing It Fair. In so expanding our awareness—appreciative of both the faith-meaning/theological significance and the historical aspect of Jesus' death—we also play it fair with the biblical data.

Paul and John. 'Death in atonement for sin' is the theology which has one-sidedly dominated our faith-understanding for centuries. This can happen when one makes Paul, John and the Letter to the Hebrews the total framework for the Jesus-story. For many centuries our Christian theology has been heavily Pauline and Johannine. Paul, in his letters, says next to nothing about the pre-crucifixion life of Jesus, much less about the historical causes for Jesus' death. Paul focuses almost entirely on the atoning significance of Jesus' death.

And John? Even though he does talk about the ministry of Jesus, his gospel is so heavily overlaid with later theological reflection that we no longer meet the Jesus of Galilee. Rather, for John, Jesus is the Eternal Word who, from the first moment of his public ministry, is at once the 'Lamb of God' who takes away the sin of the world (Jn 1:29). Jesus is not presented as the proclaimer of the Kingdom. Already in the very first chapter of the gospel, on his first public appearance, Jesus is introduced by John the Baptist as he who will die on the cross for our sins!

---

[81] The formula 'Kingdom and its justice/righteousness' I borrow from Mt 6:33.

Thus today, although it is true that in our liturgy we read about Jesus' ministry in the gospels of Matthew, Mark, and Lukc, too many of us subconsciously and inaccurately treat Jesus' life as merely a preparation or prelude to his death.

Matthew, Mark, and Luke. We have to find a balance. We have to supplement Paul and John by giving full value to the story found in the evangelists Matthew, Mark and Luke. It is the life-story of one who 'died, was executed, for the Kingdom and its justice.' It is a story which calls into question our own life-story. Is mine a life-story where a death-*bed* at the end of the road is taken for granted? Or, toning down the melodrama: is it a story of being comfortable with the way things are, rather than devoutly wishing and perilously working for the demise, for example, of the World Trade Organization?

Postscript One: the Mission of Jesus Revisited.

We can now return to a question we asked in the beginning: 'What was the mission of Jesus?' and give a fuller answer.

Mission to Die for Sin. Once again, is the statement, 'Jesus' mission was to die for the atonement of sin' correct and biblical? Yes, it is correct. It is biblical, as Mother Teresa and Padre Pio have just guided us to see. There are numerous biblical references to this. Together with Jesus' resurrection, Jesus' death is the centerpiece of Paul's gospel (1 Cor 15:3 ff). But Archbishop Romero and Evelio Javier tell us we cannot put a full stop here.

Mission Before the Cross. The mission of Jesus *before* the cross was to proclaim and to actualize final-and-definitive salvation: the Reign-Kingdom of God, healings, exorcisms, liberation and justice to the poor and oppressed (Mk 1:14-15; Mt 11:2-6; Lk 6:20).

Vantage Point: Post-Easter or Eternity. It is true that certain biblical statements present Jesus' mission in terms of his death (and resurrection): He came to die for our sins (1 Jn 4:10). Here and in similar instances, the narrator has taken either a post-Easter vantage point or a vantage point of eternity (Mk 10:45; Mt 1:21; Rom 5:6-10; Jn. 3:16; 1 Tim 1:15). Thus we have such expressions as: 'God's plan from all eternity is that Jesus should die for our sins.' Of course, from the same vantage point, one may as validly say anything, including: 'God's plan from eternity is that Jesus should proclaim the Kingdom.' At any rate, speaking from the vantage point of eternity one may, of course, validly say: 'Jesus came to die for our sins.'

A Look Inside History. But a 'look inside history' will contribute to a fuller and differentiated view. Before the moment of awareness that his Kingdom-work and conflictive activity would involve an expiating death, Jesus' life-purpose was the proclamation of the Kingdom of God. We can and should speak, therefore, of the mission of the pre-crucifixion Jesus.

When Did Jesus Know? At what precise moment did Jesus become aware that his Kingdom proclamation would entail his atoning death? Right at the start when he first took up his Kingdom task? Much later on in his career when the forces of destruction were catching up with him? It does not matter. What is important is that within history there is, primarily, Jesus' awareness of a mission to proclaim the Kingdom of God in word and deed. Subsequently (or concomitantly), soon or late, he becomes aware of his consequent death and its atoning significance.

Various Perspectives. We need a key for understanding biblical texts about the mission of Jesus. Here is the key: there are various biblical statements about Jesus' mission and they were written from *various vantage points or perspectives.*

Perspective A: *On the cross, or at some point before* the cross—when Jesus became aware of impending death and accepted it as an atoning death for sin—Jesus can speak of his mission in terms of an atoning death:

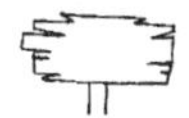

For the Son of man *came not to be served but to serve, and to give his life a ransom for many.* (Mk 10:45; 8:31; 9:31; 10:38; Cf. Also Lk 12:49-50)

Perspective B: Taking a *vantage point after Jesus' resurrection and looking back* on Jesus' life, someone like Matthew can think of the mission of the infant Jesus in terms of an atoning death:

She will bear a son, and you are to name him Jesus, for *he will save his people from their sins.* (Mt 1:21)

Perspective C: From the *vantage point of eternity*, someone like John can speak of Jesus' life-purpose in terms of an atoning death:

In this is love, not that we loved God but that *he loved us and sent his Son to be the atoning sacrifice for our sins.* (1 Jn 4:10)

Perspective D: But *inside history*, his mission initially and originally was to proclaim the Kingdom of God in word and action. Or: inside history, his initial and original mission was the proclamation of final salvation in terms of the Reign-Kingdom of God.

Now after John was arrested, *Jesus came to Galilee, proclaiming the good news [gospel] of God*, and saying, 'The time is fulfilled, and *the kingdom of God has come near;* repent, and believe in the good news.' (Mk 1:14-15)

A Word about Jesus' Baptism. It is claimed that at the very beginning of his ministry, Jesus was aware of his mission to die for sin. At his baptism in the Jordan, God's voice from heaven said: 'You are my Son, the Beloved; with you I am well pleased' (Mk 1:11; Mt 3:17; Lk 3:22). It is claimed that the 'Son' refers to the Suffering Servant who makes himself an offering for sin (see Isa 53). This conclusion is arrived at by saying that the voice at the baptism is quoting Isaiah 42:1, which, together with Isaiah 53, is one of the Servant Songs.

What to say about this claim? In the first place, with or without the baptism episode, it is possible for any person, embarking on a controversial prophetic mission, to foresee a possible death. But in the case of Jesus, did this happen at his baptism?

Well, we should, in the second place, take note of the mythical nature of the baptism account. It is full of symbolic details: the heavens opening, the dove, the voice from heaven. Although nothing prevents the evangelists from using myth to present a historical fact, still one should proceed with caution.

Thirdly, what can be said about the view that the 'beloved Son' in the baptism scene is to be identified with the Suffering Servant? Well, there are two steps here actually. The first step is the identification of the Son with the '*Servant*' (connect Mk 1:9-11 with Isa 42). The second is the identification with the *Suffering* Servant (connect Isa 42 with Isa 53). Without tiring the reader with more technical details, I would say that neither of these two steps are air-tight certain. They carry, however, some real probability. It is very important to note that the identification with the *Servant* is direct (connect Mk 1:9-11 with Isa 42) whereas with the *suffering* Servant, it is indirect (connect Isa 42 with Isa 53).

Does the 'Son' of the baptism then point to the Suffering Servant? Well, with some probability, as I have just said. And here we must insert an important 'but.' BUT one must not be too quick to *jump to* the *suffering* Servant who offers his life for sin (Isa 53), *skipping over* the *Servant who proclaims justice to the nations* (Isa 42). The italicized words below indicate the contact between Isaiah's Servant and the Son mentioned in the baptism. (This is based on the analysis of the Greek translation of the Old Testament.)

The Servant in Isaiah	The Son at the Baptism
Here is *my servant, whom I uphold,* *my chosen, in whom my soul delights;* *I have put my spirit upon him;* *he will bring forth justice (mishpat) to the nations.* He will not cry or lift up his voice, or make it heard in the street; a bruised reed he will not break, and a dimly burning wick he will not quench; *he will faithfully bring forth justice.* He will not grow faint or be crushed *Until he has established justice in the earth; and the coastlands wait for his teaching.* (Isa 42:1-4)	In those days Jesus came from Nazareth of Galilee and was baptized by John in the Jordan. And just as he was coming up out of the water, he saw the heavens torn apart and the spirit descending like a dove on him. And a voice came from heaven, *'You are my Son, the Beloved; with you I am well pleased.'* (Mk 1:9-11)

If and when one has tarried long enough to recognize the 'beloved Son' as one whose assignment is to 'bring forth justice[82] to the nations' (Isa 42), then one may proceed to jump to the suffering Servant[83] who offers his life and death for sin (Isa 53).

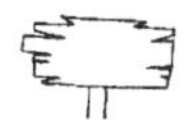

See, my *servant* shall prosper, he shall be exalted and lifted up (Isa 52:13) ... and the LORD has *laid on him the iniquity of us all* (Isa 53:6).... Yet it was the will of the LORD to crush him with pain. When you *make his life an offering for sin* (Isa 53:10) ... *He bore the sin of many, and made intercession for the transgressors.* (Isa 53:12)

If we follow this trajectory, then we have, in the baptism words, a terse but weighted statement of Jesus' life-purpose. It is the life and mission of one who lived the life of a prophet and died the death of a martyr.

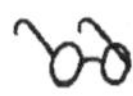

Kingdom Not Heaven. The mission statements of the pre-crucifixion Jesus (e.g., Mk 1:14-15; Mt 11:2-6; Lk 6:20-21) concern themselves not so much with heaven as with Kingdom. Jesus spoke not so much about 'going to heaven after death' as about 'entering the Kingdom of God.'

Human Being, Not Soul. The mission statements of the pre-crucifixion Jesus concern themselves not so much with the disembodied soul as with the total human person: the blind, the lame, the leprous, the poor, the sinner.

Life Includes Grace. The mission statements of the pre-crucifixion Jesus concern themselves not so much with grace-for-the-soul as with *life* (sight, health, life, joy, justice, liberation) for the *human being*.

My Catholic tradition tends to automatically associate Jesus with '(sanctifying) grace.' This is true, of course, of the crucified-and-risen Christ, assuming for the while that '(sanctifying) grace' is good theological language. It is salutary, however, to heed the appeal of the pre-crucifixion Jesus whose deeds were more '*life* giving' than they were '*grace* giving.' Jesus was concerned with total well-being for humans.

The Jesus before and after the cross would certainly be for 'life.' It is more comprehensive and more inclusive than 'grace.' 'Life' comprehends all human blessings, including the gift of the Spirit, which sometimes goes by the less fecund expression, 'grace.'

---

82 It is perhaps worth taking note that Isaiah talks of *mishpat*, justice, not righteousness in general, as some interpreters have it.

83 Originally, in Isaiah, the suffering servant most likely referred, not to an individual person, but to the nation of Israel.

Postscript Two: The Principal Gospels in the New Testament.

We are very accustomed to the word 'gospel.' Usually our gospel today is centered only around the saving death (and resurrection) of Jesus. Let us take a look at the principal gospels which the New Testament proclaims.

On the one hand:

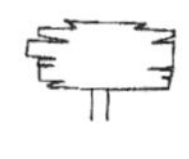

Now I would remind you, brothers and sisters, of the *good news* that I proclaimed to you ... For I handed on to you as of first importance what I in turn had received: that *Christ died for our sins* in accordance with the scriptures, and that he was buried, and that he was raised on the third day in accordance with the scripture.... (1 Cor 15:3-4)

On the other hand:

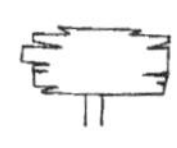

Now after John was arrested, Jesus came to Galilee, proclaiming the *good news [gospel]* of God, and saying, 'The time is fulfilled, and the *kingdom of God* has come near; repent, and believe in the *good news.*' (Mk 1:14-15)

'Go and tell John what you hear and see: the blind receive their sight ... and the *poor have good news (gospel) brought to them.*' (Mt 11:2-6; Lk 7:18-23)

Paul's Gospel; Jesus' Gospel. On the one hand: for *Paul* the word gospel or 'good news' is applied to the *death (and resurrection)* of Jesus (1 Cor 15:3-4).

On the other hand: the gospel which *Jesus* proclaims is, first, the gospel of *the Reign-Kingdom of God* (Mk 1:14-15), and second, the gospel—*of justice and liberation—to the poor.* This gospel to the poor is one of the principal blessings of the Kingdom (Mt 11:5; Lk 7:22).

The principal gospel(s) in the New Testament:

(1) the good news of the *saving death of Jesus* (Paul)

(2) the good news of the *Reign-Kingdom of God* (Jesus)

(3) the good news of *liberation and justice for the poor* as one of the Kingdom-blessings (Jesus)

Whereas the 'gospel' of Paul was about the death and resurrection of Jesus (1 Cor 15:1ff), the gospel of Jesus was not about that at all! Rather, the 'gospel' of the pre-crucifixion Jesus was about the (1) Reign-Kingdom and (2) justice and liberation to the *'anawim* (Mk 1:14-15; Mt 11:5; Lk 4:16; 6:20)! There is no need to be schizophrenic about this. Anything worthwhile can be good news or gospel. By Paul's time and that of the early Christians a few years after the death and resurrection of Jesus, the good news had become the salvific death and resurrection. For the pre-crucifixion Jesus, the good news was, in the first instance, the good news about the Reign-Kingdom of God.

The Gospel to be Proclaimed Today. Normally today, we, particularly the Second Look generation, are familiar almost exclusively with *Paul's* gospel. A highly popularized version of it is what portable loud-speakers proclaim on the street-corners of Cubao and in many buses.

The First and Third Looks challenge us to also proclaim *Jesus'* gospels.

One is the gospel of the Reign-Kingdom of God. And here, first, I remind you of an old insight: the proclaimer (Jesus) is not the proclaimed (Kingdom of God). Second, that in general we priests and pastors have been good at proclaiming the proclaimed, but not as good in proclaiming what the Proclaimer proclaimed. Much of our proclamation of Christianity has been a proclamation of Jesus rather than a proclamation of the Kingdom. This observation takes on a sharper bite if we realize that, strictly speaking, the main focus of Jesus' own proclamation was not himself, but the Kingdom of God! Jesus did not proclaim himself; he proclaimed the Kingdom of God.

The other gospel of Jesus is liberation and justice for the poor. The First Look summons us to proclaim this gospel. PCP II has taken the lead in this.

But more.

Then there is also the *gospel for our time*. I refer to the good news that we must announce in our time. I propose that the content of such a gospel is the following: the dialogical interaction of Jesus' and Paul's gospels on the one hand, and *our historical situation today*, on the other hand. Thank God, the Church has begun to proclaim this gospel today. We can use more of it, much more.

Evangelization. Another household word in Christian vocabulary is 'evangelization.' 'Evangelization' means 'proclamation of the gospel.' What gospel do we proclaim in the Church today? How do we 'evangelize'? How close is our evangelizing to that of Jesus? In certain parishes I know, evangelization has truly taken on the shapes and colors of integral evangelization. The sacraments, the eucharist, the homilies are vibrant and are linked with the life-concerns of the community and the world. The seminars, organizations, movements have a wide range of interests—from personal sanctification, folk religiosity to inter-religious dialogue, human rights advocacy and protest rallies. Clearly these parishes are concerned for life and life-before-death. Sadly, however, there are parishes where evangelization is confined to the teaching of prayers and songs, of old-style doctrine and morals—primarily in preparation for death and life-after-death.

Take Up Your Cross.

The cross of Jesus provides a good opening to talk about suffering. There seems to be an ambivalence about how a Christian should view human suffering. On the one hand, the beatitudes clearly show that Jesus wanted liberation from poverty and hunger. On the other hand, we follow a suffering and crucified Jesus. The following 'catechism' might help:

To put it plainly, is human suffering—hunger, poverty, sickness—a good or an evil?
It is an evil.

But is it not part of the human condition?

Yes. But it remains an evil. Being a part of the human condition does not make it a good.

But did not Jesus embrace suffering?

No, not right away. Remember the anguished semicolon.

But eventually he did embrace it.

Yes, when it became clear that such was to be his life-flow ... or the will of his Father. Remember again the 'thy will be done' *after* the anguished semicolon.

Therefore, we are to embrace suffering when it is the will of God, or better, the Father's will?[84]

Yes, of course, when and if it is—*clearly and after due discernment,* I repeat, *clearly and with due discernment*—perceived to be the Father's will.

The 'will of God' does not, of course, mean that a sadist God takes pleasure in seeing us suffer. Rather, we dimly intuit that the table of life, as it is set before us, includes the bitter cup and bitter herbs—the design of which only God can fathom.

Or to use another metaphor: the flow of life may rest in placid, blue lagoons but it may and will also be dashed against ugly crags and boulders—for reasons kept in the heart of God and the universe. Tragedies, death of loved ones, excruciatingly painful sicknesses, malformed babies....

We must, however, be slow to assign certain calamities and disasters to the will of God, when they are rather the result of human folly and greed. Floods that destroy lives and precious belongings in our day are to be charged to human rather than divine agency.

Further, suffering as part of the table of life is there not as an invitation to passive surrender, but as unique summons to creativity.

May we not embrace suffering in imitation of the crucified Savior?

Yes, if it is clearly discerned to be our life-flow. But if it is a suffering that we invent for ourselves, proceed with caution.

Does not the Church teach that suffering is a ticket to heaven?

A Second Look Church may. Jesus never did.

Did not Jesus challenge us to 'take up your cross and come follow me'? (Mk 8:34; Mt 10:38; 16:24; Lk 9:23; 14:27)

Yes, but that statement must be understood in context. That statement was made *before Jesus died on the cross*. The cross did not as yet have a religious meaning. If

---

[84] See page 192.

anything, it had a political meaning. Crucifixion was a punishment meted out by the Romans on rebels and slaves.

In the case of Jesus, the cross was a consequence of – a punishment for—his proclamation of the Kingdom. When we spell out his Kingdom practice, it reads: He was to be a defender of human life, the poor, justice. He was an enemy of tradition and law. He was a non-conformist, a heretic, an apostate. He was a critic of the establishment and the aristocracy. He attacked the cathedral of his time. He threatened authority and the power-holders. Jesus' cross was the 'reward' for that kind of Kingdom practice.

For the Jesus-follower, taking up one's cross means at least to take up that Kingdom proclamation which led Jesus to his cross, whether or not it leads to one's own cross. Further, it means doing the Kingdom practice which could lead to one's own cross – arrest, torture, death?—at the hands of a threatened establishment. In his time, Jesus' challenge had these (over)tones: 'Be a rebel! Risk the cross and come follow me.' That is a cross which we do not invent. Here is an ancient formulation of it:

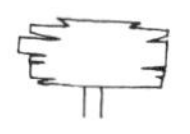

> ... They will hand you over to councils and flog you in their synagogues; and you will be dragged before governors and kings because of me ... and you will be hated by all because of my name.' (Mt 10:16-22; cf. also Acts 14:22.)

Is it possible for us Christians to invent our crosses and skirt around the cross that makes us truly follow in the footsteps of Jesus?

Yes, indeed. In fact, we do not have to think big and heroic. A prosaic example would be a person who devises an abundance of mortifications (like giving up ice cream during Lent) and is indifferent to the abuse of women and children; or a person who can marshal various forms of self-punishment (like giving up a movie) and be blind to structural economic punishments to countries and peoples imposed by the World Bank and transnational corporations.

After *Jesus died on the cross, should not we Christians, in imitation of Christ, value and accept bitter cups that come our way? Did not Paul say that he fills out what is lacking in the sufferings of Christ (Col 1:24)? And did not 1 Peter (1 Pet 2:21) say that we follow a crucified Savior?*

Yes, we should value and want to carry our cross – but again, as in the case of Paul, we value the kind that is truly what God asks of us. Moreover, remember that Paul's sufferings—imprisonments, floggings, stoning, shipwrecks, bandits, danger from brothers and sisters, etc.—were all for the sake of the gospel (2 Cor 11:21-33).

Further, while we appreciate the reflections of Jesus-followers like Paul and 2 Peter, we should also give importance to what Jesus himself said and did before he died on the cross.

What did Jesus say and do before he died on the cross?

Well, briefly, suffering was a condition to be liberated from rather than a cross to bear or a necessary ticket to heaven. The beatitudes, for example, were resounding proclamations of liberation from poverty, hunger, and misery. And his practice? When he encountered the sick and the hungry, he did not say that sickness and hunger were their certificate for heaven. No. He healed. He gave to eat.

Meaning of the Statement: 'Take Up Your Cross' – Before and After Jesus' Death. To return to the statement 'take up your cross,' what is the proper way to understand it?

People who live *after* Jesus' crucifixion may and do accept their portion of the bitter cup 'because they follow a crucified Savior.' In this instance, we may legitimately enough use the language 'taking up one's cross.' But it is good to know that this is a transferred and secondary meaning.

The *original* meaning, as Jesus spoke it before his own death on the cross, would seem to be: 'Risk the cross! Proclaim the blessings of the Kingdom. Announce and defend life. Promote justice. Stand with the oppressed. Prophesy against the powers. Denounce. Be an irritant! Risk the cross!' To dodge this cross while setting up dummy crosses, substitutes, is a way to miss the good fight that 2 Tim 4:7 speaks about.

Listen now to Jesus himself say it simply:

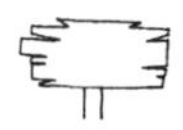

'Are you able to drink the cup that I drink, or be baptized with the baptism that I am baptized with?' (Mk 10:38)

A Closer Look at 'Take Up Your Cross.'

Jesus' words	Commentary or Paraphrase
If any want to become my followers,	If you want to be a Jesus-follower,
let them take up their cross	risk the cross … take up the Kingdom-task.
let them deny themselves	This entails repudiating self-interest and even self, or better, the ego.
for those who want to save their life will lose it, and those who lose their life … will save it …	For, Jesus-following entails a paradox: promote ego and ego-interest and you lose; repudiate ego-interest and ego and you are saved.
… for my sake, and for the sake of the gospel.	Why? For my sake and the gospel, i.e., the good news of the Kingdom.
For what will it profit them to gain the whole world …	Consider this: If you are in business, is it profitable to rake off the whole world …
… and forfeit their life?	… and suffer bankruptcy of your life?
Indeed, what can they give in return for their life?	Indeed, what can people give in exchange for your life?

There is another paradox in this saying of Jesus which we may briefly advert to. We have seen that 'life' is a high priority for Jesus. In fact 'saving life' could very well summarize Jesus' whole life. Yet here he says that the attempt to save life is to lose it! Of course, there is a particular use of language here: 'saving life' has the connotation of promoting self-interest. The statement is striking nonetheless.

Be Still and Know …

Stopover 17

In the Bosom of the Universe (Resurrection of Jesus)

OUR HOST: St. Francis

Our next stop, believe it or not, is the bosom of the universe. Our hosts are the risen Jesus himself and Francis of Assisi. Our planet earth, the stars, the galaxies, the supernovas—these make up our universe(s). And where is the center? Surprisingly, according to post-Newtonian physics, there is no one physical center. Rather each of us is the center. The core in each of us is also the bosom of the universe. There, according to our Faith, is also where the Spirit of the risen Lord, our present host, abides. He is our best guide for the signposts about his resurrection.

A Kind of 'Knowing'. How can we pierce through the veil that separates us from the next dimension? What awaits after one steps into the reaches of the after-death? Re-incarnation? Survival of the soul? Resurrection? Non-existence? Different religions and different 'no-religions' have different answers and no-answers. Or are the answers *really* different? Do they have a commonality that is beyond the ken of our simplistic laws of contradiction? I will not be one to 'prove' that they are or are not, they do or do not. But one thing does seem certain to me—the answers, or glimpses of them, will come less from rational speculation or from 'blind faith' than from a 'knowing' that 'knows without knowing.' For here we have set foot on a terrain which is beyond philosophy, beyond apologetic theology. Beyond poetry even.

I say all this only to make known how, I suggest, we may regard the resurrection of Jesus. Anyone, like myself, who accepts Jesus' resurrection, need not prove it. Nor even believe *in* it. How much personal engagement is there in deep religious 'truths' which you either 'prove' or believe *in*? In the long and short of it, it is neither a matter of apologetics nor (blind) faith. Rather, does it ring true? Does it resonate with the tuning fork of our best and *deepest* selves. Ironically perhaps, in this kind of knowing, what at first appears not to be part of the real world, turns out to be the most real.

He Is Risen

There are testimonies to the resurrection of Jesus. And the testimonies are simple, straightforward, almost matter of fact: He is risen. He is not here. He was raised on the third day.

> As they entered the tomb, they saw a young man, dressed in a white robe, sitting on the right side; and they were alarmed. But he said to them, 'Do not be alarmed; you are looking for Jesus of Nazareth, who was crucified. *He has been raised*; he is not here. Look, there is the place they laid him.' (Mk 16:5-6)
>
> For I handed on to you as of first importance what I in turn had received: that Christ died for our sins in accordance with the scriptures, and that he was buried, and that *he was raised on the third day in accordance with the scriptures*, and that he appeared to Cephas, then to the twelve. (1 Cor 15:3-5)
>
> They said to each other, 'Were not our hearts burning within us while *he was talking to us on the road,* while he was opening the scriptures to us?' (Lk 24:32)

The testimony can also be very personal, deep and mystical. 'It is no longer I who live, but it is Christ who lives in me' (Gal 2:20).

The Risen Jesus: God's Vindication

Several meanings were attached to the resurrection of Jesus. The *first meaning* entails the adversative 'but.' You killed him; *but* God raised him. For the first Christians, the Father's act of raising Jesus from the dead was an act of vindication. It is the Father's 'yes' to the stances and workings of this extraordinary person. Above all, it is the OK seal that validates the death of Jesus and invalidates the death-prone thoughts and machinations of the people who killed Jesus.

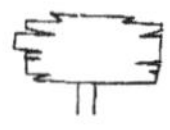

We are witnesses to all that he did both in Judea and in Jerusalem. *They put him to death* by hanging him on a tree; *but God raised him* on the third day and allowed him to appear, not to all the people but to us who were chosen by God as *witnesses, and who ate and drank with him after he rose from the dead.* (Acts 10:39-41)

And being found in human form,
he humbled himself
and became *obedient to the point of death—*
even death on a cross.
Therefore God also highly exalted him
and gave him the name
that is above every name. (Phil 2:8-9)

The Risen Jesus: the First Fruits of the New World

The *second meaning* stimulates images and hopes. They are hope-images of Jesus and of a deathless and ever-youthful world in which Jesus is the first. They are clips of a biblical scenario. Here is a replay: Is there not a future where each day will rouse us to a new world where the last enemy, death, will have been destroyed? Is not the Kingdom of God a new world where those who once slept in death would rise to new life? Well, Jesus is the *firstborn of that new world*! Is not the Kingdom of God like a *harvest*? (Mt 13:30) Well Jesus is the *first fruits*!

But in fact Christ has been raised from the dead, *the first fruits* of those who have died. (1 Cor 15:20)

He is the head of the body, the church; he is the beginning, *the firstborn* from the dead, so that he might come to have first place in everything. (Col 1:18)

The Risen Jesus: the Indwelling Spirit

The risen Jesus is the life-energy that dwells in our deepest selves. That is the *third significant meaning* of Jesus' resurrection. Jesus no longer has to play by the rules and regulations of our kind of materiality. He is freed from all the limitations of *our kind* of flesh-and-blood existence. Thus untrammeled, he can be the most intimate guest of our hearts. He is the indwelling Spirit. He is the divine element that works the alchemy of our divine sonship and daughtership. And cradled in our once-base hearts, he can – and we – utter the simple cry: 'Abba, Father!' That cry is worth infinitely more than all the valued metals in the universe. And if we let him, he can break through our opaqueness and impermeability and change us 'in his likeness from one degree of glory to another.' And if we are thus truly rooted in Christ, our loving is not an exertion but a natural fruit, a spontaneous happening. And finally, when our own days have grown older and after we too will have tasted death, 'he who raised Christ Jesus from the dead will give life to your mortal bodies also through his Spirit who dwells in you.'

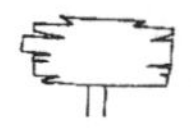

And because you are children, *God has sent the Spirit of his Son into our hearts, crying, 'Abba! Father!'* (Gal 4:6)

And all of us, with unveiled faces, seeing the glory of the Lord as though reflected in a mirror, are being *transformed into the same image from one degree of glory to another;* for this comes from the *Lord, the Spirit.* (2 Cor 3:18)

and that *Christ may dwell in your hearts* through faith, as you are *being rooted and grounded in love.* (Eph 3:17)

But you are not in the flesh; you are in the Spirit, since the *Spirit of God dwells in you.* Anyone who does not *have the Spirit of Christ* does not belong to him. But if *Christ is in you,* though the body is dead because of sin, the Spirit is life because of righteousness. If the Spirit of him who raised Jesus from the dead dwells in you, he who raised Christ from the dead will *give life to your mortal bodies also through his Spirit that dwells in you.* (Rom 8:9-11; also Phil 1:19; 1 Cor 15:45)

Keeping Intact the Kingdom Perspective

Cross and Resurrection. Sometimes the resurrection is paired with the cross to form one important saving event. This is a *fourth meaning* of Jesus' resurrection. Through his death and resurrection, Jesus has obtained atonement for sin and has given humanity the Spirit. The cross-and-resurrection of Jesus has been called the paschal mystery. Just as the paschal lamb and its blood on the doorposts saved the ancient Hebrews from Pharaoh's terror during their march out of Egyptian slavery (Ex 12:11-13), so the sacrificial blood of Jesus brings salvation from sin. For 'Christ, our paschal lamb has been sacrificed' (1 Cor 5:7). The salvation that Jesus has wrought consists in (1) the atonement for sin; (2) the outpouring of the Spirit; and (3) the consequent attainment of eternal life and salvation.

who was handed over to *death* for our trespasses and was *raised* for our justification. (Rom 4:25)

For he was *crucified* in weakness, but *lives* by the power of God. For we are weak in him, but in dealing with you we will live with him by the power of God. (2 Cor 13:4)

For to this end Christ *died and lived again,* so that he might be Lord of both the dead and the living. (Rom 14:9)

Old and Central. The cross and resurrection of Christ is central in Christian faith and theology. And its centrality is rooted in very ancient tradition. Even before Paul, we already had a formulation of faith: For I handed on to you as of first importance what I in turn had received: that Christ died for our sins in accordance with the scriptures, and that he was buried, and that he was raised on the third day in accordance with the scriptures (1 Cor 15:3-4). We also find it in the very ancient hymn, expressing belief in Jesus' obedience unto the cross and his exaltation by God quoted by Paul in Phil 2:6ff.

The Kingdom-Focus. In contemporary Philippine Christianity, however, we must not let the prominence accorded to the paschal mystery obscure another and older focus of the Christian faith. In the history of Jesus and early Christianity, there was a focus which pre-dates the paschal mystery. This is the Kingdom-focus. The heart of Jesus' pre-crucifixion mission and message was the Kingdom or the new world where God, justice, peace, joy, full life reign.

Elbow Room for Jesus. There is a form of narrow Christian spirituality which focuses almost exclusively on Jesus' death. Thus: 'Jesus died for my sins and he is the indwelling and sanctifying Spirit in my heart. He is my personal savior.' This spirituality, though good and biblical, as far as it goes, is too narrow. It does not give Jesus enough elbow room. It ignores the Jesus who proclaimed a new world, a new history, a new humanity already begun and culminating at the consummation of history; the Jesus who proclaimed good news to the poor; the Jesus who identified justice-compassion-fidelity as the weightier matters of religion; in short, the more complete Jesus who poses questions to our Christian living today. The Second Look spirituality I used to know was of this kind.

The Fundamentalist Jesus. This kind of spirituality is at the base of certain fundamentalist sects today. 'God loves you and me. Jesus died for you and me. He is my personal savior and yours. Believe in the Lord Jesus and you will be saved.' Around this one hub spins the whole of religion and life, salvation and damnation, making a caricature of the biblical message and revelation. Some go further and give the label 'atheists and communists' to other Christians who, like Jesus, proclaim good news to the poor. Frequently, these sects, knowingly or unknowingly, have financial support from the economic and political goliaths of the First World.

Before the specter of complacency slips in, we may reflect that fundamentalist theology is by no means the monopoly of so-called fundamentalist sects. It is also the possession of our institutional Church – with a difference. The fundamentalists often exhibit zeal, concern for persons and a sense of community belonging which are not always found among us.

Kingdom-Religion: Inner World and Vast Stage of History. The almost-exclusive preoccupation with the paschal mystery has given birth to a certain type of religion. Religion is played out only in individual souls, doing good and avoiding evil, hoping one day to scale the heights to heaven. It is a psycho-spiritual drama of the individual soul seeking personal salvation. And Christian ministry is understood by them as helping others to seek the same salvation. Jesus' religion, the Kingdom-religion, is very different. It is played out, yes, in my inner being, but also in the vaster stage of history, of the socio-political order, of people, of life-blessings, of our earth, in fact, of the universe....

The Risen Jesus: The Cosmic Christ

He Fills, Animates and Binds All Things. The risen Jesus has shaken off the shackles of mortality. The Pauline epistles unveil another profile of the risen Jesus. The risen Jesus, now having ascended back to the bosom of the Godhead, is the Cosmic Christ. Based on the Greek word for the universe, 'cosmos,' we speak of the risen Christ filling the entire universe as the Cosmic Christ. This is a *fifth meaning* of Jesus' resurrection. Thus the letter to the Ephesians:

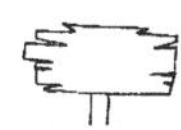

> He who descended is the same one who ascended far above all *the heavens, so that he might fill all things.* (Eph 4:10)
>
> ... which is his body, the *fullness of him who fills all in all.* (Eph 1:23)

Having broken loose from the limitations that our flesh is heir to, he has passed on to another dimension. There he has become the divine Energy that permeates and compenetrates all of reality. Just as a room can be saturated with sounds or colors or odors, so the Cosmic Christ *fills the vast, vast universe with his animating presence*. What is said of Yahweh is now said of Christ. 'Do I not fill heaven and earth?' saith Yahweh (Jer 23:4). 'One God and Father of us all, who is above all and through all and in all' (Eph 4:6).

The Energy 'fills all in all.' The universe *vibrates*. It is *alive*.

Early Christian hymns also celebrate the Cosmic Christ as the cohesive energy that holds things together, without which they cannot stand.[85]

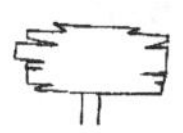

> He himself is before all things, and *in him all things hold together.* (Col 1:17)
>
> He is the reflection of God's glory and the exact imprint of God's very being, and he *sustains all things by his powerful word.* When he had made purification for sins, he sat down at the right hand of the Majesty on high. (Heb 1:3)

One Ocean of Energy. There are at least three significant groups that celebrate a beautiful reading of life in our vast universe. They say that all things in heaven and on earth are one ocean of energy. The universe is alive. So attest the eastern religions, the indigenous religions and contemporary physics.

The First Look joins this chorus. For us Christians, one name for the ocean is either God himself (1 Cor 15:28) or the Cosmic Christ. It is this Spirit-Lord that binds and bonds us and the rest of creation, 'all things in heaven and on earth.'

---

[85] The Book of Wisdom had earlier spoken in the same vein of God's wisdom: ...The Spirit of the Lord has filled the world, and *that [wisdom] which holds all things together* knows what is said (Wis 1:7).

With telescopes, contemporary science looks up and sees the energies of our present universe in uninterrupted communion with the energies of all reality, beginning with the present *homo sapiens*—back through the first mammals, to the first living cell, the birth of the sun, the birth of the milky way, the first elements in the galaxies—to the original burst of stupendous energy 15 or so billion years ago. We are connected! The same contemporary science, this time with microscopes, looks down and peers into the sub-microscopic world, inquires into the basic building block of reality and discovers not lifeless bits of matter but living energies; the universe is made up of relationships of energies, forming one continuous communion of energies, or simply, energy. We are connected!

Eastern mystical religions report the experience of the interrelatedness, interdependence, and basic oneness of all things and events.

Many indigenous communities know we are all part of the web of life. 'We are all connected to each other'—as a popular song goes—'in a circle, in a hoop that never ends.' The earth is not just a dead commodity with a price-tag; every rock and tree and creature has a life and a name.

Francis of Asisi, our host, *did not believe in this. He knew it.* Brooks, butterflies, mice, flowers, weeds and humans—brothers and sisters are. And the earth, our mother.

So why 'conquer' nature? Why use and abuse it for recreation or profit?

Reconciliation and Harmony of Creation. Not only is the universe animated and upheld by the Cosmic Christ, it is also reconciled through him. Jesus' saving death not only brings about salvation and reconciliation between God and humans (Rom 5:10-11; 2 Cor 5:18-19) and among humans, making Jew and non-Jew into one body (Col 3:11; Gal 3:27-29; Eph 2:13-16); it also brings about harmony and reconciliation to the rest of creation. The blessings of salvation and well-being are meant not only for us humans but also for our mother, the earth; for our ancestors, the rocks; for our relatives, the mammals.

So why abort nature's right to well-being? Why pollute the rivers and the air? Why kill the fingerlings and the corals? Why rape the forests and the seas?

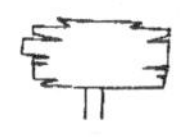

... and through him God was pleased to *reconcile to himself all things, whether on earth or in heaven, by making peace through the blood of his cross.* (Col 1:20)

This harmony in nature is probably to be correlated with the defeat of evil powers, which biblical religion speaks about. It is tempting to find incarnations of these evil powers in our time. The neo-liberal ideology of globalization and its minions perhaps?

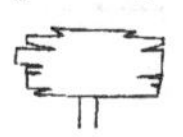

He *disarmed the rulers and authorities and made a public example of them, triumphing over them in it.* (Col 2:15)

... who has gone into heaven and is at the right hand of God, with angels, authorities, and *powers subject to him.* (1 Pet 3:22)

Song(s) of Creation. Before the final and complete rout of those 'principalities and powers,' the created universe is '*groaning* in labor pains' until it is 'set free from its bondage to decay and obtain the freedom of the glory of the children of God.' (Rom 8:18-23)

Many indigenous peoples hear the voices of the mountains.

Our host, Francis of Asisi, *must have heard them too.*

Modern science, particularly physics, has an ear for the 'music in the spheres.'

Eastern religions listen to sounds in their way of communing with the universal unity.

Paul hears the plaintive song of creation.

I wonder, are they hearing similar songs? Or are they hearing the same song? Different parts of the same song? Are they parallel adventures or are they converging experiences? It may take a few years or a few millennia for us to realize that they converge. But they have to.

Past and Future. The Cosmic Christ, who presently animates, upholds and reconciles the universe has a past and a future. In the past, he had a hand in the birthing of the universe. In the future he will bring the universe to its final consummation.

In Creation at the Beginning. The Hebrew Scriptures had earlier waxed enthusiastic about Wisdom as the intimate partner of God in the creation of the universe. When he had not yet made earth and fields ... when he established the heavens, I was there ... when he made firm the skies above ... when he established the fountains of the deep, then I was beside him, like a master worker ... (see Prov 8:22-31).

Now, it is Christ that the New Testament exalts. In and through him the universe came to be.

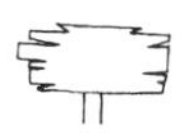

> He is the image of the invisible God, the firstborn of all creation; for *in him all things in heaven and on earth were created,* things visible and invisible, whether thrones or dominions or rulers or powers—*all things have been created through him and for him.* He himself is before all things, and in him all things hold together. (Col 1:15-17; Rom 11:36)
>
> In the beginning was the Word, and the Word was with God, and the Word was God. He was in the beginning with God. *All things came into being through him,* and without him not one thing came into being. (Jn 1:1-3)

In the Consummation at the End. Finally, at the climax and closure of human history, 'after he has destroyed every ruler and every authority and power' (1 Cor 15:24), the grand design of God will be realized: to sum up all things in the heavens and on the earth in Christ, with the cosmic Christ as head of all creation (*ana,* up; *kephalē,* head). Francis, our host, will be there. So will the littlest quark. So will the most mammoth of galaxies. And we will not only be together. We will be one – as we always have been and are.

he has made known to us the mystery of his will, according to his good pleasure that he set forth in Christ, as a plan for the fullness of time, *to gather up all things in him, things in heaven and things on earth.* (Eph 1:9-10)

Not 'Theology' But Contemplative Sightings. What are we talking about? Here we are not talking about the 'theology of the Cosmic Christ,' if by 'theology' is meant a disquisition by the rational mind. So understood, the Cosmic Christ is 'explained,' psychologized, analyzed with conceptual constructs, not to mention speculative ones. No. First, it is best to take the four experiences we have described above—eastern religions, indigenous spirituality, contemporary science, the Cosmic Christ —as sources of wisdom. Then their testimonies are best taken as sightings of the contemplative spirit. These sightings, gifts of non-rational contemplation, are second nature to eastern spirituality. And they grasp more of the essence of reality than the surface ruminations of Western philosophy.[86]

[86] In passing: equipped with semester units of Western philosophy, we venture into the world. Just when we thought we had all the answers, the questions have changed. Or, the questions have not changed. They are just different out there where the people are –- unless we persuade them that ours are the right questions, thus setting the wheels of cultural colonialism grinding again.

Stopover 18

At the Closure with Mary the Mother of Jesus (Parousia of Jesus)

OUR HOST: Mary, the Mother of Jesus

THE FINAL SALVIFIC EVENT

All stories have a closure. Jesus' story has. For the First Look, the closure occurs at the 'coming again' of Jesus. The Kingdom that was inaugurated at his first coming will be consummated at his second coming. Mary the mother of Jesus is our host and guide. She is the mother of the proclaimer. She is a person who, with a sword-pierced heart, witnessed the earthly closure of his mortal life on the hill of the skull. She is the person, according to Catholic tradition, who has already experienced the full redemption that we expect to be ours only at the 'coming again' of Jesus.

Call to God's Kingdom. Paul writes to his Thessalonian community: God calls us to his glorious Kingdom. In the meantime we lead our lives in anticipation of the coming (again) of our Lord Jesus. When he does come, in apocalyptic glory or not, we look up because our final redemption will have come.

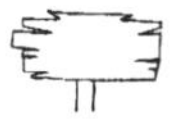

> As you know, we dealt with each one of you like a father with his children, urging and encouraging you and pleading that you lead a life worthy of God, who calls *you into his own kingdom and glory* (1 Thess 2:11-12). . . . And may he so strengthen your hearts in holiness that you may be blameless before our God and Father *at the coming of our Lord Jesus* with all his saints. (1 Thess 3:13)
>
> "There will be signs in the sun, the moon, and the stars, and on the earth distress among nations confused by the roaring of the sea and the waves. People will faint from fear and foreboding of what is coming upon the world, for the powers of the heavens will be shaken. Then they will *see 'the Son of Man coming in a cloud' with power and great glory. Now when these things begin to take place,* stand up and raise your heads, because your *redemption is drawing near.*" (Lk 21:25-28)

In Search of the Christ-Event. There was a time when I used to see the *death* of Christ as *the* Christ-event, for it was at his crucifixion that he redeemed me. Good Friday was the Christian feast for me. Later, with a little more theological sophistication, I waved the banner of Jesus' *resurrection* as an equally significant event. Salvation took place through his death and resurrection. I was taught to call this the 'paschal mystery.'

Neglected and Feared Event? At this stage, the 'second coming' of Jesus was hardly part of my religious consciousness. It was something to which I made passing reference when reciting the creed: '... he ascended to heaven, sits at the right hand of the Father, from thence, he shall come to judge the living and the dead.' I hardly understood anything about that event, except that it was something to be feared. Was I ready to face my Judge and make an exact accounting of every thought, word and deed? This, by the way, is a favorite fundamentalist way of using the *parousia*. So went my Second Look at the *parousia* of Jesus.

***Parousia:* An Event of Salvation.** A closer look at the Bible reveals the privileged place that Jesus' coming again occupied in the awareness of the early Christians. It was an *event of salvation.* All throughout the course of the 100 years or so of the New Testament era (30-120 C.E.) and even later, the *parousia* of Jesus was an important event in Christian consciousness. And why? Because that is the Victory-Day, *the day of the coming of the Kingdom!* When Jesus comes again, then will also dawn that new world where humankind will know no more mourning, nor pain, nor suffering, nor death—because all things will have been made new! Mary, the mother of the Proclaimer, *will be there to celebrate.* My childhood catechism missed out on all the vibrant joy of biblical hope.

Your Redemption Is at Hand. There is an interesting little phrase in Luke which mirrors the consciousness of the early Christians. My catechetical upbringing, and perhaps the upbringing of the average Christian today, would associate the word 'redemption' with Jesus' death or his resurrection, or with any other event, except the *parousia*. And yet, Luke says quite matter-of-factly: Then they will see 'the

Son of Man coming in a cloud' with power and great glory. Now when these things begin to take place, stand up and raise your heads, because your *redemption* is drawing near (Lk 21:27-28).

The Eucharist and the Parousia. Today, the eucharist is largely a memorial of the sacrificial *death* of Jesus. Our average Christian consciousness would not readily associate the eucharist with the *parousia* of Jesus and the coming of the new world. By contrast, Paul's Corinthian community, as often as they ate the bread and drank the cup, proclaimed the Lord's death 'until he comes' (1 Cor 11:26). As the Corinthians lived out their days and celebrated the Lord's death in the eucharist, their eyes were focused on the *parousia* and the Kingdom, as if to say: Come soon, and let the Kingdom and its blessings break into our lives today! Their prayer was, *'Maranatha*, come, Lord Jesus!' Hurry up! (cf. 1 Cor 16:22b)

Joyful Pledge for a New World. Fear, rather than anticipation and joy, used to be our feeling towards the *parousia*. After centuries of that, it is refreshing that at last in our modern liturgy we 'wait in joyful hope for the coming of our Lord Jesus Christ.' Do we know that we are proclaiming the possibility and the certainty of the new world of the future, and hopefully, our commitment to it?

Action Today. The apocalyptic imagery—'coming in a cloud' (Lk 21:27), 'sound of God's trumpet' (1 Thess 4:16)—need not be taken literally. Nor do we know exactly the shape and form of this 'coming.' What is said is that God or his Christ will put a closure to our history. And what is important is that today, as we 'wait in joyful hope for the coming of our Lord Jesus Christ,' we cannot just passively wait and pray for his coming and the Kingdom. In his first coming, he gave a mandate to his followers: "As you go, proclaim the good news, 'The kingdom of heaven has come near.' Cure the sick, raise the dead, cleanse the lepers, cast out demons" (Mt 10:1-8). With those words ringing in our ears, the *parousia* and the future Kingdom take on the guise of a finish line which summons us to action today.

Be Still and Know ...

Stopover 19

A Riverside Chat with Matthew, Mark, Luke, Paul and John (The Total Story of Jesus)

The Story of a River

The River of My Childhood. The telling of the Jesus-story is like the story of a river. The river is the river of my childhood. Flowing at the foothills of the Sierra Madre, its water gurgled blue and white on the shallow riverbed, and rested, a sleepy green, in deep lagoons in summer time. In monsoon and typhoon seasons, the river was an angry swirl of brown. A sure-fire formula for nirvana on hot summer days: brown young bodies plus prickly heat plus immersions into nature's most pristine liquid. The bliss of that ritual of daily, nay, hourly, baptisms!

The River Today. Today the riverbed is still there, but the once robust river is gone. A body of water, no larger than a stream, still courses along, an anemic shadow of what it was in my childhood. No, it is not chemical pollution. It is not human rubbish. There is just less water from the mountain. Fewer trees on the mountain.

The Story of Jesus. The story of Jesus is like the story of a river. The Jesus-story as told by my Second Look catechism is a pale shadow of the robust First Look story as told by the New Testament writers.

A Rite of Passage: From Second Look to First Look

If you have the time and patience, dear co-traveler, let me take you briefly through the paces of my passage from my Second Look catechism to the First Look story. Who knows, it might be the story of your passage too.

My Good Friday. Although, of course, the Christmas story never ceased to enthrall me, it was *Good Friday* that ran my spiritual motor. Jesus died for me. The graces he gained, and received by me in baptism and confirmation, I must continue to keep and increase in confession and holy communion, until the day when, having avoided sin and the snares of the world, I attain heaven and beatific vision.

I do not mean to hold up the mirror to anyone except myself. Nor do I intend a caricature (which it is not) of anyone except myself. It was my life, lived by me then and still appreciated today, in all seriousness, for what it was.

My Easter. The next stage in my development was a ray of light that came from *Easter Sunday*. The Vatican II Church began to reclaim the resurrection of Jesus. Jesus did not just die. He also rose. The Jesus of my life began to resemble crucifixes in many churches: on the cross hung no longer the suffering Jesus but the glorious Christ. More joy was infused into my spiritual life. More of the virtue of hope. More positive – although, of course, the risen Christ was still made to do apologetics.

A Personalist Jesus. At about the same time, there appeared a complementary spark from another source. *Personalist and existential theology* shed light on the total human person. Not just soul, also body. Not just spiritual, also psychological. Not *animal rationale* but the inner child. My 'I' learned to relate to your 'thou.' Concomitantly my Jesus became a personalist and existential Jesus. An updating. An advance.

Two Shoves with a Message: He Had a Life to Live as Well. Up to this point in my development, the Christ-event consisted in the death and resurrection of Jesus. Two contacts gave me a shove back to the Jesus of the First Look: (1) contact with the poor and (2) contact with biblical studies. These, like good teachers, gave me the push and the discipline.

Contact with the poor raised the question: Is there more to Jesus than the Jesus of paschal mystery and the Jesus of personalist theology?

Biblical studies showed me that there was and is an untold story of Jesus. He did not just die and rise. He had a life to live as well. There was that portion between his Jordan baptism and the cross.

Sure, as a Second Looker, I knew there was a 'public life of Jesus' and the 'ministry of Jesus.' But it did not have a life of its own. It was just a preparation for the cross. It did not deserve to be a story by itself. And in the Church's liturgical calendar, it was merely 'ordinary time.'

Biblical studies told me that it *was* a story. Sure, a more sophisticated theology began to talk about the 'words and deeds' of Jesus. But somehow, it was not the way Matthew, Mark and Luke said it. From these gospel testimonies we learn of a person who had a mission, not of dying, at least, not right away. It was a *mission obsessed with a new earth, with food for the hungry, with land, with healing, with forgiveness of sin, with justice* – things which mean a lot for my people in the Third World. It was a mission, clung to with passion, even in the teeth of the enemy and of death. But I will tarry here no longer. The biblical roadsigns we paused to ponder will have done a better job of telling the story.

I will permit myself one remark addressed to our liturgists and mass goers. After the consecration, we acclaim: 'Christ has died, Christ is risen, Christ will come again.' I wonder, before we allow him to die, could we let him live and say his piece? After all, the records say that before his death, 'Jesus proclaimed the Kingdom of God.'

The Closure. So then biblical studies taught me to piece together the Kingdom-proclamation, the death and the resurrection. Jesus proclaimed the Kingdom, he died, he rose. That is not yet the total Jesus-story, biblical studies hastened to say. There still remains the closure. The Kingdom, *begun in the first coming, is consummated in the second.* 'He will come again' has ceased to mean simply 'to judge the living and the dead.' It is no longer a moment of fearful judgment. It is a salvific event. It is a moment of salvation. It is the time when you look up, for 'your redemption is at hand.' The Kingdom of God is fully at hand!

Not just the seer of old, but all of us, with uncovered eyes, will see the new heaven and the new earth. God will dwell among us on this earth. Creation will have ceased groaning. The cosmic Christ will have united all things in heaven and on earth and God will have become all in all.

The Total Story of Jesus. The story of Jesus is complete, or at least the core of it. The total story of Jesus includes (1) the proclamation of the Kingdom, (2) his death, (3) his resurrection, and (4) his coming again. The one thread that binds all four is the Kingdom of God.

In his lifetime he proclaimed the Kingdom. He died for the Kingdom; atonement for sin is a Kingdom blessing. His resurrection is a vindication of his life and death for the Kingdom. As the risen one, he is the first fruits of the Kingdom. His indwelling in our hearts is the seed of our own future resurrection in the final Kingdom. His coming again is the consummation of the Kingdom.

The core:

Kingdom Proclamation ⟶ Death ⟶ Resurrection ⟶ Parousia

One Salvific Event. All this forms one unity, one salvific event. In this perspective, the saving event does not consist only in his death and resurrection. Accordingly, salvation is not limited to this: Jesus came and died for my sins, gained grace and merited eternal life and heaven for me. The following would be a fuller and biblical understanding: Jesus proclaimed in word and act the Kingdom of justice, peace, and life. Because of that salvific Kingdom proclamation, he was killed, executed. Through his sacrificial death we have atonement for sin and the gift of divine life. He rose from the dead as the firstborn of the Kingdom of God and as the saving Spirit that dwells in our hearts. Finally, he will 'come again,' at the close of history, to usher in the crowning point of salvation, the final, full and definitive Kingdom.

Blessings of Salvation. Accordingly, the blessings of salvation are not limited to sanctifying grace in this world and beatific vision in heaven. Rather, we should say: *In this world*, sight to the blind, healing to the leper, health to the lame, life to the dead, rice to the hungry, land to the poor, justice to the worker, forgiveness of sin, the Spirit in the hearts of people. In short, LIFE. *In the final Kingdom*: a new world, a new history where God will be all in all. In short, FULLNESS OF LIFE.

Introductory Portion. What about our perennial favorite, Christmas? Well, in the total picture, Christmas or infancy is part of the introduction. Preceding that is John's account of the pre-existence of the eternal Word that became flesh. Still part of the introduction would be the baptism of Jesus and his temptation in the desert. The introduction:

Introduction				Core			
Pre-existence (Jn 1:1-18)	Infancy (Matthew 1-2 and Luke 1-2	Baptism (Mk 1:9-11)	Temptation in the desert (Mk 1:12-13)	Kingdom proclamation	Death	Resurrection	Parousia

As We Part

Hats Off. Hats off to biblical studies. These, together with the poor, as I had earlier mentioned, were my tutors.

Hats off likewise to the poor.

In my experience, these two – biblical studies and the poor—always go together. One cannot be without the other. Jesus research without contact with the poor runs the risk of missing out. This is so, not only because we happen to be in and of the Third World. This is so, if you pardon the possible irreverence, because of the nature of the beast. The core-Jesus and his message are so steeped in the *'anawim* that in order to discover it, we too have to be in touch with the lives of our poor. I make this claim for Jesus research. It can be made for theological studies as whole. But this is not the place to explore this.

More Wonders. Wonders never cease! I thought I was done with teachers on Jesus when more presented themselves: indigenous nature religions, eastern spirituality and contemporary physics. They opened the New Testament and showed me those pages where the risen Lord is not only the indwelling Spirit but also the Cosmic Christ. One need not however go this route. With or without these three teachers, the Cosmic Christ and the indwelling Spirit are in the New Testament, waiting for moments of recognition and re-acquaintance. In fact, with the New Testament open or closed, at any moment, like this present one, we can connect with that Energy which fills the infinitely personal and the infinitely cosmic spaces in the universe.

It Is Not Difficult. We can all re-discover the total Jesus. It is not all that difficult. I hope that our journey together says as much. The river of my childhood is not likely to ever come back. But the Jesus of the First Look is always available, waiting to be re-discovered. How to go about it? Books? Seminars? Lectures? Perhaps, perhaps not.

I recommend still another river. At least to start. That river is the life and struggle of the poor. Jesus is there. He always has been. The waters of that river are there to cleanse, to bathe, to refresh, to nourish the seeker. In addition, trace the Source of that river. It is a Silent Spring 'way up the mountain, near the heavens. I recommend that too. That goes without saying. Drink to intoxication.

Salamat Po. Thank you for traveling and exploring with me. I hope your Third Look eye-glasses served you well. Indeed, I hope they have become permanent fixtures. Like implanted lenses. Nay, more, new retinas. You can use them for reading not only the Scriptures but life in general. You will not always be comfortable with the view, but it will be a priceless view, and it will be Jesus' view.

Carlos H. Abesamis

Appendix 1

(Titles of Jesus)

Titles of Jesus. During his lifetime, Jesus shied away from titles and honorifics. After his death and resurrection, certain realizations became clearer to Jesus followers, that: (1) he is the agent of God's definitive salvation; (2) he died for our sins; and (3) he belongs to the divine sphere. Titles—a good number of which Jesus or He may not have given to himself—were applied to Jesus. Some of the more familiar titles are described below.

Christ The most familiar to us is '*The Christ,'* the anointed one. 'Christ' has become not only a title but a personal name for Jesus: 'Jesus Christ' or simply 'Christ.' Paul took the lead in this regard. In biblical history, specially set apart and specially commissioned people were anointed with special oil. These were kings and priests, and also prophets. This title was most likely seen as apt for Jesus, because he was from King David's genealogical line, which, according to certain ancient prophets, was the provenance of king-saviors, Of course, Jesus was not a king-savior but one who died for the forgiveness of sins. One remarkable Third Look discovery is the 'anointed one' in Luke 4:18. He is one anointed, again, not in order to die for sin but 'to proclaim good news to the poor.' Similarly Acts 10:38 associates God's anointing of Jesus with 'going about doing good and healing all that were oppressed by the devil, for God was with him.'

Servant. Another title, not so popularly known by us is '*Servant.'* Chapters 52:13-53:12 of the book of Isaiah speak of a 'servant' who 'was wounded for our transgressions ... was bruised for our iniquities ... upon him was the chastisement that made us whole ... the Lord has laid on him the iniquity of us all ... he shall divide the spoil with the strong; because he poured out his soul to death ... he bore the sin of many.' The servant in this original Isaian context most likely referred not to an individual person, a savior-figure, but rather to the Israelite people. In the course of the many centuries of suffering at the hands of mighty empires like the Assyrians and Babylonians, Israel is seen as 'bearing the sins of the many.' The text is eminently suited to Jesus and his atoning death. Jesus then carries the title 'servant.' Another striking yet generally neglected fact is that in Isaiah 42, the servant is one who 'will bring forth justice to the nations;' 'he will faithfully bring forth justice,' 'he will not fail or be discouraged till he has established justice in the earth.' Yahweh upholds him. He is the chosen one. God delights in him. (Isa 42:1-5). The evangelists probably had this text in mind in connection with the baptism of Jesus. And Matthew is so impressed by it that he quotes it at length and uses it as a closure to one of the main sections of his gospel.

Son of Man. According to the gospel writers, the pet title that Jesus liked to use most was '*Son of Man.'* It is also a title which only Jesus and no one else uses. In the culture of the time, the phrase simply meant *The* Man. It meant something like 'Someone who represents what it is to be human.' In the Book of Daniel it has a special meaning. The 'Son of Man' is a symbolic designation for the people of Israel, who are contrasted with four beasts, a symbolic representation of foreign empires. Yahweh destroys the beasts and gives victory and glory to the Son of Man. This might be the best background for the New Testament use. But whereas, the Son of Man is a title of glory in Daniel, in some of the sayings of Jesus, it is rather associated with suffering and death (and resurrection).

Titles of Divinity. The principal titles that confess the divinity of Jesus are, of course, Son of God, God, Lord. Before Jesus' death and resurrection, *Son of God* need not mean divinity, for it can be used of anyone who has a special adoptive relation with God. After his death and resurrection, 'Son of God,' on the lips of those who confessed Jesus' divinity, would more definitely mean his natural divine sonship. Similarly, *Lord* could in that culture simply mean 'Sir.' But since *Lord* is the translation for Yahweh in the Greek version of the Hebrew Scriptures, it connotes divinity when applied to Jesus. Another designation of Jesus in John's gospel, referring to his divinity, is *The Word.*

Other Significant Titles. Surprisingly, although the New Testament speaks of 'redemption' and the 'redeeming' work of Christ, the title '*Redeemer*,' current among us, is hardly ever used of Jesus. On the other hand, *Savior* is sometimes used, with more or less the meaning we attach to it today. Since *Savior* is used of Yahweh in the Hebrew Scriptures, it also connoted divinity when applied to Jesus.

Personal devotion has generated other titles through the centuries. Brother, friend, counsellor, consoler, bride groom, lover. All this is fine, especially if such a Jesus is identical with that of the First Look.

Appendix 2

(Salvation)

Salvation, in the Judaeo-Christian tradition, is about a story. It is the story of the journey of humankind and the world—from the first creation (Gen 1:1) to the new creation (Rev 21:1-5). It encompasses the story of Israel's beginnings (Gen 12 - Judges), the subsequent story of the Israelite people (1 Samuel – Ezra), the perceived story of prehistorical beginnings (Gen 1-11).

The overarching theme in this story is not, as is sometimes believed, the spiral of humankind's sin and the hope to be redeemed from it. Rather it is about the drive for LIFE and life-blessings, e.g., land, progeny, liberation from slavery, alliance with God, harvests, secure homes, etc. (e.g., Dt 7:12-16). Because the exodus is the key event, the most significant life-blessing in this story is justice (e.g., Dt 24:17-22).

The classical prophets carry the story further by planting seeds of hope. The hope is for a better and definitive history in the future. Again, that history is about life-blessings and justice (e.g., Isa 65:17-25). It is the prophets who started to move the story towards expectations of eschatological salvation.

Salvation—eschatological salvation—in the New Testament is about the coming about of a new world and a new history with life-blessings. Jesus' preferred name for it is Reign-Kingdom of God.

The Reign-Kingdom of God, according to Jesus, based on his re-contextualization of Isaiah, is a new human situation with such life-blessings as health for the sick (blind, lame, lepers, deaf), life to the dead, good news of liberation to the poor, release to captives, liberty to the oppressed, jubilee year, justice to the nations (Mt 11:2-6=Lk 7:18-23; Lk 4:16-21; Mt 12:18-21; Lk 6:20-21 Mk 1:14-15).

The second part of each beatitude provides another window to the biblical meaning of Reign-Kingdom of God or eschatological salvation. Again, it is a new earth with a new history, where the following blessings are envisioned: divine filiation (Mt 5:9), seeing God (Mt 5:8), experiencing compassion (Mt 5:7), inheriting the earth (Mt 5:5), laughter and joy for the sorrowing poor (Lk 6:21b), food for the hungry poor [in Luke, satiation of real hunger (Lk 6:21a); in Matthew, of hunger for righteousness] (Mt 5:6), liberation for the *'anawim,* i.e., poor and oppressed (Lk 6:20).

Other noteworthy blessings of eschatological salvation are: destruction of satanic powers (Mt 12:28; 1 Cor 15:24-28); resurrection from death (Lk 20:34-36), the unity of all things in Christ (Eph 1:9-10) where 'God is all in all' (1 Cor 15:28).

Other significant names for eschatological salvation are: 'new heaven(s) and new earth' (Rev 21:1), in other words, a new world or a new creation, and, 'age to come;' in other words, a new and different alternative history in the future (Mk 10:29-30).

Biblical salvation is seen as having both a future aspect (Lk 13:29) and a present aspect (Lk 17:21). As a future reality, the Reign-Kingdom of God will be realized at the 'close of the age,' that is, at the end of our present history. Although, therefore, there is a life soon after the death ('going to heaven') of each individual, our *ultimate* destiny is not heaven but rather that new world and new history at the close of the present ongoing history. As a present reality in Jesus' time, it took the form of life-giving blessings through Jesus' actions. In our time, it should likewise take the form of life-giving blessings enfleshed in a humane social order.

The principal Christ events associated with this Reign-Kingdom of God are:

(1) The *ministry/practice* of Jesus where the Reign-Kingdom of God was first proclaimed and inaugurated (Mk 1:14-15);

(2) The *death of Jesus* (a) this was a consequence of his conflictive Kingdom-proclamation (Mk 14:1-2); (b) its mystical meaning is reconciliation and atonement for sin, a life-blessing par excellence in the Christian economy of salvation (1 Cor 15:3-5; Col 1:20);

(3) The *resurrection of Jesus* (a) this was a vindication of Jesus' Kingdom practice and death (Phil 8:2-9); (b) the risen Jesus is the first fruits and first born into the Reign-Kingdom of God (1 Cor 15:20); (c) the risen Jesus has become the indwelling Spirit that guarantees our own resurrection in the final Kingdom (Rom 8:9-11); and (d) he is the Cosmic Christ that binds all things (Eph 1:9-10).

(4) The *parousia of Jesus* is the closure. The Reign-Kingdom of God will have come in its fullness (Lk 21:25-28).

Biblical salvation therefore is not for souls but for persons and people, for the natural world (Rom 8:19-23) and the universe. The blessings of salvation encompass everything that gives life, including, but not limited to, divine life, sanctifying grace or beatific vision. It is not narrowly limited to the private sphere of the individual person but has to do also with the social, political, economic and other dimensions of life. One may not limit the Christ-events to the paschal mystery (death and resurrection) but must encompass his whole career, beginning with the ministry and culminating in the *parousia*. The pre-existence and infancy narratives, the baptism and temptation narratives—serve as introductions.